AN RTI GUIDE TO
IMPROVING THE PERFORMANCE
OF
AFRICAN AMERICAN
STUDENTS

D1484679

This book is dedicated to Deshawn Williams, Malachai Ward, Jada and Jazmin Price, Dwayne II, and Noni Williams. This book is also dedicated to Evan and Ian Byrd, Leaoance Williams III, Harper T. Williams III, and Alexandra M. Paul. I want you all to know and remember that education is power.

Your uncle, father, and friend, respectively

Dwayne D. Williams

AN RTI GUIDE TO
IMPROVING THE PERFORMANCE
OF
AFRICAN AMERICAN
STUDENTS

DWAYNE D. WILLIAMS

CORWIN
A SAGE Company

A SAGE Company

FOR INFORMATION:

Corwin

A SAGE Company

2455 Teller Road

Thousand Oaks, California 91320

(800) 233-9936

www.corwin.com

SAGE Publications Ltd.

1 Oliver's Yard

55 City Road

London EC1Y 1SP

United Kingdom

SAGE Publications India Pvt. Ltd.

B 1/I 1 Mohan Cooperative Industrial Area

Mathura Road, New Delhi 110 044

India

SAGE Publications Asia-Pacific Pte. Ltd.

3 Church Street

#10-04 Samsung Hub

Singapore 049483

Acquisitions Editor: Dan Alpert

Associate Editor: Kimberly Greenberg

Editorial Assistant: Cesar Reyes

Production Editor: Veronica Stapleton Hooper

Copy Editor: Gillian Dickens

Typesetter: C&M Digitals (P) Ltd.

Proofreader: Sally Jaskold

Indexer: Sheila Bodell

Cover Designer: Michael Dubowe

Marketing Manager: Stephanie Trkay

Copyright © 2015 by Corwin

Printed in the United States of America.

Library of Congress Cataloging-in-Publication Data

A catalog record of this book is available from the Library of Congress.

ISBN: 978-1-4833-1973-5

This book is printed on acid-free paper.

SFI® Certified Sourcing
www.sfiprogram.org
SFI-00453

15 16 17 18 19 10 9 8 7 6 5 4 3 2 1

Contents

A Note to the Reader

As a school psychologist, I have had the wonderful opportunity to work at every level of the response-to-intervention (RTI) process—from providing consultation to teachers and working with students directly to qualifying students for special education services who did not respond to Tier 2 and Tier 3 interventions. I have been afforded the great experience to help shape an RTI model at the high school level, where I facilitated RTI meetings and chaired annual review and 3-year reevaluation meetings for students who qualified for special education services because they failed to respond to interventions. In addition to working at every level of the RTI process—from prevention to special education eligibility—I have dedicated every year of my professional career to studying culture within the context of education and RTI. In particular, I have studied and conducted research on characteristics that have been associated with African American culture and have put research to practice at both the primary and secondary levels.

Throughout this book, I share my experiences working with students and parents of color, educators, and grade-level team members. I do not intend to leave readers with the belief that all students and parents of color will act similarly to the students and parents I have worked with or with the belief that all teachers will practice similarly to those discussed throughout this book. Practical stories and examples are shared within this work as opportunities to learn; they are intended to be used as case studies and teachable moments.

This book is divided into three parts. Part 1 lays the foundation for understanding RTI and culture, including theory and science that support culturally relevant RTI models. Part 2 includes practical examples of working with students and parents of color at the primary through secondary levels; this section of the book details their concerns surrounding race relations and cultural differences they experienced within the classroom. The final part of this book—Part 3—brings all chapters together to provide concrete examples of how educators may increase engagement among African American students by implementing culturally relevant

RTI models, including culturally relevant instruction. Part 3 shows how culturally relevant RTI models should look, starting at the Tier 1 level. While reading this book, it is important that readers remain cognizant of the variability that exists within and between all groups. No two people are exactly alike. No two people have the same worldviews. All people are different—even if they share cultural values, preferences, and interests— and just because a student is Black does not mean he or she will value characteristics that have been associated with African American culture. To ignore the research on variability that exists within and between all groups is to ignore the individuality among all people.

Acknowledgments

I am grateful for the many minds who have labored over this work.

I give honor to God for instilling a passion within me, a passion to research, write, and apply practices that address the needs of all students, including students who come from culturally diverse backgrounds. Without this passion, I would not have the motivation to research and write for hours at a time.

To my wonderful wife, Toni Williams: I thank you for understanding the importance of this work and being patient with me throughout the writing process. I thank you for being patient with what seemed to be disorganization—my scattered papers, sticky notes, books, articles, and even napkins, which included ideas for this book that piled up in many places within our home.

To my son, Dwayne D. Williams: You have inspired me by your imitation. When you put your suits on and act as if you are "teaching teachers" (as you call it) and writing and selling books—"just like your daddy"—you show me the impact of observational learning.

To my daughter, Noni D. Williams: Thank you for helping me balance writing and playing. When you thought I spent enough time writing, you were sure to let me know that my writing time was up and that it was time to play some games. Thanks for helping me balance things out.

To my mother, Mildred Mason: I thank you for your ongoing support and always reminding me of the source of my strength.

To my father, Willie B. Williams, I thank you for the talks that you had with me during the writing process. I am most inspired by your passion to hear me present on this work and your encouraging words.

To my brother, Lashawn Williams, and sister, Tabatha Price: I am always thankful for your love and support.

To my stepfather, Mark Mason: I thank you for your encouraging words. I am inspired by your strength to encourage me. No matter what you experienced with your health, you had a word from the Lord for me, and I want you to know that I appreciate that.

To editor Dan Alpert: I am grateful that you saw the need for RTI models that emphasize cultural diversity and were moved to work with me to get this book published.

To editor Cesar Reyes: I thank you for assisting with this work and keeping me in the loop with the publication process.

To the reviewers of this work: Thank you all for your feedback. Thanks for encouraging me to include more content about the basic principles of RTI. This book would not be what it is if it were not for your scrutiny and constructive feedback. Your questions, inquiries, and feedback made this edition much more detailed than the original edition. Thank you for your thoughts!

PUBLISHER'S ACKNOWLEDGMENTS

Corwin gratefully acknowledges the contribution of the following reviewers:

Lydia Adegbola
Assistant Principal, NYC
Department of Education
Elmsford, NY

Julie Esparza Brown
Assistant Professor in Special
Education, Portland State University
Portland, OR

Cindy Lawrence
Curriculum Coordinator/RTI
Coordinator, Lumberton ISD
Lumberton, TX

Rufus Thompson
Retired Educator and Technology
Coordinator, Independent Education
Consultant
Fayetteville, NC

Velda Wright
Associate Professor, Lewis University
Romeoville, IL

About the Author

Dwayne D. Williams is a school psychologist, educational consultant, and certified success coach. He provides training to school districts on how to create culturally relevant educational models, including RTI models. He earned a bachelor's degree in psychology (BA) from Fairmont State University; he earned a master's degree in psychology (MA) and an Educational Specialist degree (EdS) from Marshall University Graduate College. Dwayne received training in the area of life coaching from Youth and Family Guidance, Inc. and received board-certified life coaching credentials through the Center for Credentialing and Education (CCE). Dwayne is the founder of Tier 1 Educational Coaching and Consulting Services—a firm that provides urban educational and psychological consultative services to stakeholders, including administrators, teachers, community leaders, and parents. Dwayne is a first-generation college graduate and is devoted to shedding light on the importance of integrating cultural activities and instruction in the classroom. He was raised in housing projects in Springfield, Illinois, and often speaks on the need to connect with families and community leaders from underrepresented backgrounds. Dwayne is married to Toni Williams, and together they have two beautiful children: Dwayne II and Noni Williams.

Email Dwayne D. Williams at dwayne@tier1education.com

Website: www.tier1education.com

Follow Dwayne on twitter: @dwaynedwilliams

Introduction

The purpose of this book is twofold: (1) to examine response to intervention (RTI) in the context of culturally relevant instruction and (2) to discuss how educators might incorporate an RTI model that fits the cultural needs of most African American students.

RTI is a problem-solving model that emphasizes the importance of using scientifically based instruction and interventions to increase academic performance among all students (Brown-Chidsey & Steege, 2005). There is an array of research on culturally relevant instruction and RTI, but very few resources integrate culturally relevant pedagogy with the practice of RTI and other problem-solving models. To this end, my hope is that this book will encourage educators and researchers to collect data on culturally responsive activities in the classroom and to consider culturally relevant instruction and interventions prior to referring students for special education services.

The process of providing education is as sociocultural as it is psychological and emotional. Although sociocultural factors play a significant role in academic achievement, the education system in America has paid little attention to the social aspect of culture that teachers transmit into their classrooms (Bodrova & Leong, 2007). This is unfortunate, considering a vast amount of research points to cultural discontinuity as a key contributor to academic disengagement among students of color. In place of sociocultural factors, schools in America focus primarily on cognitive and emotional factors that shape learning.

An effective response-to-intervention model will not only ensure that educators and practitioners will research evidence-based instructions and interventions but will also identify cultural ethos within their classrooms; an effective RTI model will ensure that educators identify which students respond well to those cultural ethos and which students are unresponsive to those same cultural characteristics. Identifying cultural values within one's classroom and determining which students respond well to those values fit perfectly within an RTI model. In fact, this is an example of problem solving based on a culturally responsive approach.

PART 1

Culturally Relevant Response to Intervention (CR-RTI)

How Did
We Get Here?

1

Response to intervention (RTI) is arguably one of the most popular initiatives within school districts across the country. Some educators are well versed with implementing RTI, while others are becoming more familiar with the process. The good news about RTI is that components that comprise the model have been used in the classroom for years; in fact, most educators have been implementing principles related to RTI throughout their teaching career (Brown-Chidsey & Steege, 2005). Although key components of RTI have been used for years, important questions surround the model:

- Why did RTI become so popular two decades ago?
- What's the big idea about RTI?
- Why are states implementing this process now?
- How did we get to this point in education?
- What is the relationship between current educational policy and RTI?

A discussion on how we have gotten to this point in education—with regard to accountability measures and emphases placed on scientifically based instructional strategies—begins with the *Nation at Risk* (The National Commission on Excellence in Education, 1983) report, perhaps the most devastating report on education in America's classrooms that was issued in the 1980s.

A NATION AT RISK REPORT

All, regardless of race or class or economic status, are entitled to a fair chance and to the tools for developing their individual powers of mind and spirit to the utmost. This promise means that all children, by virtue of their own efforts, competently guided, can hope to attain the mature and informed judgment needed to secure gainful employment and to manage their own lives, thereby serving not only their own interests but also the progress of society itself.

—*The National Commission on Excellence in Education (1983, p. 4)*

In 1981, the secretary of education, T. H. Bell, instructed the National Commission on Excellence to examine the performance of students in schools nationwide and to create a report based on its findings. Secretary Bell requested that the commission make the report accessible not only to him but also to the American people. He recommended that the commission publish the report no later than 18 months from his request. By 1983, the report was ready for publication, and T. H. Bell and the American people had to bear the devastating news. The United States was a nation at risk (The National Commission on Excellence in Education, 1983).

The commission's report confirmed the beliefs of most Americans that the education in our school systems was not adequately preparing our children and youth to compete with their peers globally. The report showed that approximately 13% of our 17-year-old students were functionally illiterate, SAT scores were decreasing, and students entering college were required to take a number of remedial courses to prepare them for postsecondary education (The National Commission on Excellence in Education, 1983).

As indicated as a risk factor, the report explained that perhaps 40% of minority students were functionally illiterate at the time the report was released. From the data that showed how poorly students of color performed, accountability factors were created to ensure that all students, including students from diverse backgrounds, achieve and thrive in the classroom. Although researchers spoke to the need to improve performance among African American students prior to 1983, it was the *Nation at Risk* report—and the standard and accountability movement—that generated nationwide discussion around setting goals and improving performance among students of color. The federal government's response to the commission's report has created a paradigm shift in the field of education, a shift that had begun gradually but has made marked changes in the way educators are required to provide instruction in the classroom. To be sure, the *Nation at Risk* report did not singlehandedly change the discourse of education in America; rather, it was the impetus that catapulted change.

EDUCATION LEGISLATION

The No Child Left Behind Act of 2001 (NCLB) and the Individuals With Disabilities Education Act of 2004 (IDEA) are important educational laws that explain, in part, how we have gotten to this point in education.

No Child Left Behind Act (2001)

The NCLB is a policy initiated by the federal government to hold educators accountable for the educational success of not only high achievers but also of low achievers, students with disabilities, and students who come from low-income and culturally diverse backgrounds. The intent of the NCLB legislation is to implement a comprehensive educational strategy to bring all students to a "minimum level of competency" (Kirk, Gallagher, Coleman, & Anastasiow, 2012, p. 36), in an effort to leave no child behind in the process. The mandate holds educators accountable by measuring the success of students—based on test scores—who attend public schools; schools that do not demonstrate academic gains over time run the risk of losing federal funds. To this end, all states require public schools to assess student progress in the areas of reading and math in Grades 3 through 8 and at least once during Grades 10 through 12; schools must measure student progress in science at least three times—once during Grades 3 to 5, Grades 6 to 9, and Grades 10 to 12 (National Center for Education Statistics, 2003).

As mentioned, the intent of NCLB is to ensure that all students, including those from low socioeconomic and diverse backgrounds, will achieve high standards. Moreover, this mandate was to change the culture of America's schools by emphasizing accountability and scientific, research-based instruction. But for many parents of color, the NCLB initiative has become another medium that shows how poorly students of color perform in relation to many European and Asian American students.

Individuals With Disabilities Education Act (2004)

The IDEA is the reauthorization of the Education for All Handicapped Act of 1975 (Public Law [PL] 92–142), which is the original law that required schools to provide specialized services for students with disabilities (Kirk et al., 2012). This act (PL 94–142) emphasized six key service provisions: (1) zero reject, (2) nondiscriminatory evaluation, (3) individualized education program, (4) least restrictive environment, (5) due process, and (6) parental participation.

1. Zero reject

Zero reject explains that all students with a disability should receive a free and appropriate education (FAPE). This means that the education must be provided free of charge to the student and must address the student's needs as appropriately as possible (there have been many debates and court cases regarding what is *appropriate* for students with disabilities).

2. Nondiscriminatory evaluation

Nondiscriminatory evaluation means that all students have the right to receive a full evaluation surrounding all areas of suspected disabilities, including academic, social-emotional, and cognitive functioning, prior to being placed into special education services. An essential component of nondiscriminatory evaluation includes testing students with instruments and tools that are appropriate for the student's age, culture, and language.

3. Individualized education program

All students who qualify for specialized services must be provided an individualized education program (IEP). This document must specify the identified disability, goal(s), and strategies on how to help the student achieve in the classroom.

4. Least restrictive environment

Least restrictive environment explains that students with disabilities must be educated, to the greatest extent possible, in classrooms and spaces with students who do not have disabilities.

5. Due process

Due process refers to legal procedures that take place to ensure fairness when making decisions about specialized services.

6. Parental participation

Parental participation explains that all legal guardians/parents have the right to participate in the decisions of special education services; parents are a part of the educational team and assist with making decisions about IEPs. The law explains that parents have the right to access student records.

The Education for All Handicapped Act (PL 94–142) is now called the Individuals With Disabilities Education Act (IDEA); the above six components (of PL 94–142) remain key provisions of the IDEA and continue to lay the foundation for specialized services for students who require additional support in the classroom (Jacob & Hawthorne, 2007).

RTI PRINCIPLES ARE NOT NEW

Although the NCLB and IDEA of 2004 are federal regulations that high-light instructional strategies consistent with RTI principles, the idea of conceptual grouping based on student needs did not arise from these legis-lations. Rather, conceptual grouping strategies based on student needs were foundational in Deno's (1970) cascade model. Deno's model was used as a special education service delivery initiative during the 1970s and 1980s. In his model, Deno emphasized appropriate instruction in the least restrictive environment, with additional support provided to students who continued to demonstrate limited growth (Brown-Chidsey & Steege, 2005).

Throughout the 1980s, instructional strategies included placing students in increasingly smaller groups and tailoring academic instruc-tion based on student needs. Deno's (1970) cascade model emphasized grouping strategies, but the NCLB and IDEA of 2004 are responsible for the emphasis placed on accountability, scientifically based practices, and appropriate instruction in the classroom.

EDUCATIONAL POLICY AND RTI

For years, educators have used components of the RTI model, including differentiating instruction by skill level. But RTI, as a scientific problem-solving model and identification system used to determine special educa-tion eligibility, did not gain momentum until the NCLB and the reauthorization of the IDEA of 2004. These two educational policies place emphases on *scientifically based instruction* to increase performance among all students and support the use of RTI within the classroom (Meyers, Meyers, Graybill, Proctor, & Huddleston, 2012). For example, the reauthorization of the IDEA of 2004 places great emphases on evidence-based instruction, "including (1) a requirement for the use of scientifically based reading instruction, (2) evaluation of how well a stu-dent responds to intervention, and (3) emphasis on the role of data for decision making" (Brown-Chidsey & Steege, 2005, p. 18). In addition, the IDEA of 2004 places emphases on using evidence, scientifically based instruction, reliable data, and a student's response to instruction to understand achievement and performance.

Consistent with the language in the IDEA of 2004, many school dis-tricts now refer to response to instruction and intervention to identify and determine the need for special education services surrounding learning disabilities rather than relying solely on IQ and achievement tests to deter-mine eligibility. Thus, educational policy—the NCLB, with its emphasis on scientifically based instruction, and the IDEA of 2004, with its emphasis on evidence-based and appropriate instruction—has changed the way educators provide services for students in the classroom, and educators nationwide are using RTI principles, including prevention and intervention, to provide the greatest support for students the moment they enter the classroom. Moreover, when considering learning disabilities, special education team members can now make students eligible for special services based on how students respond to evidence-based strategies—or appropriate instruction—over time, rather than by IQ and achievement scores that are usually determined within a few hours.

CHAPTER SUMMARY

During the 1980s, the American people received devastating news: The United States was a nation at risk. *A Nation at Risk* (The National Commission on Excellence in Education, 1983) shed light on the poor performance among children in America's classrooms, including students of color. The report showed that many students were functionally illiterate, SAT scores were decreasing, and students enrolled in college were unprepared to take college-level courses. In addition, this report showed that the process of teaching and learning in the classroom required drastic changes. Two of the most significant educational policies that are responsible for making changes to the ways educators are required to teach in the classroom—if they are to receive federal funds—are the No Child Left Behind Act of 2001 and the Individuals With Disabilities Education Act of 2004. These two policies place emphases on *accountability, data-based decision making, scientifically based instruction,* and *appropriate instruction* in the classroom. States are now referring to RTI principles to provide best practices in the classroom and to meet the requirements set forth in the NCLB and the IDEA of 2004; also, states are now using student response to instruction over time to make decisions about special education eligibility—rather than relying solely on IQ and achievement scores.

In the next chapter, I define RTI, discuss the basic idea and components of the model, and provide concrete examples of how the process should look within the classroom, using scientific and evidence-based instructions and interventions.

Response to Intervention 2

Let yourself be guided by your pedagogic interventions, especially by the observations you have made on the results of the former intervention.

—*Alfred Adler*

RTI is the topic of discussion in most school districts across the country. When I go to school psychology and special education conferences, RTI is discussed more than any other topic. In fact, the best way to start a conversation with someone at these conferences, after having introduced yourself, is something like this: "So how is the RTI process in your district?" This question could easily lead to an hour-long conversation.

In the first edition of this book, I did not go into great detail about the process of RTI. I believed that there were enough books on the market that explain the process of RTI, including important components that comprise the model. For many reasons, I believed that teachers were tired of hearing about the "triangle" and components that make up the model. I was wrong! Superintendents, principals, teachers, school psychologists, and professors from across the country responded to my initial work with questions surrounding basic principles of RTI. I have received an array of emails with questions about Tier 1 instruction, along with Tier 2 and Tier 3 interventions. In addition, educators have asked for concrete examples of how to integrate culturally relevant instruction at the Tier 1 level; they have also requested step-by-step approaches to creating culturally relevant RTI models. Important questions surrounding response to intervention include the following:

- What exactly is RTI?
- What are the basic components of RTI at each tier?

- How many tiers should RTI include?
- Are RTI principles effective at identifying students who might have a learning disability?

From my initial work, my inbox was flooded with questions about basic principles of RTI and how to use the model to support the needs of culturally diverse students. For example, the following is an email from a school psychologist who practices in New York:

> I've been very intrigued by RTI and have tried to learn about it. Also, my district's student body has consisted of more children learning English as a second language as well as larger numbers of African-American children in the past 15 years. Again, it's something I strive to learn more about.

Emails such as the one above are invigorating for me because they show that educators are buying into RTI and seeking additional support in creating effective strategies for all students, including African American students and students who are learning English as a second language. This edition, in part, is a response to the many questions I have received surrounding RTI and creating culturally relevant models. The many responses imply that there is great need to flesh out the concept of culturally relevant RTI models and to provide step-by-step approaches to creating such practices for teachers to implement within K–12 education and for professors to use as a guide throughout teacher training programs.

BASIC CONCEPT OF RTI

RTI is a *prevention, intervention,* and *identification* school-based support model ("Response to Intervention," 2012). Educators use RTI principles to *prevent* academic failure, to *intervene* when students show signs of being at risk for failure, and to *identify* students who may require special education supports. Although it has many purposes and definitions, the main goal of RTI is to "prevent long-term debilitating academic failure" (L. S. Fuchs & Fuchs, 2009, p. 41).

A review of books and articles on RTI will show that there is much variability in how districts implement the model across states. Most states use a three-tiered support model and consider students for special education services when data show that students have made minimal progress with intensive interventions at the third tier; special education considerations would represent a fourth tier (Berkeley, Bender, Peaster, & Saunders, 2009).

Other districts use a two-tier approach (Collier, 2010) and consider students for special education services after minimal progress after the second tier; thus, special education considerations within this framework would represent the third tier. Although the three-tiered approach (prior to special education services) is most common, some states have used as many as six tiers (D. Fuchs, Fuchs, & Compton, 2012). However, D. Fuchs, Mock, Morgan, and Young (2003) explain that RTI models lose their "potency" and effectiveness when they comprise many levels or tiers. They explain that "the greater the number of levels [tiers] the less practical RTI becomes" (p. 168).

To emphasize *instruction* in RTI, many districts identify their models as a response to *instruction* and intervention (RTII) (Collier, 2010). Nonetheless, states are consistent with the concept that approximately 80% of the general education student population will respond positively to research-based instruction, whereas 20% of the general education student population will require additional support to learn academic content, even when provided scientific research-based instruction.

As explained previously, educators have been using components that make up the RTI model for years (Bender & Shores, 2007). For example, teachers of one-room schoolhouses were challenged with teaching students of different abilities and skills, and they differentiated reading, writing, and arithmetic instruction to meet academic needs (Tomlinson, 1999). School districts across the country have emphasized the importance of reporting student progress throughout the school year, and when deficits were noted, teachers provided additional support (Moe, 2001).

The difference between one-room schoolhouse instructional strategies and current RTI practices is that educators are now required to take a much more scientific approach to teaching and learning in the classroom. Instead of providing assessments at the end of a unit, quarter, or semester, the concept of RTI emphasizes universal screenings to identify students who might be at risk for reading; educators *screen* students at least three times a year— at the beginning of the year (BOY), middle of the year (MOY), and end of the year (EOY)—monitor progress, and make educational decisions based on data collected from screenings and student progress.

IDENTIFYING STRUGGLING STUDENTS PRIOR TO RTI MODELS

Prior to the current, scientific approach to education, most students received instruction in general education classrooms, but when students demonstrated academic or cognitive (thinking) deficits, they were immediately referred for special education, administered academic and IQ tests, and usually qualified as students with a disability (Mellard & Johnson, 2008). Even more, when evaluated for special education services, if a student's academic scores (which measures reading, writing, and math skills) and IQ scores (which measures verbal and perceptual reasoning, working memory, and processing speed using cultural information) were commensurate, then he or she would not qualify for specialized support (Fletcher, Lyon, Fuchs, & Barnes, 2007).

The interpretation of such IQ achievement (ability-performance) discrepancy profiles was that students were performing up to their abilities—that since their IQs were low, it would make sense that their ability to reason using letters, numbers, and academic content would also be low; it was believed that because of their low "IQs," students processed information slower than their peers and had deficits in their ability to retain information (using working memory and long-term memory), which was believed to be evident in low reading, writing, and math skills. In other words, researchers believed that a student's IQ was an indication of how much information the student could learn. This idea became known as the *milk-and-jug thinking* (Share, McGee, & Silva, 1989).

Consider, for example, the reasoning of Cyril Burt (1937):

Capacity must obviously limit content. It is impossible for a pint jug to hold more than a pint of milk and it is equally impossible for a child's educational attainment to rise higher than his educable capacity. (p. 477)

This way of thinking influenced educational practices and provided very few opportunities for students who scored low on an IQ test. Based on their low IQ and low achievement scores, students were *expected* to perform below standards and were identified as slow learners; their low skills were directly related to their low IQs. Unlike RTI processes and current scientific approaches to teaching and learning, many educators did not consider appropriate instruction, learning styles, and cultural or environmental factors that created barriers to learning.

The problem was solely the students' inability to learn. More specifically, it was a brain capacity problem. Thus, although students struggled to read, they remained in the general education classroom without additional support—and it goes without saying that these youngsters fell further and further behind as the quarter and semester progressed.

STUDENTS WHO EVENTUALLY QUALIFY FOR SPECIAL EDUCATION SERVICES

When reassessed months or years later for special education services, many students would qualify for services because their academic scores would be well below their cognitive ability scores. The reason for the difference in their pre– and post–special education evaluation performance was, although students would use their cognitive abilities daily (which would explain the consistency with cognitive abilities), they would miss out on multiple hours of instruction due to their inability to keep up with the lessons in the classroom (which would explain their lower academic scores). This process has been described as the "aptitude-achievement discrepancy" (Fletcher et al., 2007, p. 31); others have described it as the "wait-to-fail" model (Brown-Chidsey & Steege, 2005, p. 2).

When students perform below expectations, important questions arise, questions that the discrepancy model failed to address.

- Did the student receive appropriate instruction in reading and math?
- Was instruction differentiated by content, process, and product?
- Was instruction differentiated by culture—meaning, was instruction culturally relevant?
- How long did the student receive additional support in the area with which he or she struggled?
- Was the student indeed a slow learner, or did he or she have a disability?

With RTI, students are not required to show a discrepancy between their academic skills and cognitive abilities prior to receiving intensive support. They simply need to show difficulty learning when presented with scientific, research-based instruction, and consistent with their needs, students would receive progressively intense instruction as they move through tiers.

MOVING STUDENTS THROUGH TIERS: A THREE-TIER APPROACH PRIOR TO ELIGIBILITY

The process of implementing RTI begins with high-quality instruction provided to all students within the general education classroom (Mellard & Johnson, 2008). Actually, "RTI activities begin and end in general education," which is why the model has been phrased a "general education initiative" (Brown-Chidsey & Steege, 2005, p. 10). In this sense, Tier 1 is synonymous with general education, and all students within the classroom receive the same research-based, *core* curriculum.

Consider the following scenario to understand how RTI would look within an elementary classroom upon the start of the academic school year. Pay particular attention to the difference between the RTI approach and the aptitude-achievement discrepancy approach described above.

Scenario

Upon her return from summer break, Ms. Johnson, a third-grade teacher at Springhill Elementary School, began instruction in her classroom with get-to-know-you activities for her students. She allowed her students to share experiences from their summer break. Eventually, Ms. Johnson integrated math, reading, and writing instruction throughout the day. Instruction was aligned with state standards, was research based and appropriate, based on her knowledge of the students. She implemented a research-based reading program as her "core" reading curriculum. Her program was evidence based and was shown to be a highly effective reading curriculum for third-grade students (as evidenced by What Works Clearinghouse [WWC]).

Ms. Johnson was careful not to screen her students in the areas of reading and math during the first few weeks of school; she understood that screening students immediately upon return from summer break might falsely identify students as at risk. After all, many of her students were vacationing and enjoying their break with families and friends; they probably dedicated very little time to reading and computing numbers.

Throughout the weeks, children became comfortable with each other, and Ms. Johnson continued her instruction through activities; she paid special attention to students who struggled during academic games. Her goal was to help students transition from summer break back into the learning process. As Ms. Johnson concluded her lesson for that Friday afternoon, she was both anxious and excited for the following week, in which she was required by her district to provide the BOY screening for reading fluency. Ms. Johnson looked forward to assessing her students, although she knew that some scores would reveal a false sense of academic need.

BOY Outcomes

After the BOY screening, Ms. Johnson identified students who were at risk—students who scored below the 25th percentile on the reading AIMsweb measures—and documented their performance. Interestingly, Ms. Johnson did not refer these students for Tier 2 services immediately. Rather, she

(Continued)

(Continued)

provided rigorous interventions within the classroom, aligned to their needs (based on her screening), and monitored their progress weekly for 5 to 6 weeks. From this practice, she noticed that many of her students who read below standards (from the BOY screening) made tremendous progress within weeks; other students continued to show very little progress at the end of the 6 weeks. Ms. Johnson shared with her problem-solving team (grade-level team) the lack of progress among students who continued to struggle. Based on the students' BOY and 5 to 6 weeks of progress monitoring data, the team made the recommendation to provide Tier 2 supports for these students.

Key components at Tier 1:

1. Rigorous (research-based) core curriculum (WWC provides many evidence-based programs)

2. Universal screening to identify skill levels and students at risk: curriculum-based measures (CBMs) and Dynamic Indicators of Basic Early Literacy Skills (DIBELS)

3. Tier 1 intervention within the classroom: repeated readings with appropriate text to supplement core curriculum; classwide peer tutoring

4. Progress monitoring to identify gains made from core curriculum and intervention: CBMs

5. Data-based decision making to determine if student needs are met or if additional support is needed

Recommended screening dates (Chidsey & Steege, 2005, p. 67):

- BOY assessment date range: September 15 to October 15
- MOY assessment date range: January 1 to 31
- EOY assessment date range: May 1 to 31

Question to consider: Why didn't Ms. Johnson immediately recommend Tier 2 services the moment she noticed that her students were performing below standards?

Answer: She wanted to ensure that their underachievement was not due to lack of instruction during summer school break but was a real indicator of a possible risk factor. She provided interventions for these students, and when they did not respond, she brought them to the attention of her grade-level team members and made decisions based on data.

Tier 2 Supports

Because Ms. Johnson's students did not respond well to the core curriculum at the Tier 1 level and supplemental reading instruction, Ms. Johnson and her team decided to provide Tier 2 supports. It is important to note that, although students often leave the classroom to receive additional instruction, Tier 2 should not be viewed as a place or location. Rather, Tier 2 supports should be viewed as additional services—sometimes 30 additional minutes of intervention time—that are paired with the core curriculum. To be sure, Tier 2 is a level of support in which students receive rigorous interventions, within small groups, consistent with their skill deficits.

Tier 2 Intervention Outcomes. From the 12-week research-based reading intervention offered at this level, paired with the general education "core" curriculum, half of Ms. Johnson's students made tremendous progress. They attained their goals and met grade-level reading fluency benchmarks. Based on their progress, the team decided to discontinue Tier 2 interventions within small groups and return these students to the Tier 1 level, where they would continue to receive the core instruction only. One student within the group made steady progress, but his progress was not significant enough to return to Tier 1, so the team members decided to continue with Tier 2 interventions.

Other students who were receiving Tier 2 interventions within small groups for 12 weeks made very little progress over time. Some of these students remained at Tier 2 but were provided a different intervention, while others were moved on to Tier 3 supports.

Key components at Tier 2:

1. Core instruction from Tier 1 aligned to standards

2. Appropriate, research-based intervention (9–12 weeks in duration; at least 3 weeks)

3. Small instructional group three to four times a week for 30 to 40 minutes per session (two to five students per group)

4. Progress monitoring (twice a month; recommendations vary)

The goal of Tier 2 is to develop skill deficits (based on progress monitoring data) and to assist students with meeting grade-level benchmarks (return to Tier 1).

Tier 3 Supports

Based on progress monitoring data from Tier 2—which consisted of 9 weeks of intense interventions (two different interventions provided within groups of five students)—Ms. Johnson and the grade-level team agreed to move a few students to Tier 3, where they would receive highly intensive and targeted support. After rounds and rounds of highly intensive intervention support within a small group (one to two students), progress monitoring data showed very little progress. Based on the data, the team made the decision to refer these students for special education services. The team considered eligibility for special education services within the area of reading fluency disability (specific learning disability).

Based on the evaluation results, including RTI data, the team created an individualized education program (IEP) for these students and identified academic goals, accommodations, and modifications based on the needs of the students.

Key components at Tier 3:

1. Core instruction from Tier 1 aligned with standards

2. Appropriate, research-based intervention (9–12 weeks in duration; at least 3 weeks)

3. Small instructional group three to four times a week for 60 minutes per session (one to two students per group—or two separate groups of 30-minute sessions; districts vary on how many students are placed in groups at the Tier 3 level)

4. Weekly progress monitoring

5. Possible special education referral

The above scenario provides examples of how teams could move students through a three-tiered RTI model prior to referring students for special education services. As mentioned, some states endorse two-tiered models and refer students for special education services if progress monitoring data show that students have not made appropriate gains with Tier 1 supports and Tier 2 interventions.

Compare the above RTI approach to the discrepancy model approach discussed earlier. With RTI, students receive intensive support while moving through tiers, whereas with the discrepancy approach, if students demonstrate commensurate skills and abilities—such as low reading skills and low IQ—then they are regarded as slow learners and do not receive specialized support. With RTI, team members provide a core reading program, along with increasingly intensive interventions in the areas of concern. From this process, team members usually have a wealth of data surrounding a student's response to research-based intervention, along with core instruction in the classroom, and are better able to determine if a student is merely a slow learner or if there might be a presence of a specific learning disability. This process also helps team members determine if the cause of underachievement is related to poor instruction.

CONTROLLING FOR CULTURE PRIOR TO CONSIDERING SPECIAL EDUCATION SERVICES

Notice how, in the above model, Ms. Johnson and grade-level team members did not integrate culturally relevant instruction at the Tier 1 level or across tiers prior to referring students for specialized services. This is an important point to consider as it sets the tone for discussion questions in subsequent chapters regarding appropriate and inappropriate instruction for students of color. In addition, this point is worth considering as most RTI models emphasize *skill-focused* interventions, such as in the case above (reading fluency), and place little emphasis on *process-focused* interventions, a concept that we will address in later chapters.

CAVEATS PRIOR TO MOVING AFRICAN AMERICAN STUDENTS THROUGH TIERS

In this book, I encourage educators to adopt the three-tiered approach to RTI when considering culturally relevant models and when putting students of color through tiers. The reason is educators must provide ample opportunities for students to learn. As mentioned, the basic concept surrounding RTI is that approximately 80% of the general education student population will respond well to scientifically based instruction, whereas 20% of the general education student population will require additional support. A critical question is, within the 20% of students who do not respond well to Tier 1 instruction, what percentage have learning issues and processing deficits that truly require specialized support?

The Individuals With Disabilities Education Act of 2004 (IDEA), which is law that governs special education eligibility (see Chapter 1 for a review of IDEA), allows team members to qualify students for a learning disability in the areas of basic reading, reading fluency, reading comprehension, mathematical calculation, mathematical problem solving, written expression, oral expression, and listening comprehension. Of the 20% of students who did not respond well to Tier 1 instruction, it is assumed that 5% or less will be identified as students with learning disabilities. That is, it is believed that approximately 15% of the 20% might respond well to evidence-based interventions, whereas 5% of the general education student population will require specialized support, including accommodations and/or modifications in the classroom to account for their learning deficits. They will require an IEP with goals aligned with their academic deficits.

When considering the 20% of students who do not respond to Tier 1 instruction, important questions are the following: Why are these students nonresponders? What are their needs? How could instruction be differentiated for these students to increase academic motivation and engagement in the classroom?

From my experiences, problem-solving team members believed that certain students had learning disabilities without sufficient data to support their conclusions. The most common response I would hear was, "Dwayne, look at his scores. He is performing below grade level." My responses to these statements were always the same: "Okay, now that we know he is performing below grade level, let's seek to understand why." This is perhaps the most common response I provide to team members when a member explains that a student might have a learning disability. As I often explain to team members, underachievement does not always indicate the presence of a disability. It is critical that educators and team members do not predetermine special education eligibility without data that show the need for specialized services. This practice is both inappropriate and against the law (IDEA).

Most students who struggle academically do not need drastically different supports in the classroom than their general education peers; rather, they need more time to learn instruction (hence, the emphasis on a three-tiered approach prior to referrals), in smaller groups. In addition, they need instruction tailored to their learning styles. Hierck and Weber (2014) sharpen this point. They explain that when students struggle in the classroom, specialists and assistants may aid teachers by providing interventions that are "qualitatively different from the initial instruction" (p. 7); they explain that "the key to this step is not teaching slower and louder, but rather using an alternative instructional approach and allocating more time" (p. 7). Their feedback is key to RTI implementation.

RTI models that incorporate a two-tiered level of support may include a 9- to 12-week intervention duration (Mellard & Johnson, 2008), whereas a three-tiered level of support may include 10 to 20 weeks (D. Fuchs et al., 2012) or more of an intervention duration prior to considering students for specialized support. Although school districts and states vary regarding the duration of support throughout tiers, students are usually referred for special education services or identified as needing specialized support when the data show that they have made minimal progress with intensive support.

One concern that I address with moving students through tiers is that, no matter how long we provide support, if the support is not catered to the students' sociocultural needs, interventions may not be effective. African American students place a high premium on relationships, harmony, and cooperation (Seiler & Elmesky, 2007). In a study conducted by Hamre and Pianta (2001), students who were rated negatively by their teachers performed worse in the classroom, whereas Stewart (2008) found that students performed better in math when their teachers praised them and provided positive interactive experiences. In addition, researchers have reported increased performance among African American students when movement and rhythmic activities were paired with instruction (R. T. Cunningham & Boykin, 2004).

If students are moved through tiers and receive interventions that focus on building academic skill in the absence of relationships, entertainment, and movement-expressive interventions, then they may not respond to skill-focused interventions at their highest potential. That is, they may not engage themselves at a level needed to learn and process information. Consequently, these students may move through tiers—because they are not engaged and motivated to learn from the skill-focused interventions—and eventually get referred for special education services. Engaging students at the earlier tier levels is critical because once they are referred for specialized services, they usually qualify as students with disabilities (D. D. Williams, 2012). For example, when school psychologists administer achievement tests and/or CBM to students who demonstrate academic deficits, students usually perform poorly on the test or measure in the areas with which they struggle. If students are not provided intensive instruction that is engaging to them, they will not apply themselves at the extent needed to learn the new material. This is one reason why many students who are referred for special education become eligible for services. Achievement tests do not measure potential; they measure current knowledge in a particular skill area, which, for many students of color, is usually underdeveloped because of prolonged periods of disengagement, not because of neurological problems.

When I administer achievement tests to students who are suspected of having a math disability, I often notice that many make simple mistakes, like confusing basic math facts. In other cases, they do not know basic math facts. As I watch them compute and write down the wrong answer, I usually wonder if these students received instruction surrounding math computation that was entertaining and stimulating—rather than receiving mundane, skill-focused interventions alone. I have evaluated high school students who have the ability to solve higher level thinking and reasoning questions in advanced math classes but will qualify for services because they have difficulty with simple math facts. At eligibility meetings, team members strongly agree that these students have math calculation disabilities based on math scores, other state standardized scores, and history of underachievement with calculating numbers. I always wonder at these meetings, What if these students were provided a math tutor who taught consistently to the students' needs and provided entertaining activities to assist with building math fact fluency? Would they be in this predicament? These questions are difficult to answer at most eligibility meetings because most interventions focus on skill-based interventions rather than process-focused interventions.

RTTR—RESPONSE-TO-TEACHER RELATIONSHIP

When a student does not respond to interventions, educators are encouraged to document the outcome and use a different intervention, move the student to another tier, or refer the student for specialized support. What most interventions do not address is the amount of time it takes to build and maintain relationships among teachers and students. Moreover, academic interventions do not measure the quality of relationship that teachers and students share; they do not measure student perceptions of their teachers. This point is important, considering research shows that there is a correlation between how students perceive their teachers and how they perform in the classroom (Hamre & Pianta, 2005; Hughes & Kwok, 2007; Murray, 2009). This is definitely the case with many African American students (Hamre & Pianta, 2001; Iruka, Burchinal, & Cai, 2010).

Students who have solid relationships with their teachers usually are compliant and apply themselves during instructional time; students who have poor relationships with teachers usually disengage during instructional time and demonstrate oppositional behaviors toward their teachers. Even more, some of these students do not care about referrals, detentions, suspensions, or phone calls to parents.

When asked what is the underlying problem that is causing them to perform poorly in the classroom, many have stated, "I can't stand [don't like] my teacher, she always. . . ." I have worked with many students with disabilities across grade levels who attribute their poor performance to dislike toward their case manager or resource teacher. As educators, we often ask, "Why would you let how you feel about your teacher determine your performance in the classroom?" We ask this question, but their responses are consistent with research in that the performance of students is often related to how they feel about their teachers. Thus, when we review data during problem-solving team meetings, are we reviewing a student's response to skill-focused instruction—as we usually think is the case—or are we reviewing a student's perception of his or her teacher?

"The numbers don't lie" is a common saying. Regarding performance in the classroom, are numbers—the data—actually reflective of poor relationships rather than ability and skill? If we do not address the quality of relationship between the student and his or her teacher, we cannot answer this question, and if this question is not considered prior to moving students through tiers, it is possible that we will continue to believe the student is oppositional and lacks skills. Stated differently, it is possible to refer to *deficit thinking* and *deficit models* when we do not consider the quality of relationship between the student and his or her teacher.

Considering many African American students place a premium on relationships, if their relationship with teachers is negative, then it does not matter how scientifically based a skill-focused intervention is; students may remain nonresponsive toward their teachers. This shows that, instead of documenting students' responses to interventions, the data might reflect students' responses to the relationship they have with their teachers. If team members document student responses to their poor relationship with teachers, RTI—for African American students—will be similar to using the discrepancy model: ineffective at addressing the root cause.

Effective culturally relevant RTI models require at least a three-tiered approach framework because it allows educators to identify learning styles, allows educators to implement culturally relevant instruction and interventions—such as relationship building and activities that incorporate movement-expressive activities that are aligned with student deficits—and provides needed time to respond to the support.

In the above examples with Ms. Johnson, special education team members qualified students for specialized services and created IEPs for these students, but prior to making students eligible, team members must ensure that the primary reason for underachievement is not due to cultural factors (IDEA). An important question is, what criteria should team members use to determine if underachievement is not a primary result of cultural factors when considering special education services for African American students? What kind of problem-solving model could team members use to compare traditional instruction with culturally relevant instruction to determine progress and effect sizes?

When considering culturally relevant RTI models, which is the focus of this book, differentiating for culture in the classroom is a critical component of appropriate instruction. Subsequent chapters speak to the need to create culturally relevant RTI models and the need to integrate research-based, culturally relevant instruction throughout tiers to engage all students behaviorally, emotionally, and cognitively. The pages that follow provide examples of important components to creating RTI models that integrate characteristics associated with African American culture, including step-by-step examples to guide you through the process.

CHAPTER SUMMARY

RTI has many definitions, but a common one is that it is a *prevention, intervention,* and *identification* model. RTI principles begin in the general education classroom, with general education teachers providing appropriate and evidence-based instruction. There are many types of RTI models, in that some states use more tiers than others. A commonly used multitiered approach is the three-tier model, in which students are referred for special education services if they do not respond to evidence-based interventions throughout the three tiers. Core components of the RTI model include the following:

- High-quality and appropriate instruction—including culturally relevant instructional strategies and scientifically based core reading programs
- Universal screening (at least three times a year)
- Evidence-based interventions
- Progress monitoring
- Fidelity to plan
- Data-based decision making

An essential feature of RTI is additional time. The idea is that most students who struggle academically do not require special education supports. Rather, they need more time to learn, in smaller groups, and provided solid instruction. In addition, many students may need to establish relationships with their teachers and feel valued among peers to engage themselves in the classroom at a high level.

In the next chapter, I discuss and define culturally relevant RTI (CR-RTI) models and discuss whether CR-RTI and traditional RTI models are similar or different. In addition, I provide a formula for creating CR-RTI models and shed light on three common myths that are associated with race and culture. I explain why it is most important for educators to identify and debunk these myths prior to creating CR-RTI models.

Culturally Relevant Response-to-Intervention (CR-RTI) Models

3

We try to make things relevant to the lives of our students culturally and by teaching timeless truths. This allows us to be on their field, their turf.

—*Jayson Samuel*

If you are like most administrators, educators, and parents, you may have heard of culturally relevant models but may not know exactly what they are or how they should look in the classroom. Important questions when considering culturally relevant RTI (CR-RTI) models include the following:

- What is the big idea surrounding CR-RTI models?
- Are CR-RTI models the same or different from traditional RTI models?
- What steps must I take to make my instruction culturally relevant?
- What key components are needed to begin this process?
- What knowledge must I have prior to creating these models?

PLAYING ON THEIR FIELDS—THEIR TURF

The quote that introduced this chapter speaks to the importance of entering the space of our students—being on their field and playing, or teaching, on their turf. Creating culturally relevant instructional models and strategies requires educators to identify the values, interests, and passions of their students and to use those characteristics as the foundation for learning; creating such models requires that educators teach on their students' turf—meaning making instruction student centered and using their values and passions to increase engagement. Often, when many students who come from culturally diverse backgrounds enter the classroom, they enter space where they are required to learn, interact, and adjust to cultural norms, values, and rules. They often are required to learn and play on the fields of their teachers, as teachers often create norms and rules based on their own cultural values.

Defining Culturally Relevant RTI Models

Culturally relevant RTI models, then, are models that integrate the values and cultural interests of students at the Tier 1 level, using their passions to empower and engage them throughout tiers. Because RTI is not a set of interventions but an evidence-based method of providing appropriate instruction to students, the cultural values of students—those values and interests that are embraced most—must be at the center of instruction, considered when problem solving, and documented as having been implemented *prior* to moving students through tiers. Thus, the practice of creating culturally relevant RTI models extends beyond simply creating academic strategies and interventions that might be relevant to the lives of students. Rather, CR-RTI is a process of problem solving within the context of the student's culture. This is in contrast to problem solving using one's own cultural values and worldviews and making sense of the student's behaviors from one's own background experiences. The latter is what often takes place during problem-solving meetings, when moving students through tiers, and when disciplining students for what we may call *behavioral infractions*—negative behaviors demonstrated during the school hours.

Considering RTI is an evidence-based method of providing appropriate instruction to all students, educators who implement CR-RTI models must pay particular attention to not only the cognitive aspect of engagement—such as processing information—but also the affective level (which deals with feelings), including creating an environment where students of color feel that they belong, feel that they are valued, and feel that relationships are as important as turning in assignments or doing well on tests. These concerns should be addressed prior to moving students through tiers and prior to referring them for special education services. This concept is consistent with the proverb that says, "You must first touch the heart before you can touch the mind."

To be sure, creating CR-RTI models requires teachers to get to know students on a personal level, a level that extends beyond traditional "teacher-student" relationships. This means teachers must be willing to work at creating relationships not only with students in the classroom but also with the parents and relatives of students, becoming interested in affairs of students—such as community activities and sports—and periodically asking the student how his or her family is doing. These interactions, for many students of color, and students in general, are how relationships are created and maintained.

CR-RTI MODELS ARE NO DIFFERENT FROM TRADITIONAL RTI MODELS

Having basic knowledge of the traditional framework of RTI is a prerequisite to creating culturally relevant models. The reason is CR-RTI models are no different from traditional RTI models. For example, the essence of RTI is providing *appropriate* and high-quality instruction for all students. An important question is, What does this mean? For culturally diverse students, appropriate instruction includes having opportunities to learn within the context of evidence-based, culturally relevant activities. Therefore, providing research-based instruction that focuses on improving academic skills—apart from culturally relevant instruction—may not be enough to engage culturally diverse students.

Rather, many African American students may require activities that integrate movement expressiveness, bonding, interdependence, sharing, and variability in the classroom to increase academic motivation and engagement. Moreover, some students may require classroom learning environments that emphasize communalism; they may require solid relationships with peers and teachers prior to learning.

Within any RTI framework, appropriate instruction includes scientific research-based, *skill*-focused instruction that is delivered in a manner that connects students to the lesson, based on the students' learning styles, prior knowledge, and cultural values. This definition places students at the center of teaching and learning by differentiating content based on their learning styles, interests, prior knowledge, and cultures. Notice that the definition does not focus only on scientific research-based instruction but also includes research-based practices that have been shown to engage students throughout the learning process. In other words, the definition highlights the need to differentiate instruction by culture and process (how instruction is delivered in the classroom). An emphasis is placed on culture, considering students learn through cultural lenses (Rogoff, 2003).

The latter definition is important, considering some districts interpret appropriate instruction by focusing primarily on providing scientific research-based reading and math "skill-based" instruction—instruction that is rooted in the five big ideas of reading and instruction, which are rooted in basic problem solving and calculation skills (Illinois State Board of Education [ISBE]). Such instruction focuses on skill-based instruction and interventions but does not place enough emphasis on the process of delivering such instruction in culturally appropriate ways. How teachers deliver their lessons is just as important as research-based instruction (D. D. Williams, 2012); delivery is key when engaging most students of color. In their article regarding culturally relevant RTI models, Klinger and Edwards (2006) state, "Our position is that we must ensure that children have received culturally responsive, appropriate, quality instruction that is evidence-based, but in order to be deemed appropriate, quality instruction and evidence based, it should be validated with the students with whom it was applied" (p. 109). Their position shows that simply providing scientific research-based instruction is not enough to be considered appropriate instruction.

There is no question surrounding the notion of scientific research-based instruction. More emphasis must be placed on *culturally relevant appropriate* instruction; in addition, as Klinger and Edwards (2002) explain, quality instruction should be based on whether it is evidence based and validated with students similar to those who were reported in the scientific study. In other words, if a "scientific research-based" program is shown to improve reading and math skills among 200 second-grade White students who come from middle-class backgrounds, we cannot be sure that this same "evidence-based" program will have the same effect on Black and Latino students—even if the program is implemented with fidelity and even if these Black and Latino students also come from middle-class backgrounds.

From my experiences with working in K–12 education, problem-solving coaches, principals, and team members have placed great emphases on evidence-based practices. Instead of glamorizing all evidence-based practices and believing that all programs will work with *all* students, from *all* backgrounds, we must ask with whom were the evidence-based practices effective? This requires an additional step prior to determining an intervention during problem-solving meetings. This question should also be addressed before determining that culturally diverse students are not responding to interventions and moving them through tiers. If this question is not addressed, it is possible that students will be moved through tiers and placed in special education services without having received appropriate instruction—instruction based on their own cultural, instructional, and learning styles.

Although districts focus on the five big ideas of reading when referring to appropriate instruction, if culturally relevant activities are not integrated with instructional practices, then we cannot say that we are providing services consistent with best practices. The reason is that "all practice needs to be culturally responsive in order to be best practice" (Moje & Hinchman, 2004, p. 321).

CULTURALLY RELEVANT INSTRUCTION

As CR-RTI is a process of placing the cultural values of students at the center of problem solving, *culturally relevant instruction,* within the context of CR-RTI, is a process of using the cultural values, interests, and passions of students to increase behavioral, cognitive, and affective engagement throughout tiers (see Chapter 7 for more on behavioral, cognitive, and affective engagement levels).

When I discus culturally relevant instruction during seminars, I usually ask educators if they integrate culturally relevant instruction in their classrooms and, if so, if they are willing to share with others what their instruction consists of. In response to this question, educators often explain that they never really thought about the impact culture plays in academic engagement. Educators who explain that they provide culturally relevant instruction often state that their instruction consists of talking about African Americans in a positive light and selecting books about Black characters written by Black authors.

These experiences usually lead to engaging discussions on the difference between (1) appropriate, culturally relevant instruction and (2) instruction that integrates Black characters and Black authors. Reading about Black characters and reading books written by Black authors are not examples of culturally relevant instruction. It is essential that, when considering culturally relevant instruction, we are careful not to conclude that race and culture are synonymous. Providing culturally relevant instruction is not synonymous with talking about Black people or reading the works of Black authors. Many Black authors have perspectives and worldviews that are consistent with Eurocentric values, values that may be in stark contrast to characteristics that are valued within the African American community.

The race of a teacher or author does not determine cultural relevance. For example, educators could present lessons on European philosophy and make the instructional theme culturally relevant. Thus, an important determinant of culturally relevant instruction would be based on how teachers provide the lesson and whether they integrate the instruction with characteristics that are valued within their students' culture(s). Notice that, in the latter example, the content surrounded European philosophy; the determinant of whether the lesson would be culturally relevant is based on how the lesson is delivered and the methods educators use to engage students. Questions that speak to the cultural relevance of the lesson include the following:

- Will educators require all students to work independently?
- If students become excited about a fact or draw a connection with the instruction and speak without raising their hands, will they receive a verbal consequence?
- Will students receive consequences for working with and helping their neighbors better understand a philosophical concept?
- Will students have to ask for permission every time they leave their desks?
- Will students be written up if, during independent seat time, they listen to music through their earpieces or headphones?
- If a student stands up and engages in a dance during independent seat work, will he receive a negative consequence?
- If a student makes a beat with his fingers on the desk, while working, will he receive a negative consequence?

Likewise, educators could provide a lesson on African philosophy and discuss the achievements of African American men and women—but if students are required to learn the content in ways that bore them, the instruction is not appropriate and is not culturally relevant. The content alone—African American achievements—does not make the instruction culturally relevant. Although racial group members may share similar skin complexions, hair textures, and vernaculars, they indeed have different experiences and values. Believing that we present culturally relevant instruction for African American students by simply presenting on African Americans is believing that racial group members are monolithic.

I have also found that many teachers believe that culturally relevant instruction is about creating an environment where students have opportunities to play, run around the classroom, dance while reciting facts, bop around in their seats, and interrupt teachers during instructional time. These are completely contrary to the research on culturally relevant instruction. Although students may demonstrate these behaviors, culturally relevant instruction should be orderly, structured, and purposeful.

Integrating culturally relevant instruction does not mean that the environment should be a place for chaos or that teachers should ensure that they create opportunities for students to play with peers while learning. This sort of environment could easily become disruptive. In fact, such an environment could become extremely dangerous, and students could injure themselves as they engage in entertaining, highly stimulating activities. If there is a myth surrounding culturally relevant instruction, it would be the belief that such instruction is nonstructural and without purpose.

FORMULA FOR CREATING CR-RTI MODELS

With RTI models, educators implement research-based instruction at the Tier 1 level, as well as research-based interventions throughout tiers; the same occurs with CR-RTI models. The integration of characteristics that are valued within students' cultures is what makes RTI models culturally relevant and most appropriate for engagement and learning. Thus, the formula for such models is as follows: *valued cultural characteristics among students + RTI framework = culturally relevant RTI (CR-RTI) models*. This model speaks to providing scientific research-based instruction *plus* differentiating instruction by the cultures of students. It is important to note that, when content is differentiated by culture, the interests of students are usually increased, as culture includes valued experiences, interests, and preferences among cultural group members (Diller, 2007).

Prior to considering culturally relevant models, educators must debunk myths that are related to race and culture to ensure that they do not create classroom practices that are stereotypical and prejudicial toward students of color. In addition, educators should be careful not to create practices with the mind-set that all Black students have the same cultural experiences, come from the same cultural backgrounds, and value the same characteristics. Prior to considering culturally relevant models, educators must acknowledge that there is much variability within all cultures and groups (Gottlieb, 2007; Sattler, 2008), including African American culture (Belgrave & Allison, 2014) in general and among African Americans in particular (Oyserman, Coon, & Kemmelmeier, 2002).

MYTHS RELATED TO RACE AND CULTURE

Boykin and Noguera (2011) highlight the following three myths that are associated with race and culture:

Myth 1: Race and Culture Are Synonymous

The first myth is the belief that race and culture are interchangeable such that if a student is Black, then she must come from Black culture. In the above example, teachers stated that their interpretation of culturally relevant instruction was consistent with the practice of reading books about Black people and/or reading books written by Black authors. As stated, just because a student is Black does not mean her cultural experiences will be synonymous to the Black characters that are in books written by Black authors; likewise, just because she is Black does not mean she will have the same cultural experiences as Black people within nonfiction books.

Race does not determine culture. Although race has been used to explain differences among people, social scientists now refer to culture to explain the variability that exists among human groups, including cultural variability, rather than referring to race alone (Diller, 2007). To be sure, race has many definitions, but most commonly, *race* has been defined as a "family, tribe, people, or a nation belonging to the same stock" (Merriam-Webster, 2003). Belgrave and Allison (2014) explain that the most identifiable characteristics of race include "skin color, facial features, and hair texture" (p. 104). Culture, on the other hand, encompasses beliefs and values that are shared and passed from one generation to another (see Chapter 7 for a discussion on culture and to learn how culture has been defined).

Myth 2: The Belief in Essentialism

The second myth is the belief in essentialism—the idea that group members have internal, innate traits that make them act in certain ways. An example of essentialism is believing that all Black people have rhythm, can dance, and prefer group membership over independence. Another example is believing that Black people are loud. These are myths in that some Black people have no rhythm, some can't dance, and some prefer to work in isolation and prefer autonomy over group bonding and group identity. Although it is true that some Black people are extremely loud and obnoxious, many are quiet and reserved. D. D. Williams (2012) provides an example of a problem-solving team member who was curious to know why Black students are so loud. The team member explained that in all of his years of teaching, the Black students he worked with were always loud and obnoxious. When we believe that students from certain racial backgrounds act in certain ways, we engage in essentialist beliefs (D. D. Williams, 2012).

To illustrate essentialist beliefs, consider the movie *White Men Can't Jump*. Throughout this movie, Billie Hoyle (actor Woody Harrelson) and Sidney Deane (actor Wesley Snipes) were street ball hustlers; they hustled people on the basketball court. It was the belief, among ball players in the movie, that White men were no good at playing basketball and that they "could not jump."

Although Billie hustled other ball players on the court, he initially had difficulty slam dunking a basketball. Throughout the movie, Billie made several attempts to prove that, although he was White, he could jump; ballers equated the term *jump* with being able to dunk a basketball. He failed on many attempts at dunking the basketball and lost tons of money in the process. By the end of the movie, he finally jumped high enough to dunk the basketball. His dunking the basketball debunked the myth that "White men could not jump." This movie beautifully portrayed the myth of essentialism—the belief that all group members have internal qualities within them that make them act a certain way or prevent them from doing certain things. Like the men in this movie, it is possible to hold essentialist views about students of color (as racial group members), their abilities, skills, and achievements. Thus, it is vital that team members receive professional development training and engage in book club readings surrounding the research on race and culture.

Myth 3: Culture Determines Behavior

The third myth refers to cultural determinism, which is the belief that culture determines how a person will think and act. Because culture is complex, it is common practice to associate behaviors with cultural values. For example, it is common to hear educators say that certain parents do not attend parent-teacher conferences or show up for individualized education program meetings because "their [family] culture does not value education." Similarly, theories have been created that explain that students who come from impoverished backgrounds think and act in ways that are consistent with the culture of poverty (Payne, 2001).

If educators do not identify and debunk myths related to race and culture prior to creating CR-RTI models, then it is possible that their practices and models will reflect stereotypes and prejudicial practices. If educators do not debunk these myths, it is possible that they will abuse culture, believe that all Black students will respond the same to certain instructional practices, believe that underachievement is a part of Black culture, and focus directly on skin color rather than learning styles and effective instruction.

CHAPTER SUMMARY

CR-RTI models place the values, passions, and interests of students at the center of instruction and problem solving. One of the most important components of RTI is the emphasis placed on "appropriate instruction." Thus, if RTI models do not integrate the cultural values, interests, and passions of all students—interests and values that have the potential to increase engagement—then such models cannot be defined as appropriate. Thus, although they are not distinct models, RTI and CR-RTI models are synonymous so long as they place students and their cultural values at the center of problem solving. It is inappropriate to move students through tiers without documenting that they have received appropriate instruction; moreover, it is inappropriate to move students through tiers and qualify them as students with disabilities without documenting that they have received instruction that has been culturally relevant and without placing their cultural values at the center of problem-solving models.

In the next chapter, I discuss theory that is associated with CR-RTI models and show the relationship between theory and best practices. In addition, I make connections between CR-RTI and Charlotte Danielson's evaluation system.

Theory and Culturally Relevant Models

4

There is nothing more practical than a good theory.

—*Kirk Lewin*

Prior to the 20th century, educators implemented models and provided instruction in the classroom based on personal preference and interest. Educators provided instruction consistent with their own learning styles and taught consistent with how their own teachers taught them. They also consulted with their colleagues to see what worked for students in other classrooms and attempted to integrate those strategies into their own practices (Moe, 2001). Long gone are the days when educators are allowed to teach reading, writing, and math based on personal opinion of what might work and opinions of what students should learn. States now require educators to teach based on standards, and the No Child Left Behind Act of 2001 (NCLB) calls for teachers to implement high-quality and scientific, research-based instruction. Thus, the emphasis placed on science within the teaching profession (high-quality instruction) has made drastic changes to how educators are required to approach teaching and learning in the classroom.

Often, when I present on culturally relevant RTI (CR-RTI) models, audience members ask questions surrounding whether such models are supported by research and whether there are studies that show the effectiveness of integrating cultural characteristics with instruction. Most educators explain that they are interested in learning such models, but although they have heard of culturally relevant instruction, they have not found evidence-based instructional practices that they could implement in the classroom. In addition to questions that surround evidence-based studies, educators have asked what theoretical framework supports culturally relevant models. This chapter addresses the importance of understanding theory that supports culturally relevant instructional models. Important questions surrounding theory within the context of CR-RTI models are the following:

- Does theory support the use of culturally relevant instructional models?
- Why must I become familiar with theory surrounding culturally relevant models and African American cultural characteristics?

IS THEORY PRACTICAL?

German psychologist Kirk Lewin was fond of saying, "There is nothing more practical than a good theory" (Lewin, 1952, p. 169). What Lewin meant was best practices begin with theory. Let's use psychology and education as examples. We now know the effectiveness of positive reinforcement and negative reinforcement based on theories surrounding animal and human behavior. The principle of positive reinforcement states,

> If, in a given situation, someone does something that is followed immediately by a positive reinforcer, then that person is more likely to do the same thing again when he or she next encounters a similar situation. (G. Martin & Pear, 2007, p. 30)

Research is replete with studies that show the effectiveness of positive reinforcement on behavior. In fact, although we may be unaware of it, most of the habits that we demonstrate were shaped and strengthened through positive reinforcers—things that reinforced our behaviors. We know the effectiveness of positive reinforcement based on theories that have been studied over time. From research, we know that, in most cases, the best way to maintain behavior is by reinforcing it.

Most educational theory and practices are rooted in psychology and behavior modification. This means that most of the practices that we enforce in schools—whether these are disciplinary or instructional—have theoretical roots in psychology. This makes sense, considering psychology is the study of human behavior, and as teachers and practitioners, our goal is to motivate and teach students by introducing reinforcers—entertaining strategies, praise, attention—in the classroom. At other times, our goals might be to modify behaviors that interfere with learning. Essentially, all that we call *best practice*—cooperative learning, peer tutoring, buddy reading, mentoring, repeated reading, positive reinforcement—is rooted in theories that were shown effective. Considering that our practices should be rooted in theory and research, an important question is, What theories support culturally relevant instruction? Although many theories pertain to culture and instruction, I will focus on the (1) constructivist approach to teaching and learning and (2) sociocultural-historical theories.

CONSTRUCTIVIST APPROACH

This book includes studies that show that when students of color are provided learning opportunities that integrate their interests, learning styles, and cultural values, their academic motivation increases, they become engaged academically, and their learning is enhanced. One reason for these positive outcomes is understood within the context of (1) *constructivist theory*, which is associated with the work of psychologists Lev Vygotsky and Jean Piaget, and (2) *cultural-historical theory*, which is primarily associated with Vygotsky's work.

Although Piaget and Vygotsky differed in their beliefs about how students construct knowledge, they both believed that students are active participants in their own learning (Bodrova & Leong, 2007). Students do not sit passively at their desks while teachers pour knowledge into their minds. Rather, students are active *constructors* who contribute to their own learning. Consistent with the idea of constructivism, when students are engaged in the learning process—or spend time constructing their own learning—they become engaged and achieve at high levels (Danielson, 2007).

A CLOSER LOOK AT VYGOTSKY'S AND PIAGET'S VIEWS ON CULTURE

Vygotsky believed that culture is at the heart of learning (cultural-historical theory). He placed an emphasis on culture and social interactions when constructing knowledge, an emphasis Piaget did not highlight. According to Vygotsky, students develop and learn through interacting with people within cultural environments and frameworks. Contrary to Vygotsky's views, Piaget placed emphases on objects, rather than people and culture.

In his later theories, Piaget acknowledged the importance of "social transmission" in development (Bodrova & Leong, 2007, p. 30), which emphasized the importance of people and culture in the process of cognitive development. Although he acknowledged the importance of culture,

Piaget believed people were secondary to objects, and he placed less emphasis on social and cultural factors to learning. Because Vygotsky's work placed emphases on people, social interactions, and culture, in the process of cognitive development and learning, his views lay a foundation to understanding the role culture plays in learning. The following is an example of implementing culturally relevant instruction from a sociocultural, constructivist approach.

1. Present information in a culturally relevant manner.

2. Allow students to use cultural experiences and prior knowledge to best understand and retain the information.

3. Help students construct more meaning from the information, using *their* personal and cultural experiences.

CR-RTI models are consistent with Piaget's constructivist theory, only as it applies to students constructing their own knowledge and being active participants in the learning process; CR-RTI models are consistent with Vygotsky's theories that place emphases on culture and social interactions that shape learning. In Vygotsky's views, students construct their own knowledge, and their construction is a sociocultural process that facilitates learning. As you will notice in the chapters that follow, when students were active participants in their own learning, and when their instruction was paired with cultural characteristics that reflected their values, students engaged and experienced success in the classroom.

CONSTRUCTIVIST THEORY AND CHARLOTTE DANIELSON'S EVALUATION SYSTEM

Danielson (2007) explains that much of the work involved in her evaluation system stems from constructivist teaching and learning. She says this about the constructivist approach:

> This orientation has become de rigueur in education circles and is reflected in many of the curriculum standards promulgated by both professional organizations and many states. (p. 15)

Many districts have adopted Danielson's teacher evaluation model. When I provide workshops for teachers and administrators, I explain that teachers who understand the constructivist approach to teaching and learning and who are able to teach students using this theoretical method are more prone to receiving high evaluation ratings when evaluated. The reason is clear: Danielson's evaluation model is rooted in this theory of academic engagement. For example, Danielson (2007) encourages teachers to involve students in their own learning and to use student background information to enhance engagement. She contrasts hands-on learning with "minds-on" learning and explains that students who retain knowledge are those who are cognitively engaged in the instructional task (p. 17); these students do not merely work with their hands to perform a task but rather engage their minds to construct knowledge and meaning. To this end, she places emphasis on students using their minds as tools to construct meaning from classroom instruction.

When students activate cultural knowledge while learning, they pull from their memory experiences with which they are most familiar. For example, if students are learning about science and chemicals, if they are encouraged to consider chemicals they use in their households—and chemicals that are used in barbershops and beauty salons—they may become more engaged cognitively because they would have background information to pull from. Their background knowledge will make the lesson more relevant and personal. In other words, the lesson will go from a simple standard to practices that are pertinent to family and racial group members. Now that we have addressed the importance of theory, let us now consider the concept of scientific, research-based instruction and how CR-RTI models fit within this paradigm.

CHAPTER SUMMARY

All good instruction begins as theories. Once theories are researched and shown effective, over multiple studies, they are then applied in the classroom. German psychologist Kurt Lewin said it this way: "There is nothing more practical than a good theory" (Lewin, 1952, p. 169). This means that theory and practice are interconnected; they are inseparable. CR-RTI models derive from constructivist theories, which explain that students learn best when they *construct* their own models using their interests, passions, learning styles, and worldviews. Students learn best when they use their minds to construct, or shape, their learning by using prior knowledge (cultural knowledge). This method of learning contrasts learning new ideas apart from their cultural experiences—or learning ideas solely from ideas and examples provided by teachers or examples that are provided at the end of book chapters. Charlotte Danielson's evaluation system embraces the constructivist approach to teaching and learning.

In the next chapter, I discuss and define scientifically based instruction and evidence-based instruction. I distinguish between these types of instruction and discuss how CR-RTI is both scientific and evidence based.

Scientific Research- 5
Based Instruction
and CR-RTI

Science is a way of thinking much more than it is a body of knowledge.

—*Carl Sagan*

There is no doubt about the stance the federal government takes on using scientific, research-based instruction for schools that receive federal funds. To be sure, researchers have counted the phrase "scientifically research-based instruction" over 100 times in the No Child Left Behind Act of 2001 (NCLB) (Hood, 2003; National Center for Education Statistics, 2003, p. 3).

Educators have questioned if the concept of culturally relevant RTI (CR-RTI) includes scientific research- and evidence-based instruction, and considering the importance NCLB places on research in the classroom, an answer to this question is warranted. This chapter addresses scientific and evidence-based instruction related to African American cultural values. Important questions surrounding scientific research-based instruction and strategies that integrate African American cultural values include the following:

- What is scientific research-based instruction?
- What is evidence-based instruction?
- What is the difference between scientific and evidence-based instruction?

- Have African American cultural characteristics discussed within this book been studied scientifically?
- Are there evidence-based studies that show the effectiveness of integrating African American cultural characteristics with instruction?

CULTURALLY RELEVANT RTI AND SCIENTIFIC RESEARCH-BASED INSTRUCTION

Are culturally relevant models truly scientific, or are these models perfect examples of pseudoscience—theories and ideas that do not have a scientific basis? To address these questions, let's consider how the NCLB legislation defines scientific research-based instruction and identify how culturally relevant models fit within the definition. To be considered "scientific," according to the NCLB, research must (Stanovich & Stanovich, 2003)

- employ systematic, empirical methods that draw on observation or experiment;
- involve rigorous data analyses that are adequate to test the stated hypotheses and justify the general conclusions;
- rely on measurements or observational methods that provide valid data across evaluators and observers, as well as across multiple measurements and observations; and
- be accepted by a peer-reviewed journal or approved by a panel of independent experts through a comparatively rigorous, objective, and scientific review.

The above criteria show that, according to the NCLB, simply because educational studies are published within journals or shared at national and state conferences does not mean they are scientific; a plethora of studies placed in journals and shared at conferences are pseudoscientific (Stanovich & Stanovich, 2003). To determine if a study is indeed scientific, according to the NCLB standards, Stanovich and Stanovich (2003) explain that educators should ask the following questions:

- Has the study been published in a peer-reviewed journal or by a panel of independent experts?
- Have the results of the study been replicated by other scientists?
- Is there consensus in the research community that the study's findings are supported by a critical mass of additional research?

In addition to scientific research-based studies, the use of evidence-based practices (EBPs) has received a tremendous amount of attention in education since the NCLB. Considering the importance of scientific research-based studies and the need to identify programs that have evidence of effective results, the U.S. Department of Education has funded the What Works Clearinghouse (WWC) to evaluate programs and to identify what works—that is, if studies have met the scientific research-based criteria associated with the NCLB and if they have produced effective and reliable outcomes for students (Hood, 2003). Although many programs and instructional strategies are considered evidence based, it is vital that teachers identify not only what works but also what works "with whom, by whom, and in what contexts" (Klinger & Edwards, 2006, p. 108). Important questions include the following: What students were involved in the study, and how did the students respond who were similar—in terms of race, class, gender, culture, and socioeconomic status—to the students in my classroom? Were African American students involved in the study that was determined effective? Were English language learners involved in the study?

SCIENTIFIC RESEARCH-BASED RESEARCH AND RTI

Now that we have background on how the NCLB defines scientific research-based instruction, let us determine if culturally relevant RTI models are scientific and evidence based. To be sure, we cannot answer this question without using criteria set out in the NCLB, for the standard by which we define instruction as scientific is determined by the law.

Prior to determining whether culturally relevant models are scientific, we must first determine if RTI is an evidence-based approach to increasing performance among students. We must consider the scientific basis of RTI because culturally relevant models are not stand-alone models. Rather, they are methods of delivering appropriate instruction within an RTI framework. To be sure, RTI is indeed an evidence-based approach to increasing performance in the classroom and reducing the number of students referred for special education services (Burns, Appleton, & Stehouwer, 2005; VanDerHeyden & Burns, 2005). Moreover, researchers found a significant difference in students who responded to early interventions and those who had difficulty responding; students who had difficulty responding to early interventions had severe deficits in phonemic awareness and fluency (Stage, Abbott, Jenkins, & Berninger, 2003; Vellutino, Scanlon, & Jaccard, 2003; Vaughn, Linan-Thompson, & Hickman, 2003). RTI was an effective approach to predict who would need intensive support with instruction.

RTI is not a canned program that educators implement within their classrooms. Rather, it consists of principles and components that are rooted in theory and research. At its core, RTI is all about differentiating instruction to meet the needs of all students by providing scientific research-based instruction through a multitiered approach (Hierck & Weber, 2014). Carol A. Tomlinson, who is the leading researcher on differentiated instruction, explains that differentiation is "a flexible approach to teaching in which the teacher plans and carries out varied approaches to content, process, and product in anticipation of and in response to student differences in readiness, interests, and learning needs" (Tomlinson, 2000, p. 10). In this context, *content* refers to what students are expected to learn; *process* refers to how teachers deliver instruction—the method in which teachers teach the content; and *product* refers to measuring what students learned from the instructional lesson (Tomlinson, 1999, 2000, 2001).

Often, all students are required to learn in the same fashion and are required to demonstrate mastery of learning by the same methods; they are rarely permitted to learn based on their own interests and demonstrate mastery of learning in culturally relevant ways (Boykin, Albury, et al., 2005). This was certainly the case for a sophomore student with whom I worked closely. This particular student, whom I will refer to as Anthony, was amazingly gifted and talented in the areas of writing music and making beats. He wanted to become a music artist. Upon hearing his recorded music, I told Anthony that it was interesting to learn that he didn't enjoy literature, considering he writes music well. His response: "Mr. Williams, I always try to incorporate music into my assignments and classes. I always ask my teachers if I could take the literature and write rhymes from the assignments to show that I understand the chapter content. My teachers won't let me. This is why the stuff is so boring—and to be honest, I could write something to the whole lit book in no time!" Although this young man was amazingly gifted with writing and confident in his ability to integrate his talents with instruction, he failed his literature courses. He was not engaged and grew to dislike literature. It is important to note that allowing students to demonstrate mastery in nontraditional ways does not mean that teachers should eliminate "testing" or "assessing." It simply means allowing students to demonstrate learning based on their interests, "in addition" to traditional testing and assessments.

When students are able to include their passions with learning, they will engage themselves during instructional time. Anthony is not alone in desiring differentiated instruction in the classroom; many of my students who struggle academically explain that they would "do more" if they could integrate music with their writing and lessons. As another example, during a cultural awareness book club session that I facilitated, I presented the concept of "differentiating by culture." Group members agreed that the majority of their African American students desired to listen to music in the classroom and to integrate hip hop within their writing. One teacher explained that she allows the students to integrate these interests only when the students demonstrate appropriate behavior in the classroom. The teacher explained, "We have a rule that if students enter the room quietly, get prepared to work, and work throughout the classroom period, I let them listen to music the last 15 minutes of the lesson and let them integrate hip hop with their homework assignments." Rather than rewarding students with music, educators could possibly prevent disengagement by allowing students to integrate their interests with instruction the moment they enter the classroom.

Notice that differentiating instruction is not RTI; it is a component of RTI. It is an evidence-based practice that should take place throughout tiers to meet the needs of students and extend beyond tiers to meet the needs of students who have disabilities that interfere with learning. Similarly, culturally relevant instruction is not RTI; it is a component of RTI. It is an evidence-based process of differentiating *what* we teach, *how* we teach (based on learning styles, interests, and cultural needs), and how we *measure* mastery of content.

Culturally relevant RTI, then, is a process of consciously identifying cultural values among students and differentiating instruction by content, process, and product to increase academic motivation. One way to look at this, and how I usually describe it to teachers is, culturally relevant RTI is a process of differentiating instruction by culture, within an RTI model. It is a process of cultural differentiation. When teachers differentiate their instruction by culture, they do not haphazardly throw together instructional strategies they believe might work for Black students (see myths associated with race and culture in Chapter 3), Latino students, or students who come from impoverished backgrounds. They do not make assumptions about what will work, and they do not rely on what worked with their previous Black and Brown students; rather, teachers invest in understanding their students on a personal level, including understanding their backgrounds, cultures, values, interests, and learning styles. They then integrate these experiences with instruction. This is the basic premise of RTI, which is a prerequisite of differentiating instruction. We cannot teach who we do not know (Belgrave & Allison, 2014). And we cannot establish and maintain solid relationships with students we do not value.

During seminars, when I ask educators to explain their thoughts on culturally relevant RTI, most refer to differentiating instruction by content. Many explain that it is a process of integrating books and lessons that focus on people of color, with a specific focus on the achievements of African Americans. I often explain that such practice is differentiating by *race*, not culture, unless these Black and Brown authors share the same experiences as the students in the classroom and if these experiences are highlighted in the books. There are many books written by Black authors who demonize those who value characteristics that are associated with African American culture; these "Black authors" do not identify certain characteristics as honorable and valuable.

Students must read books from Black authors and receive instruction surrounding African American contributions to science and the arts, just as they should read books that speak to their own cultures and ways of life. Because most educators would agree about the need to differentiate lessons by race (i.e., contributions of African Americans), I often focus on the process and product of differentiation for students who come from backgrounds that value characteristics that have been associated with African American culture.

I would argue that *cultural differentiation*—providing instruction in the classroom consistent with the cultural values of students—is perhaps the most difficult for educators for many reasons. Scholars who study education and equity explain that one reason is many teachers have limited training surrounding multiculturalism and are unprepared to serve culturally diverse students in the classroom (Gorski, 2009; Milner, Flowers, Moore, Moore, & Flowers, 2003). In addition, prior to entering the classroom, many new teachers have never occupied the same space—including attending the same school and living in the same neighborhood—as people of color (Reiter & Davis, 2011).

In his article "Cultural Applications: Ideas for Teacher Education Programs," Michael Bartone (2010), a White male teacher, provides examples of his experiences as a teacher unprepared to teach culturally diverse students. He explained that, prior to attending college in North Carolina and taking a teaching position at a school near Atlanta, Georgia, he had very little contact with people of color and lacked information surrounding African American culture. Michael initially attempted to teach consistent with Eurocentric classroom management strategies but soon found that they were ineffective. Initially, he did not differentiate by culture because he was unfamiliar with the cultural values of his students; rather, he taught based on his own understanding of what they might enjoy (Bartone, 2010). Because many educators are unfamiliar with the experiences of culturally diverse students, professional development is recommended to increase knowledge surrounding multicultural values.

DIFFERENTIATING INSTRUCTION BY CULTURE

Throughout this book, I highlight the need to differentiate instruction by culture and process. This simply means that within our RTI models, we must create activities that integrate cultural characteristics that are valued among all students, including students of color. Considering the emphasis placed on scientifically based research, best practices with regard to implementing RTI call for educators to refer to scientific research-based studies that not only speak to the culture(s) they wish to differentiate but also find research-based studies that are scientific—that is, studies that have undergone rigorous scientific procedures, including appropriate methodologies that meet the criteria associated with the NCLB as described above.

A. WADE BOYKIN

Because scholars explain that many educators are unfamiliar with culturally relevant instructional models (Howard, 2001) and the cultural experiences of African American students (Delpit, 1995/2006), I refer to Dr. A. Wade Boykin's work in this book as a key component to creating culturally relevant RTI models, as his work has undergone the rigorous and systematic processes that the NCLB speaks to and has been peer reviewed and replicated by other educators and researchers as indicated throughout this book. Through rigorous and systematic procedures, Boykin and colleagues have conducted repeated studies on the relationship between (1) academic engagement and (2) cultural characteristics that are valued among African American students.

Their research shows that academic engagement among African American students increased when culturally relevant approaches were integrated with instruction (Boykin, Coleman, Lilja, & Tyler, 2004; Ellison, Boykin, Tyler, & Dillihunt, 2005; Hurley, Allen, & Boykin, 2009; Hurley, Boykin, & Allen, 2005); their research also showed that the cultural values of many African American students clashed with the cultural values, rules, and norms of the school system (Boykin, Tyler, & Miller, 2005).

EVIDENCE-BASED PRACTICES USING CULTURALLY RELEVANT INSTRUCTION

Educators engage in EBPs when they refer to scientific research-based studies that address effective ways to engage students. EBPs refer to both (1) problem solving and (2) providing best practices in the classroom

(Hood, 2003; Muellen & Streiner, 2004). Thus, when educators review scientific research-based studies to learn about cultural characteristics that have been shown to increase engagement among culturally diverse students, they engage in evidence-based practices as they pertain to problem solving; when they *integrate* these cultural characteristics with instruction to increase engagement, they provide best practices. This two-part process—problem solving and best practices—of providing EBPs is essential to providing high-quality instruction and increasing engagement among culturally diverse students, especially when students are unmotivated and avoidant learners.

Although the concept of culturally relevant instruction is a new idea to many educators, Howard and Terry (2011) say, "There are at least three decades of theoretical and empirical work on culturally responsive teaching" (p. 347). Among other areas, scientific-based studies have examined the relationship between culturally relevant instruction and *mathematics* (Civil & Khan, 2001; Ensign, 2003; Gutstein, Lipman, Hernandez, & de los Reyes, 1997; D. B. Martin, 2000; Terry, 2010); *literacy, language arts, and reading* (Bell & Clark, 1998; Ladson-Billings, 1995b; Lee, 2001; Tate, 1995); and *construction of identity and academic achievement* (Nasir, 2000).

MOVING STUDENTS THROUGH TIERS WITH EVIDENCE-BASED PRACTICES

When moving students through tiers, it is critical that team members refer to EBPs that pertain to problem solving with culturally relevant strategies and interventions. Although there have been many changes to law and emphases on scientific and evidence-based instruction, very little has changed in how school districts serve students of color, including African American and Latino students. For example, when team members move students through tiers, they often use interventions without considering culturally relevant approaches to delivering the interventions. If students work more productively when listening to music, working interdependently, or having opportunities to move around while learning, these approaches to instruction should be used prior to determining that students have difficulty retaining information. It would be helpful to determine the kind of instruction students failed to respond to and compare their response to culturally relevant interventions. Culturally relevant instruction and interventions should definitely be used over time, prior to referring students for special education services.

CHAPTER SUMMARY

Researchers have counted the phrase "scientifically research-based instruction" more than 100 times in the NCLB law (Hood, 2003; National Center for Education Statistics, 2003). This shows that the federal government has placed great emphasis on using instruction that is supported by science. An important question surrounding CR-RTI models is, Are these models supported by science and research? The answer is yes, in that CR-RTI models are not stand-alone models. To understand how science supports CR-RTI, it is important to understand research that supports RTI. First, it is imperative to know that culturally relevant practices are not examples of RTI. Differentiated instruction is not an example of RTI. These are scientific and evidence-based *strategies* that have been shown to increase engagement among all students—which should be applied throughout the RTI framework. RTI, on the other hand, as defined as a problem-solving model that integrates differentiated, culturally relevant instruction, is indeed a scientific and evidence-based approach to increasing performance among students in the classroom. In other words, RTI is a framework that consists of evidence-based practices that have been shown effective in increasing performance among all students. It consists of differentiated, scientifically based instruction; ongoing screenings; goal setting; progress monitoring; and culturally relevant approaches to teaching and learning, among other evidence-based strategies. Many teachers explain that they desire to read articles that refer to culturally relevant instruction in the classroom. A good place to start with such articles is the works of A. Wade Boykin and colleagues.

In the following chapter, I provide a step-by-step approach to creating CR-RTI models and discuss the importance of ethnographic research in creating such models.

Step-by-Step Approach to Creating CR-RTI Models

6

Plan your goals and move step by step. Make your dreams true by action, passion, persistence, and dedication.

—*Anil Sinha*

Ihave received a tremendous amount of phone calls and emails from teachers, assistant principals, department chairs, and superintendents who have all asked where to start with creating RTI models that are culturally relevant for African American students. In response to this question, I always emphasize that, prior to creating models that consider cultural factors and culturally relevant instruction, educators must ensure that they do not create models that are stereotypical and prejudicial; they must identify and celebrate differences within racial group members and within cultures. Because the above question is common among emails and phone calls, this chapter provides a step-by-step approach to creating culturally relevant RTI (CR-RTI) models, which consist of five levels. Each level or component is rooted in best practices with working with students in the classroom. Important questions when creating culturally relevant models include the following:

- What steps are needed to create effective RTI models that consider African American cultural characteristics?
- Do race and culture play a factor in academic engagement?

- Is race a predictor of reading performance in elementary school?
- Why is it necessary to work through each component of the five levels?
- Why is it critical that we refer to the research on race and culture and their effect on engagement rather than rely on our own beliefs and experiences?

LEVELS OF CULTURALLY RELEVANT MODELS

In order for teachers to become competent with creating CR-RTI models, they must commit to working through each of the following five levels. If educators move through levels too quickly or move to a higher level, without understanding previous levels, they will be unprepared to integrate cultural characteristics with instruction, which is the theme of Level 5. Levels include the following:

1. Awareness

2. Research on culture and cultural characteristics

3. Ethnography

4. Observation

5. Implementation

Levels

Level 1—Awareness

The awareness stage of the model consists of becoming aware of the literature surrounding culture and the role culture plays in academic engagement. It is a process of becoming aware of myths surrounding race and culture. This level requires teachers to self-reflect. It also requires that teachers learn about core characteristics that are valued within their students' cultures. Important questions for teachers to consider at this level are as follows:

- What are my current beliefs surrounding race and culture?
- Do I believe race and culture matter in academic achievement?
- Do I hold biases about African American or Latino students?
- Do I believe most Black students are disruptive and noncompliant?
- Do I hold negative stereotypes about parents of color?
- Am I successful with working with unmotivated African American and Latino students?
- Do my classroom norms conflict with my students' cultural values?

Educators could ask an array of questions at this level to reflect on personal beliefs surrounding race and culture. Many teachers with whom I have provided training did not believe that race and culture are critical factors to engagement in the classroom. These educators were adamant in their beliefs about race and culture, and their beliefs were rooted in their own understanding, rather than on research. Level 1 of this model encourages teachers to compare their personal beliefs to the research on race and culture. This level focuses strictly on teachers and the perception they hold about their students' racial and cultural backgrounds. For example, at this moment, consider this question: "Does race play a critical factor in academic success?" Take some time to consider this question prior to moving forward with your reading.

If your response to the above question was yes, then your thinking is consistent with research. In a study that shed light on the role race plays in education, researchers found that, at the first-grade level, race did not play a significant role in reading development once vocabulary skills were controlled. This means that once researchers identified their students' age and vocabulary knowledge, race did not provide any additional predictors of how well students would perform in first grade. However, race had become a significant and accurate predictor of reading performance by the end of third grade (F. B. Wood, Felton, Flowers, & Naylor, 1991).

I have worked with educators who often attributed the race factor as described in F. B. Wood et al. (1991) to deficit models and parental status variables; they explained that students of color might have performed poorly because their parents did not value education and did not have the academic skills to assist within the home. In addition, they explained that many of the students probably came from low-income backgrounds. But Wood et al. found that, even when critical factors were controlled, including "parental marital status, parental education, parental status as welfare recipient, SES [socioeconomic status], the number of books in the home, and occupational status," they "did not remove the race effect from its potency as an independent predictor of third grade reading" (p. 9). From this study and other data on race and achievement (Haycock, 2001), we know that race is a significant predictor of reading performance around the third grade and throughout middle and high school.

If educators are unwilling to compare their beliefs to, and accept the results of, research-based studies surrounding race and academic performance, they may not be prepared to move on to the next level, which is understanding and valuing their students' cultures. Some educators may not be able to move to subsequent levels because they may have a difficult time accepting studies that show that race has been shown to be a powerful and significant predictor of reading performance. When educators compare their beliefs against the literature on race and culture, their comparisons become more objective; when educators compare their beliefs against their colleagues' opinions, their comparisons are usually biased and subjective, based on their colleagues' personal experiences, rather than on research. As educators, we must get beyond our own personal beliefs and biases about education and look toward research for answers.

The purpose of reflecting on personal biases, beliefs, and knowledge of our students' cultures is to negate faulty thinking and to work toward validating or adjusting beliefs based on research. After teachers self-reflect at this level, it is important that they share their stories and reflections with other supportive teachers to discuss personal biases, fears, beliefs, and questions. Teachers should meet with colleagues who may have different beliefs from their own to be sure not to reinforce biases.

Level 2—Cultural Characteristics

A key component of creating CR-RTI models is becoming familiar with cultural characteristics that you wish to integrate with instruction. If you desire to integrate characteristics that are valued within African American culture, then you will have to become familiar with and learn about these characteristics prior to creating instructional activities. Becoming familiar with cultural characteristics includes reviewing research and literature on valued characteristics, rather than relying on feedback from friends, colleagues, and experiences. Likewise, if you desire to integrate characteristics that are valued within Latino cultures, then you will have to review available literature to become familiar with and learn about valued characteristics prior to creating instructional practices.

Level 2 of the model focuses on theory and research surrounding culture and academic engagement. Two important questions at this level are the following:

- What role does culture play in academic engagement?
- What are key characteristics associated with African American culture—or associated with other culture(s) of interest?

To answer these questions, educators must refer to research studies surrounding race and culture to ensure that they do not create stereotypes about their students' racial group members and cultural backgrounds.

When providing professional development on CR-RTI models, I often ask my audience members two important questions: "What is culture?" and "What are cultural characteristics associated with African American culture?" To the first question, audience members usually become silent and provide blank stares. After moments of silence, I usually provide a standard definition and explain the difficulty in defining culture. In one workshop, a teacher explained that she had never thought about the definition of culture and could not provide a response, although she used the term *culture* regularly. Her comment was not unique. Most teachers in general were reluctant to provide a definition of culture and would explain that it was difficult for them to speak confidently about it, although they use the term daily.

From my experiences, teachers usually have been more willing to provide feedback surrounding African American cultural characteristics than defining culture. Common responses that teachers have provided surrounding African American cultural values are the following:

- Caring for the elderly
- Soul food
- Value of music
- Family
- Emphasis on church/religion

One teacher who was comfortable providing feedback explained, "African American culture seems very interesting and entertaining. It is very lively!" Her response elicited head nods and smiles from other audience members. Because Level 2 of the model reflects research on culture and cultural characteristics associated with African American culture (or the cultures you desire to integrate with instruction), educators must invest in reading content surrounding these topics.

It is most beneficial for teachers to create book clubs where they can discuss the content as a group; in these clubs, teachers should work to form intimate bonds where they express their reading, determine their learning progress, discuss fears and goals, and address questions. The focus of these book clubs should be on culture and characteristics associated with African American culture (or the culture[s] you desire to integrate with instruction). To assist with understanding African American cultural characteristics, educators might be interested in my book *A Cultural Awareness Manual: What Every Teacher Should Know About Traditional Characteristics Associated With African-American Culture.* This book is free at our website, along with other free resources surrounding CR-RTI models.

Level 3—Ethnography

Level 3 of the model is about becoming familiar with the cultural backgrounds of your students. Notice that Level 2 requires educators to become familiar with the research on African American culture; Level 3 requires educators to become familiar with their *students'* backgrounds and values. Simply having knowledge of Level 2 will not prepare you to work effectively with your students. There is much variability within and between racial groups and cultures, and educators should create models and interventions based on their students' cultural values and learning styles rather than race.

Although there is much variability within and between race and culture, research shows that many African Americans value communalism, movement expressiveness, orality, and verve expressions (Belgrave & Allison, 2014; Boykin & Noguera, 2011). Because this is true, it is most important to identify which of your students value these cultural characteristics and which do not. Level 2 focuses on research; Level 3 focuses on students and requires you to understand their values and interests compared to the research from Level 2. The main theme of this level surrounds ethnography, which is the "study of cultural patterns and perspectives of participants [i.e., students] in their natural setting" (Gay, Mills, & Airasian, 2005, p. 15).

Many teachers have engaged in ethnographic studies at some point in their teaching career. For example, one teacher I spoke with explained that she would visit her students' communities and would attend local churches to understand how leaders in these settings engaged her students. She explained that after attending her students' churches and communities, and after understanding the behaviors within those cultural settings, she was able to incorporate interesting activities into the classroom that reflected her students' values. This is a perfect example of an ethnographic study.

To engage in ethnographic studies, educators will have to become knowledgeable about their students' values and activities within their communities. From this practice, teachers may find that some of their students attend predominantly African American churches, barbershops, and beauty salons, among other locales. Because churches and barbershops/beauty salons are important locales within the African American community and culture, teachers may want to visit local barbershops on Fridays or Saturdays and visit local African American churches on Sundays. From ethnographic studies, teachers will learn that there is great variability among African American students in that many African American students do not frequent barbershops and beauty salons; many do not attend church, although an overwhelming majority worship and believe in God. Moreover, not all African American people in general and students in particular identify as Christians, and many embrace the values of other religious beliefs.

Although there is much variability within their religious beliefs, Chatters, Taylor, Bullard, and Jackson (2009) found that African Americans value religious activities—including joining religious organizations, engaging in prayer, and reading religious resources. Chatters et al. also studied differences among African Americans, Black Caribbeans, and non-Hispanic Whites on 12 measures of religious participation, including praying, reading of religious materials, and listening to religious programs. In a similar study, the Barna Group (2009)—which is a group that conducts studies on religion, spirituality, and faith in the United States—found that Blacks were more prone to engage in religious activities such as attending Sunday school, reading the Bible, and volunteering their time at their church compared to Hispanics and Whites.

The following data were found by the Barna Group (2005):

- Typical Sunday services for churches attended by predominantly African American parishioners are 70% longer than services for churches attended by predominantly White parishioners.
- Attendance is 50% greater in predominantly African American churches compared to predominantly White churches.
- The pastor is an influential person in most predominantly African American churches.
- Sixty-five percent of African Americans in the study reported that the pastor was a significant community leader.
- Respondents reported that Black churches are places to go not only for worship but also for assistance with nonreligious, nonspiritual help.

Although the literature is replete with studies that show the significance of the church and religious activities among African Americans, it is contrary to research to believe that all African American students and parents will identify pastors and clergy professionals as valued community leaders. In addition, it is against best practices to attend "Black churches" with the goal to *understand* Black people or to learn about the *Black experience* of students. This thought process will further perpetuate myths related to race and culture and strengthen stereotypes about African Americans. It is more appropriate to place students at the center of teaching and learning and attempt to learn about the experiences of students on an *individual basis;* from this process, it is possible to learn the values of all students within the classroom and whom they respect within their communities.

Collecting Data on Students Prior to Making Decisions About Student Values. To collect information on their students, educators could have their students provide answers to the following questions: "Explain what you and your family do each day of the week." "Do you all go anywhere during the weekends—on Fridays, Saturdays, or Sundays?" "Are there things you all engage in every weekend, consistently?" From this process, educators may learn about local settings students visit. This is a better process than asking specific questions like, "Do you attend church?" or "What church do you worship at?" These questions are inappropriate, unless students express them themselves. Similarly, many students of color take pride in their hair. When students come to school with a new haircut or hairstyle, teachers could ask students who did their hair.

Barbershops and Beauty Salons. Since barbershops and beauty salons are important locales within the African American community, educators could ask their students to write a narrative about hair, barbershops, and/ or beauty salons. Within these short narratives, teachers could encourage students to write about who does their hair, who cuts their hair, and whether they attend barbershops and beauty salons. From this process, teachers will learn that not only do many African American males value getting their hair cut at African American barbershops, but so do Latino and White students. Teachers will also learn that there are many African American students who do not value barbershops and beauty salons and that many refuse to pay the financial price of getting their hair done from professional hairstylists.

If students explain that they attend barbershops or beauty salons, educators could ask students to provide a list of five barbershops where students get their hair cut—or five shops where they would go—and beauty salons where young ladies get their hair done. Educators could then set appointments with barbershop owners to explain the purpose of ethnographic studies and to request a visit to the shop to learn more about what goes on in these settings, other than cutting and styling hair.

Ethnographers—teachers, in these examples—should be careful not to make judgments about what they observe within these settings. Observation, without judging or attempting to interpret the setting or behaviors, is essential to ethnographic studies (Gay et al., 2005). The goal with these studies is to understand behaviors within cultural settings; if teachers attempt to interpret behaviors upon observing them, their interpretations would reflect their own personal beliefs and biases. Their interpretations would interfere with the purpose of ethnographic studies. When engaging in these studies, it is important that teachers identify recurrent themes. For the purpose of CR-RTI models, it would be important for teachers to attempt to identify how these settings engage communalistic bonding, movement expressive behaviors, orality, and verve.

In addition to ethnographic studies, Level 3 pertains to becoming familiar with your students' values, beliefs, fears, and goals. At this level, educators also become familiar with their students' views on race, culture, and education. It is important that teachers collect this information after forming solid relationships with their students. Students are more prone to providing meaningful feedback when they trust their teachers. Students are more honest and become less offended by questions and comments when relationships are established early.

When teachers engage in ethnographic studies, they become more skillful at identifying cultural values and less prone to categorizing students based on skin color. Scholars have expressed the need to integrate cultural assets of students of color (Boykin, Coleman, Lilja, & Tyler, 2004), which is an important component of Level 3. These include identifying strengths that teachers could use to engage students in the classroom—strengths that could potentially build academic motivation. Boykin and Noguera (2011) identify these strengths as student assets and include "existing or emerging interests and preferences, motivational inclinations, passions and commitments, attitudes, beliefs, opinions, self-perceptions, personal or collective identities, and prior experiences" (p. 69).

Teachers are much more effective at engaging and forming solid relationships when they know as much as possible about their students, including their assets. Knowing students on a personal level is a critical component of creating CR-RTI models. Getting to know students personally helps educators avoid practices that are stereotypical and prejudicial.

Level 4—Classroom Observation

Being skillful at identifying cultural characteristics is critical in creating CR-RTI models. When educators become competent with identifying behaviors that reflect communalism, movement expressiveness, orality, and verve, they learn that these characteristics are valued among people of many races and socioeconomic backgrounds; they learn that these characteristics are not exclusive to African Americans or African American culture.

From challenging personal beliefs, becoming familiar with their students' cultural values, and engaging in ethnographic studies, educators should be able to identify cultural values among their students. If educators are at this level but are unable to identify cultural values among the students they have been studying, it is vital that they revisit previous levels. At this level—Level 4—you should be able to identify students who prefer communal bonding, movement expressiveness, and vervistic activities. You may have been able to identify these students prior to moving through levels, but the levels should give you a better appreciation of cultural values.

In Chapter 18, I explain that a colleague of mine scheduled a meeting with his son's teacher because his son brought negative behavioral statements home from her. From the meeting, my colleague learned that the teacher was reprimanding his son for engaging in communal behaviors. Apparently, this teacher did not know and understand the importance of communal behaviors for many students who come from communalistic backgrounds. This example shows that the teacher had a set of rules in her classroom that clashed with her students' cultural values. Her rules were insensitive to communalistic learning styles and resulted in negative consequences for students who engaged in these behaviors. Teachers who are successful at this level are able to observe student behaviors and identify cultural meaning from the behaviors—based on ethnographic studies and interviews—and are able to integrate those characteristics with instruction to build academic motivation.

Notice that, prior to moving through levels and challenging personal beliefs about race and culture, teachers may have attributed student movement expressive behaviors to some disability—maybe attention-deficit hyperactivity disorder, for example—or to the need to draw attention. They may have identified certain behaviors as disrespectful to classroom rules; students were probably deemed noncompliant, combative, and oppositional. From moving through levels, teachers may have a better understanding of culture and the role culture plays in education. It is my prediction that when teachers are able to identify and embrace their students' cultural characteristics, they will be less prone to writing behavioral referrals for certain behaviors and will experience an increase in relationship building among their students. If these practices are embedded in positive behavior intervention support (PBIS) models, schools may see a decrease in referrals among students in general and students of color in particular. Studies using African American cultural values are warranted within the area of PBIS.

Level 5—Implementation

Level 5 is the implementation process of this model. At this level, teachers should have challenged and compared their beliefs to research surrounding race and culture. Teachers should also have a solid understanding of the role culture plays in academic engagement and have a solid understanding of their students' cultural values. From ethnographic studies and interviews, teachers should have knowledge of how to make the classroom meaningful for students who value characteristics associated with African American culture.

Teachers should also be able to create themes that are relevant in local churches, barbershops, and/or beauty salons—themes that emphasize communalism, movement expressiveness, orality, and verve. I say teachers should be able to do certain things, but teachers will have different competencies, based on their learning at previous levels. Whether teachers are competent and able to integrate instruction with valued cultural characteristics will depend on the work that was invested during Levels 1 through 4. If teachers did not study materials and content on cultural characteristics surrounding their students' values, challenge personal beliefs, and ask questions, they may not be prepared to create effective Tier 1 activities that integrate culturally meaningful instruction.

CULTURALLY RELEVANT INSTRUCTION THROUGHOUT TIERS

Once educators are proficient at creating culturally relevant models, they should implement culturally relevant instruction throughout tiers—beginning at the Tier 1 level. Such instruction should not be reserved as some special instruction used for Black children when they begin to fall behind or disengage in the classroom. Rather, educators should seek to understand their students and their cultural backgrounds—and use such knowledge to prevent disengagement. Many might question the importance of integrating culturally relevant instruction in the classroom or wonder why such instruction has been effective with increasing performance among students of color. The answer, in part, relates to emotions.

As educators, we often focus on academic and cognitive processes and place less emphasis on social emotional learning (SEL). When students (1) become emotionally connected with their teachers and peers in the classroom, (2) find learning entertaining, (3) feel that their cultural backgrounds are affirmed and valued, and are (4) comfortable within their own skin—comfortable being who they are while learning in the classroom—they become more engaged at the behavioral, cognitive, and affective levels (see Chapter 7 for a definition of these engagement levels).

Subsequent chapters in this book speak to creating culturally relevant instruction at the Tier 2 and Tier 3 levels. Is it possible for teachers to simply read the chapters that follow and attempt to implement such instruction and interventions? Absolutely. But when we become competent through the above levels, we are able to tweak instruction and interventions to boost academic motivation and engagement among our low-performing and unmotivated students. We are able to boost engagement and motivation because, from moving through levels, we become competent at creating classroom norms and instructional strategies that speak to the experiences and values of our students. From this process, students feel connected, respected, and appreciated.

CHAPTER SUMMARY

Research is clear in that there is great variability within and between groups. As such, all students are different and have unique worldviews based on their experiences and interactions with people. An essential component of creating *culturally relevant* models is student-centered teaching and learning; educators must learn about their students' interests, values, and passions, as well as integrate the cultural values of students with instruction. Although there may be an array of approaches, I present five levels—or steps—in creating culturally relevant models. These include the following:

1. Awareness

2. Research on culture and cultural characteristics

3. Ethnography

4. Observation

5. Implementation

Educators must engage in each step at a deep level prior to moving on to subsequent lessons.

In the next chapter, I discuss the relationship between culture and academic engagement and discuss how teachers and students often create classroom environments that reflect their own cultural values.

Cultural Characteristics and Academic Engagement

7

A fish only discovers its need for water when it is no longer in it. Our own culture is like water for the fish. It sustains us. We live and breathe through it.

—Stephanie Quappe and Giovanna Cantatore

Best practices, when implementing RTI, includes using scientific research-based instruction, but one body of research that is rarely considered when referring to RTI is the effect of culture on academic engagement. When most coaches discuss culture in the context of RTI, they make general statements about it. A familiar comment is, "When incorporating an RTI model, it is best practice to make sure the model is culturally relevant; we must make sure that it reaches all of our children."

When I hear these statements at conference and seminars and read about them in articles and textbooks, I usually wonder, "What does this mean?" and "What does this look like?" I ask because many educators I have trained on culturally relevant models perceived *race* and *culture* as synonymous terms, and many have stated that they honestly did not understand how to create cultural themes within their classrooms. Educators made these statements not knowing that they usually integrated Eurocentric cultural characteristics with instruction by merely teaching consistently with how their teachers taught them. Thus, most RTI models are indeed culturally relevant but usually for students who embrace Eurocentric cultural values; culturally diverse learners are often required to learn consistent with the value system of the school culture (Boykin, Tyler, & Miller, 2005), and problem-solving practices are usually implemented and progress monitoring data interpreted through the cultural lens of Eurocentric values rather than through multicultural perspectives on student engagement. Students of color are moved through tiers, often without consideration of how the classroom rules, norms, and values interfere with learning and student engagement. This is evident considering *culturally relevant* RTI models are new concepts to many educators across the country. To shed light on the role culture plays in academic engagement, this chapter includes case studies that were presented to educators during an RTI in-service. In addition, this chapter sheds light on four core characteristics that have been associated with African American culture. Important questions surrounding culture and academic engagement include the following:

- How do educators create cultural conditions within their classrooms?
- How do teachers transmit culture into the classroom?
- How do students transmit culture into the classroom?

CULTURAL CONDITIONS WITHIN THE CLASSROOM

Research shows that incorporating cultural characteristics into the classroom that students identify with increases academic engagement and student performance. This research became apparent during the 1980s and 1990s (Allen & Boykin, 1991; Gilmore, 1985), and researchers are now investigating the benefits of culturally relevant activities for students of color. Why is culture such an important variable when considering academic engagement and moving students through tiers? The following scenarios shed light on the latter question and show the need to create models that are sensitive to the needs of all students.

Scenario 1

Markisha

Markisha is a third-grade African American female student who is referred for a full case study because she is not responding to research-based interventions. Markisha barely made it through the second grade, although she would periodically pass math and spelling quizzes without any problem. Markisha's reading fluency scores show that she is performing below her grade-level peers, but her teacher believes she has the skills to do better. The beginning of the year DIBELS measure—a predictor of early reading skills—showed that she performed at the strategic range (often color-coded yellow) in oral reading fluency, which indicated some risk at the time of the measure. Starting in October, Markisha's reading scores and grades began to drop. The middle of the year assessment showed that she dropped to the intensive range (often color-coded red), which indicated severe deficits in oral reading fluency. She was provided rounds and rounds of interventions in a small group to improve her reading fluency skills, but progress-monitoring data showed very little improvement. In fact, her scores decreased when research-based interventions were implemented.

Scenario 2

Oscar

Oscar is a Latino male student in the second grade. He and his family have recently moved to a high-performing suburban school that very few students of color attend; they moved from a city in the Midwestern United States. Both English and Spanish are spoken in Oscar's home, and he is bilingual. The beginning of the year (BOY) AIMSweb fluency measure showed that Oscar performed below the 20th percentile, which indicated that he was at risk for having reading problems. Oscar's performance was interesting considering his records showed that he was a top reader in his previous school as a first grader.

Because it was the beginning of the school year, Oscar's teacher wanted to determine if his performance was a response to his return from summer break—after all, he may not have read much during vacation. His teacher also wanted to ensure that Oscar's performance was not a response to the transition to the new school. Because of these concerns, she did not consider him for Tier 2; rather, she implemented classroom-based interventions at the Tier 1 level for 6 weeks. No progress was made. Because of his BOY data and minimal response to research-based interventions at the Tier 1 level, Oscar was provided minutes of research-based interventions to improve reading fluency. The intervention used was evidence based and shown to increase fluency skills of second- and third-grade students. Thirty minutes of intervention time were included in addition to his core 90 minutes of reading instruction.

After rounds of interventions and progress monitoring, Oscar still performed below the 20th percentile; his rate of improvement was considerably low. Considering his performance over time, 30 *additional* minutes of intensive interventions were provided—which meant that he received a total 60 minutes of intervention time—and he was placed into an even smaller

(Continued)

(Continued)

group. Because Oscar's scores did not improve when provided additional time and rounds of intensive interventions, the team requested a full case study to determine if Oscar had a specific learning disability in the areas of reading and reading fluency.

During the evaluation process, the school psychologist administered the Wechsler Individual Achievement Test, Third Edition (WIAT-III)—a standardized achievement test—to gather additional information to help determine eligibility. During the eligibility meeting, the team was surprised to learn that Oscar performed in the average range in both Basic Reading (standard score of 110) and Reading Fluency (standard score of 108). Average range for the WIAT-III achievement test begins with scores of 85. At the meeting, Oscar's father became frustrated. He lamented, "I knew my son could read. He was a top reader in his previous school for first graders; he reads just fine at home. I didn't understand why he was placed in all of those low groups, and stressed out about his reading skills to begin with!"

Scenario 3

Darnell

Darnell is an African American male student who was referred for a full case evaluation because, according to his teacher, "He is always bouncing off the wall!" Mrs. Doe explained, "Darnell has a difficult time remaining still in his seat, taps his pencil on his desk throughout the day, and talks to his neighbors when, after all, he should be completing his work." Mrs. Doe explained that she moved Darnell's desk to the front of the room, directly next to her desk, and has implemented behavior modification research-based interventions. Although she implemented these interventions, Darnell's behaviors have gone unchanged.

An observation was conducted using the Behavior Observation of Students in Schools (B.O.S.S.)—a behavioral observation instrument—and it showed that Darnell was off task motorically 48% of the time during the observation (meaning that he moved around a lot during the observation) and off task verbally 30% of the time (meaning that he talked with his neighbors a lot during the observation). These data showed that Darnell tapped his pencil, made beats on the desk, and either sang or rapped music to himself during instructional and independent seat time. At one point during the observation, Darnell got the entire class involved—they sang with him as he danced around the classroom. After the observation, Mrs. Doe asked the school psychologist, "Did you see Darnell dance around the room? Did you hear him rapping to himself and tapping on his desk? He constantly disrupts the classroom. These are typical 'Darnell behaviors' and I don't know what to do with him!"

QUESTIONS

Scenario 1

What are some possible reasons why Markisha performed below grade level by midyear?

Scenario 2

What are some possible reasons why Oscar performed poorly during the intervention phases?

Scenario 3

What are some possible reasons why Darnell was "bouncing off the wall"?

When I presented these scenarios and questions at an RTI seminar, educators provided the following responses.

- Markisha probably didn't have much academic help at home.
- Maybe Markisha began to experience problems of some sort at home or within her community and the experiences impacted her achievement.
- Maybe the interventionists did not implement the interventions with fidelity when working with Oscar.
- Maybe Oscar actually had a specific learning disability.
- It sounds like Darnell had ADHD.
- Maybe Darnell had a reading deficit and would become disruptive to get removed from class so he would not have to read aloud in front of his peers.

Although these responses could have been the underlying factors, no one mentioned factors related to culture. Consistent with research that shows many students of color value engaging instruction and stimulating activities while learning (Carter, Hawkins, & Natesan, 2008), Markisha, Oscar, and Darnell could be suffering from the same condition, which is boredom in the classroom; it is possible that the instructional lessons were not engaging enough to spark their interests. It is possible that these students come from highly stimulated backgrounds and home environments that incorporate expressive movement and entertaining activities when learning and interacting with others. These students could have come from home backgrounds that place emphasis on affection, bonding, and sharing. If this were true for these students, simply incorporating research-based interventions aimed at improving reading skills might not be enough to engage them academically; rather, these students may require not only research-based interventions but also affection, bonding, entertainment, and sharing to increase academic engagement and motivation.

During the seminar, educators explained that Darnell demonstrated ADHD-like behaviors, but it is possible that Darnell is encouraged to sing, dance, and entertain when he works with his peers during the children's ministry at the church he attends on Sunday and at home when working with his siblings. The RTI process—including evaluation for special education provisions in the above scenarios—did not take into account issues related to student interests and cultural values. Also, interventions focused on improving skills, and teachers approached their problem-solving process using deficit thinking strategies. They believed that Markisha's and Oscar's reading performance was due to skill deficits; they believed these students lacked skills needed to read at a fast pace. The following are cultural factors that could have been barriers to learning in the above scenarios:

- Whether the classroom culture, including rules and norms, clashed with the students' cultural values
- Student perception of their teachers and interventionists
- The quality of relationship between the students and their teachers
- If performance would have increased with the use of scientific research-based, culturally relevant interventions that differentiated instruction by process—the manner in which instruction was provided in the classroom

UNDERSTANDING CULTURE

The study of cultural learning styles is a relatively new phenomenon. Actually, this research first became popular in the United States during the 1960s. Research on culture and cultural learning styles became of interest in response to Lyndon Johnson's "War on Poverty" and the nation's attempt to understand "cultural deprivation" (Gutiérrez & Rogoff, 2003, p. 19).

Throughout history, many articles—perceived as *scholarship*—consisted of scientific racism that attempted to prove the low-level reasoning of African Americans. These pseudo-scientific reports purported that Black people demonstrated behaviors that stemmed from cultural and cognitive deficits (Guthrie, 1976/1998; Herrnstein & Murray, 1994; Jensen, 1969). In other words, such writings attempted to explain the behaviors of Black and Brown people by suggesting that they had deficits in their ability to think and process information and that their culture was inadequate.

The "deficit culture" concept relates to a definition of culture postulated by Oscar Lewis. In 1961, Lewis wrote a book titled *The Children of Sanchez*. His book is an ethnography that depicts an impoverished community in Mexico City. Based on this study, he concluded that people from low-income backgrounds are monolithic—that, although people from low-income backgrounds vary with regard to race, ethnicity, and geographic locations, little variability exists within their behaviors and worldviews. Consistent with his research, he coined the culture of poverty theory (Lewis, 1961). This theory views culture negatively and is associated with low socioeconomic status. Although research shows that variability exists within and between groups—and that no two people are exactly alike (Marieb & Hoehn, 2013)—educators continue to receive training on how to place students who come from poverty and diverse backgrounds into Lewis's culture of poverty framework (see Payne, 2001).

Many researchers explained that Lewis's definition of culture was prejudicial. During the 1960s, Valentine (1968) was a leading voice against categorizing a large and varied group of people simply on the basis of lower socioeconomic status. Valentine explained that researchers and educators abuse culture when they perceive it as *adaptations* to environmental experiences that are debilitating. Valentine also explained that cultural responses represent positive behaviors, behaviors that group members value and transmit to others.

DEFINITION

A common definition of culture is "the conscious and unconscious content [behaviors/information] that a group learns, shares, and transmits from generation to generation that organizes life and helps interpret existence" (Linton, 1945, as cited in Diller, 2007, p. 61). Consistent with this definition, *culture* is a word that we use to express behavior patterns that are valued among group members. However, educators should not interpret behaviors demonstrated by Black students as representative of Black culture or behaviors demonstrated by Latino students as representative of Latino culture. Stated differently, educators must be careful not to assume that simply because a student is Black that he or she must come from Black culture. When educators assume that their students come from certain cultures, based solely on skin color, they engage in stereotyping behaviors (Boykin & Noguera, 2011).

CULTURAL WORLDVIEWS

Group members create cultural values through repeated behaviors; cultural values help group members cope with a host of factors, including emotional distress. Scholars argue that Africans transmitted unique cultural patterns and lifestyles to African Americans, and these valued behaviors have become known as "Afrocultural" characteristics (Boykin, Albury, et al., 2005, p. 340). The belief that Africans transmitted cultural behaviors to African Americans is a concept that rebuts early theories that explain African slaves were soulless bodies and cultureless people, that because their minds and bodies were empty, they were plastic creatures, able to be molded and subjugated by Westerners (White & Parham, 1990).

African Americans share an admixture of Afrocultural and Eurocentric values, but for many African Americans, the former dominates their perception (Belgrave & Allison, 2014). To understand the importance of cultural values on emotional and psychological functioning, it is important to begin with the concept of worldviews, which Belgrave and Allison (2014) describe as "way[s] of thinking that organizes all aspects of one's life, including intra- and interpersonal thoughts and behaviors and one's functioning in social systems and institutions in the community (e.g., family, school, job, and Church), and in the larger society" (p. 32).

Belgrave and Allison (2014) explain that *intrapersonal thoughts* refer to evaluations about life, which present in "one's attitudes, beliefs, values, and expectations" (p. 32). *Interpersonal behaviors* include interactions among people, including how teachers and students interact during the teaching and learning process. Thus, when teachers and students interact in the same space (interpersonal behaviors) but do not acknowledge and show sensitivity to each other's cultural values, clashes may manifest. Consequently, teachers may believe that students are noncompliant, disrespectful, and devalue education (*teacher intrapersonal* thoughts); students of color may believe their teachers are racist, devalue their cultural interests, and do not care for them as people (*student intrapersonal* thoughts). Because students and teachers enter the same space with different cultural worldviews, learning to respect each other's cultural values is critical to establishing and maintaining relationships.

CHARACTERISTICS ASSOCIATED WITH AFRICAN AMERICAN CULTURE

Scholars argue that integrating cultural characteristics that are valued within the Afrocultural worldview may increase performance among

African American students (Gay, 2010; Spencer, Noll, Stoltzfus, & Harpalani, 2001). Gilmore's (1985) work was instrumental at showing that integrating the cultural themes and expressions of African American culture increases engagement and learning among students of low-income backgrounds who value Afrocultural characteristics. From the early work on cultural characteristics (Akbar, 1981; Boykin, 1983; Gilmore, 1985), scholars have shed light on the role culture plays in cognitive development and learning styles.

Although many characteristics have been linked to African American culture, Dr. A. Wade Boykin, a developmental psychologist from Howard University, has collaborated with other scholars to conduct studies on four core constructs associated with African American culture. Characteristics that reflect this worldview include (1) *communalism*, (2) *movement expressiveness*, (3) *orality*, and (4) *verve* (Belgrave & Allison, 2014; Boykin, 1983; Boykin, Jagers, Ellison, & Albury, 1997; Boykin, Tyler, & Miller, 2005; Chimezie, 1998; Ramose, 2003; White & Parham, 1990). Educators interested in creating culturally relevant RTI models should consider these characteristics when moving students through tiers, while remaining cognizant of myths related to race and culture. These characteristics should be used to engage students at each tier of the RTI process.

Communalism

Communalism is a concept that is characterized by four constructs: (1) *social orientation*—a preference for social bonds and interconnectedness with people over objects; (2) *group duty*—the belief that one's duty to the group supersedes individualistic duties; (3) *identity*—viewed within the context of group membership, as opposed to individualistic, materialistic worth; and (4) *sharing*—the summation of communalistic constructs in which members share with one another to gain success (Boykin, 1986; Boykin et al., 2004).

Movement Expressiveness

Movement expressiveness comprises three valued dimensions: (1) rhythmic orientation, which is observed in dance movements, preference for percussive music, and daily activities that incorporate stylistic patterns, including speech patterns that are rhythmically vocalized; (2) a premium placed on rhythmic music that elicits movement, which is needed for one's psychological well-being; and (3) gestures such as coordinated movements (Allen & Boykin, 1992; Boykin, 1986; Boykin, Tyler, & Miller, 2005).

Orality

Orality represents the vibrancy with which group members express words. Such vibrancy is attached to meaning and sensation and depends on a "call-and-response" communication (a transactional and continuous dialogue between two or more persons, such that a person may be perceived as bored or uninterested if he or she remains quiet while waiting his or her turn to speak). Moreover, speaking is a lively performance, not restricted to simply conveying a message (Boykin, Albury, et al., 2005). Orality was a key method of conveying messages and telling and retelling stories within African tribes (Belgrave & Allison, 2014). African Americans have expressed themselves through rap, storytelling, spoken word, preaching, and teaching, which are all conveyed through orality.

Verve

Verve represents the preference for variability, which stems from expressiveness, bonding, music, movement, and percussiveness. Verve is characterized by three components: (1) lively and intensified behavior, (2) preference for variety and alternations within a given setting, and (3) preference for multiple background elements existing simultaneously in one's environment, including activities and stimulation (Boykin, Albury, et al., 2005). In addition, verve is characterized by rhythm and energy; it is represented in a person's walk, talk, and expressions (Belgrave & Allison, 2014; Jones, 2003). Afrocultural themes intermix to form what many scholars call Black culture.

Because Tier 1 includes differentiating instruction and connecting students to the core curriculum, many African American students may benefit from classrooms that have themes related to communalism, movement expressiveness, verve, and orality. When I speak with teachers about incorporating Afrocultural characteristics into the classroom, most ask if I could bring them information that explains these concepts. In most cases, incorporating these cultural characteristics into the classroom is a new concept to most educators, including African American educators.

African American educators with whom I have worked were unfamiliar with the research on communalism, movement expressiveness, orality, and verve; the mere description of each characteristic rekindled in them nostalgic moments, as they reminisced on the times they shared growing up in homes that were communalistic.

Because many educators have asked how they might incorporate cultural characteristics into their classrooms, I have included in the next chapter empirical studies that have examined the effect of cultural characteristics on academic performance of African American students.

CULTURE AND ACADEMIC ENGAGEMENT

Prior to discussing the relationship between culture and academic engagement, it might be helpful to define academic engagement so that we are working from the same definition. Although there are many definitions surrounding academic engagement and many sources to pull from to understand the term, I will refer to Shapiro's (2004) descriptions of engagement. I focus specifically on this definition because it is used by many psychologists and teachers in PK–12 education to describe on-task, off-task behaviors in the classroom. For example, when students are referred to problem-solving teams or for special education services, school psychologists usually observe the students and document engagement time based on Shapiro's definitions. I also use Shapiro's definition because, although many educators refer to it when determining academic engagement in the classroom, the definitions are insensitive to cultural characteristics that are valued among many African American students. Thus, educators, social workers, and school psychologists must consider this important caveat prior to determining on-task, off-task engagement of students who come from culturally diverse backgrounds when measuring behaviors using the B.O.S.S.

ACADEMIC ENGAGEMENT AND OFF-TASK BEHAVIORS (SHAPIRO, 2004)

Shapiro (2004) created an observation scale known as the B.O.S.S., which measures students' responses to instructional activities in the classroom. His observation scale includes active engagement time, passive engagement time, off-task motor behaviors, off-task verbal behaviors, and off-task passive behaviors.

Academic Engagement Time

Academic engagement time refers to the extent to which students respond to and participate in classroom activities. Shapiro (2004, p. 38) divided engagement into two different types: active engagement and passive engagement. Examples of active engagement, according to the manual, include the following:

- writing,
- reading aloud,
- raising a hand,
- talking to the teacher about the assigned material, and
- looking up a word in a dictionary.

Shapiro (2004) describes passive engagement time as "those times when the student is passively attending to assigned work" (p. 39). Examples of passive engagement, according to the manual, include the following:

- listening to a lecture,
- looking at an academic worksheet,
- reading assigned material silently,
- looking at the blackboard during teacher instruction, and
- listening to a peer respond to a question.

Along with active and passive engagement, Shapiro (2004) included off-task behaviors in his observation system. Off-task behaviors are of three different types: (1) off-task motor, (2) off-task verbal, and (3) off-task passive behaviors. Off-task motor behaviors are defined as "any instance of motor activity that is not directly associated with an assigned academic task" (Shapiro, 2004, p. 39). Examples of off-task motor behaviors, according to the manual, include the following:

- engaging in any out-of-seat behavior (defined as buttocks not in contact with the seat);
- aimlessly flipping the pages of a book;
- manipulating objects not related to the academic task (e.g., playing with a paper clip, throwing paper, twirling a pencil, folding paper);
- physically touching another student when not related to an academic task;
- bending or reaching, such as picking up a pencil off the floor;
- drawing or writing that is not related to an assigned academic activity;
- turning around in one's seat, oriented away from the classroom instruction;
- fidgeting in seat (i.e., engaging in repetitive motor movements for at least 3 consecutive seconds; student must be off-task for this category to be scored).

Shapiro (2004) defines off-task verbal behaviors as "any audible verbalizations that are not permitted and/or are not related to an assigned academic task" (p. 40). These may include any of the following behaviors:

- making any audible sound, such as whistling, humming, or forced burping;
- talking to another student about issues unrelated to an assigned academic task;

- talking to another student about an assigned academic task when such talk is prohibited by the teacher;
- making unauthorized comments or remarks; and
- calling out answers to academic problems when the teacher has not specifically asked for an answer or permitted such behavior.

Shapiro (2004) describes off-task passive behaviors as "those times when a student is passively not attending to an assigned academic activity for a period of at least three consecutive seconds" (p. 40) Examples, according to the manual, include the following:

- sitting quietly in an unassigned activity,
- looking around the room,
- staring out the window, and
- passively listening to other students talk about issues unrelated to the assigned academic activity.

As mentioned, educators and school psychologists must take caution when using these definitions of off-task behaviors because many of the definitions are insensitive to characteristics that have been associated with African American culture. For example, the definition of off-task behaviors, as described by Shapiro (2004), is insensitive to *movement expressiveness.* Many students who come from Afrocultural backgrounds place a premium on movement-expressive behaviors but would be considered off-task if they

- engage in out-of-seat behaviors (defined as buttocks not in contact with the seat),
- turn around in their seat,
- fidget in their seat, or
- engage in motor movement for at least 3 consecutive seconds.

Because many students of color value music and movement, they may create a beat in their heads and, while working, bob their heads to the internal beat, as well as tap their feet and pencils to the beat—all while working at their desks. In these instances, would it be accurate to say that these students are off-task? I call these behaviors—pausing to create beats or to engage in varying activities—*cognitive breaks* (see Chapter 21). Although students may come from stimulating and lively backgrounds, when observed using the B.O.S.S. in the classroom, they are expected to remain still at their desks and talk only when authorized by their teacher, if to be considered on-task. Call-and-response interactions are defined as off-task behaviors.

Shapiro's (2004) definitions of off-task behaviors are also insensitive to communalism, orality, and verve. Many students who come from Afrocultural backgrounds value bonding and sharing; they may touch their peers to show expression and to emphasize some thought or idea, or they may give their peers dap (fist bump) or a high five if they become excited. They may also engage in call-response interactions with their teachers and peers during instructional time. Although students may engage in these cultural values, they would be considered off-task when observed with the B.O.S.S. if they

- physically touch another student when not related to an academic task,
- talk with other students about issues unrelated to academic tasks,
- make unauthorized comments or remarks, or
- call out answers to academic problems when the teacher has not specifically asked for an answer or permitted such behavior.

Many of the off-task behaviors described by Shapiro (2004) are consistent with Eurocentric cultural values. Behaviors that deviate from these norms are the ones coded as off-task. Researchers describe traditional Eurocentric cultural characteristics as consisting of *individualism, competition,* and *bureaucratic orientations* and are most evident in mainstream settings, including classroom settings (Boykin, Tyler, & Miller, 2005).

Individualism

Individualism refers to a preference to work in isolation of other people; it refers to autonomy and independence of the group. Examples of individualism in the classroom include requiring students to work alone on classroom assignments and recognizing and praising individual students as opposed to praising the efforts of the overall group.

Competition

Competition refers to competing in an effort to outperform others. Competition promotes rivalry as opposed to group dependency. Examples of competition in the classroom include creating games and activities by which students must outperform their peers to achieve some goal. Educators may pit students against each other and offer rewards for those who score the highest on assignments or quizzes; they may offer rewards for students who consistently follow classroom rules—rules that are rooted in Eurocentric culture.

Bureaucracy Orientation

Bureaucracy orientation refers to a preference for strict rules and regulations within some setting. Bureaucracy orientation requires students to abide by a strict set of rules or norms, and any deviation from the rules results in disciplinary action (see Boykin & Bailey, 2000, for a review of these cultural characteristics). Examples of bureaucracy orientation in the classroom refer to establishing strict rules. A few common ones follow:

- don't walk without being told,
- don't speak without raising your hand,
- don't move around in your seat,
- don't tap on your desks, and
- don't speak when I (teacher) am speaking.

Students who demonstrate behaviors that are consistent with movement expressiveness, communalism, orality, and verve are often deemed unruly. Instead of receiving rewards and praise from their teachers, students who demonstrate such cultural values receive negative consequences and are eventually sent to the office or sent home. Often, behavior modification is used to attempt to reduce the occurrence of these culturally valued behaviors. When behavioral data show that students have not responded to "evidence-based interventions"—or when students continue to demonstrate these valued behaviors, although they have received treatment to reduce such behaviors—they are often referred as needing special education services; in these instances, special education team members may evaluate the student for an emotional disability or question the presence of ADHD. However, in many cases, the students' negative behaviors reflect frustration to the cultural clash they experience in the classroom. They become fed up with negative feedback, discipline referrals, and harsh comments about their behaviors. Consequently, they begin to disrespect teachers, become noncompliant, and learn to despise the learning experience. Eventually, when teachers complete socioemotional rating scales about the students' behaviors—which is used to help determine the need for special education services—teachers often rate their students negatively. Often, these rating scales are better measures of the relationship teachers have with the students, rather than "student maladaptive behaviors." In other words, teacher data often reflect the quality of relationship they have with their students, rather than some disability that lies within the students.

As mentioned, off-task behaviors, as described by Shapiro (2004), are insensitive to characteristics that are associated with cultural values among students of color. It should be clear by now why this is the case. Shapiro's definitions are *consistent* with bureaucracy orientation, in that students are considered off-task if they move around in their chairs or desks (defined as off-task motor), touch another peer during instruction time, or fidget in their seats. Therefore, the extent to which students are coded off-task depends on how well they can follow rules in the classroom—in other words, how well they conform to traditional Eurocentric norms.

Many children of color may prefer to interact with others while working; they may prefer to discuss nonacademic topics while completing assignments (consistent with verve); they may periodically touch their peers and teachers while interacting, as touching is a way of showing affection and is consistent with bonding (consistent with communalism); and students of color may move around or sing to themselves while sitting at their desks (consistent with movement expressiveness). Essentially, students who value verve may joke, laugh, sing, and tease their peers throughout the process of completing an assignment (Carter et al., 2008).

If students engage in movement-expressive or vervistic behaviors while being observed with the B.O.S.S. instrument, they will usually appear off-task during the observational period. Data from the B.O.S.S., then, may project misleading and invalid data when used to identify whether students who come from culturally diverse backgrounds are academically engaged or off-task. It is important to note that engagement is determined by definitions; we may refer to some behaviors as reflective of academic engagement and other behaviors as reflective of academic disengagement—and these definitions usually arise from cultural biases. The reason for the inherent bias is that it is impossible to create rules and regulations apart from cultural values (Gutiérrez & Rogoff, 2003).

Whenever we create rules or norms, we refer to cultural values to which others must adjust and conform. The cultural values of the school system are often in stark contrast to the cultural values of many of our students of color, which means that students spend enormous amounts of time not only learning content in the classroom but also learning and accommodating specific rules and values; often, when students demonstrate behaviors that are valued within their own cultural systems, such behaviors are deemed off-task, disrespectful, and unruly.

If one's definition of engagement is based on traditional Eurocentric values, such as raising one's hand before speaking or sitting still in one's chair during instructional time, then behaviors that deviate from these definitions will reflect academic disengagement. Interestingly, research shows that many African American students are more engaged academically when teachers incorporate movement-expressive behaviors with activities (Boykin & Allen, 2001).

Fredricks, Blumenfeld, and Paris (2004) describe academic engagement as behavioral, cognitive, and affective expressions. The definition of *behavioral engagement* by Fredricks et al. resembles the definition by Shapiro (2004), in that students involve themselves by asking questions and actively participating in class activities and assignments. *Cognitive engagement* refers to deeper investments in academic content, such as seeking to comprehend difficult questions and problems; with cognitive engagement, students are not merely participating but are seeking to memorize, analyze, and process relevant information. *Affective engagement* refers to emotional involvement within the learning environment, whereby students and educators tie positive emotions with learning. These definitions of engagement are interdependent.

Often, when I observed classrooms, if students became excited or stimulated while learning, educators would tell them to calm down. Because many African American students are often stimulated and value expressing emotions, educators should create opportunities by which students can demonstrate affective engagement in the classroom, starting at the Tier 1 level. Movement-expressive behaviors should be used to increase academic motivation as much as possible.

In their position statement, National Center for Culturally Responsive Educational Systems (NCCRESt, 2005) explains that, if educators do not address how culture mediates learning, "RTI models will simply be like old wine in a new bottle" (p. 1). That is, without considering how culture affects learning and engagement, RTI will be used as the new model to sort students based on deficit thinking. To be sure, classrooms are not culture free. Educators transmit culture into their classrooms based on their teaching styles, rules, and expectations of students, and students transmit culture through their interactions with their peers and their teachers. We learn culture through interacting with others. Thus, culture is transmitted in at least three different ways: "through deliberate teaching, through observational learning, and through direct participation" (Boykin & Noguera, 2011, p. 100).

CHAPTER SUMMARY

Very few books and articles on RTI go into detail about the importance of culture when considering academic engagement. Important questions surrounding RTI and culture include the following: When students do not respond to scientific evidence-based instruction, is their nonresponse related to cultural clashes? If instruction and interventions were relevant to the student's interests, passions, and cultural values, would the student engage at a higher level? These questions are critical in that students learn best when they engage at high levels; if students find interventions boring and disinteresting, they may continue to disengage and fall further behind academically. Research shows that many African American students value four characteristics. These characteristics have been associated with African American culture and include (1) communalism, (2) movement expressiveness, (3) orality, and (4) verve. These characteristics have been shown to increase engagement among African American students. Because many students have responded well when presented with instructional strategies that include these four characteristics, educators and RTI coaches should consider integrating such themes within their RTI models. In addition, researchers and scholars should conduct additional research on integrating these themes at the high school level.

In the next chapter, I shed light on effective intervention practices and differentiate between skill-focused and process-focused interventions. In addition, I explain that culturally relevant interventions are just as important as scientific and evidence-based interventions—and are needed to increase performance among many culturally diverse students.

Cultural Characteristics in the Classroom

8

Every man's ability may be strengthened or increased by culture.

—*John Abbott*

Implementing an RTI model in schools requires educators to engage in research, and consistent with the RTI approach, when interventions prove to be ineffective, and when students continue to disengage, educators must go back to the drawing board.

If you are an educator within PreK–12 education, I am sure you have heard of at least one scientific research-based intervention. Even more, I would bet that the intervention is based on building or improving skill in the areas of reading, writing, or math—such as building reading fluency and comprehension, grammar, and/or math computations and problem-solving skills. If you are at the high school level, I would bet that you have sought interventions of some sort to help your students learn the subject matter better; these interventions may be related to mnemonics or strategies to process information quickly. Such strategies are *skill-focused* or *content-focused interventions*, and I alluded to them earlier in this book. Although most educators are familiar with skill-focused interventions pertaining to reading, writing, and math, many are less familiar with *process-focused interventions* that integrate Afrocultural values. Process-focused interventions shed light on the delivery of instruction. When delivering instruction, important questions arise: "How am I supposed to deliver this particular unit or intervention?" or "How can I deliver this intervention in a way that will engage my students behaviorally, cognitively, and affectively?" Important questions surrounding process-focused instruction and interventions include the following:

- What teaching strategies do I use to increase engagement among students of color?
- How do I create process-focused instructional strategies that integrate characteristics associated with African American culture?
- Could the manner in which I present information create barriers to learning in my classroom?

THE DOMINANCE OF EUROCENTRIC CULTURAL CHARACTERISTICS

Eurocentric cultural characteristics dominate the delivery of instruction in many classrooms in our educational system. For example, in a study in which researchers observed 21 classrooms from six schools in a Midwestern part of the United States, 89% of the classroom cultural themes resembled Anglo or Eurocentric cultural values, and a mere 11% of the observances resembled Afrocentric cultural values (Boykin, Tyler, & Miller, 2005). More specifically, the movement-expressive cultural theme was observed 6% of the time (27 times out of 429 classroom observances). Interestingly, of the 27 observances of movement in the classroom, 70% (19) of the movement behaviors were initiated by students themselves, not by teachers. Communalism accounted for 3% (13 observances out of 429) of the time; verve accounted for less than 2% (8 times out of 429 observances). Students initiated seven of the eight verve themes in the classroom, which means the teacher initiated a verve theme only one time during the observational sessions.

Cultural norms that reflect individualism were the most observed and accounted for 47% (201 times of the 429 observances), competition accounted for 26% (113 times of the 429 observances), and bureaucracy orientation accounted for 15% (67 of the 429 observances). Interestingly, all educators who incorporated Afrocentric cultural themes into their classrooms were African American (see Boykin, Tyler, & Miller, 2005).

Service delivery models that focus on *individualism* consist of creating classroom environments whereby individual seatwork is encouraged over group work. With this model, students usually work alone, at their desks; teachers encourage student autonomy and usually provide praise to those individuals who meet academic standards.

Service delivery models that focus on *competition* consist of creating classroom environments whereby students are encouraged to compete against one another. With this model, students strive to outperform their classroom peers, and teachers usually praise those who outshine other students. Students in this model usually conclude that their success is based on the failure of their classroom peers (Boykin, Tyler, & Miller, 2005).

Service delivery models that focus on *bureaucratic orientations* consist of creating classrooms with strict rules and requiring students to adhere to these rules. Students who do not adhere to these rules are usually sent to the principal's or dean's office. Many of these students do not thrive academically because, while in the office, they miss an enormous amount of instructional time. Cultural characteristics such as individualism, competition, and bureaucratic orientation are in stark contrast to cultural characteristics many children of color value.

Because Eurocentric or Anglo cultural values dominate most classrooms in America's school system, researchers have conducted studies to determine the effect Afrocultural characteristics might have on African American students. Research by Gilmore (1985) was instrumental in showing the relevance of culture on academic engagement. Based on qualitative studies, Gilmore (1985) concluded that Black students' reading performance improved when "out-of-school," culturally relevant delivery models were used as opposed to using school-based, Eurocentric models.

Since characteristics that identify Black culture—communalism, movement, verve—are rarely observed within America's classrooms, studies have been conducted to understand the effect they might have on academic engagement among African American students of low-income backgrounds. For example, because African American students who come from working-class families have reported high levels of activity, stimulation, verve, and frequent engagement of rhythmic movements within their homes (Boykin, 1983), researchers have examined the extent to which these behaviors generalize to the school setting. In other words, researchers have sought to understand the level of academic engagement children of color would demonstrate in the classroom if these same characteristics were present during instructional time.

In one study, researchers used the Home Stimulation Affordance (HSA) questionnaire and the Child Activity (CA) questionnaire. Researchers measured household stimulation by asking questions such as, "How often does the radio and television remain on throughout a given day? How often do family members engage in clapping and dancing behaviors? Do you like active games that require movement such as running and jumping?" (Bailey & Boykin, 2001).

Twelve picture pairs (animal-food) were included in the study to measure students' learning performance. In the first condition, characterized by low movement/verve (LMV), children were seated in chairs and asked to learn the animal-food relationship by verbalizing the pairs directly after the presenter verbalized them: The presenter would say, for example, bear-cake, and the students would repeat, "bear-cake" (Bailey & Boykin, 2001).

In the second condition, characterized by high movement/verve (HMV), children were allowed to learn by incorporating music and hand clapping, although hand clapping was an option. Students listened to a percussive tune while standing. Researchers reported that clapping and moving in place to the sound of the rhythmic music was an automatic response from most students. In this group, words were called out in a varied, alternative fashion; either one word was called out, or a pair was called out while displaying the animal-food card. For example, if the examiner called out one word, students had to provide the corresponding mate; if the examiner verbalized the pair, students would verbalize the (animal-food) paired relationship verbatim.

Results indicated a significant effect with condition such that performances within the high-movement verve condition were better than the low-movement verve condition. Researchers concluded that students from Black working-class families may become academically engaged and perform better if cultural characteristics that are valued within their homes are incorporated in their school experiences. These include high levels of movement, as opposed to mundane, low-movement classroom activities (Bailey & Boykin, 2001).

These results confirm the study by Boykin and Bailey (2000), in which it was found that African American students from low-income working families place high value on Afrocultural characteristics that are present within the home. Students preferred learning environments that incorporated movement, music, communal learning, and vervistic orientations (Boykin & Bailey, 2000).

Because most research concerning the incorporation of Afrocultural themes in school has focused on language-based tasks, researchers have examined the relationship between cultural themes and mathematics (Hurley et al., 2005). Seventy-eight African American students engaged in mathematical estimation tasks. These tasks consisted of two learning groups: one representing communalism (high communal), the other, individualism (low communal). It was predicted that the group that engaged in high levels of communal expressiveness would be more motivated to learn and engage academically compared to the low communal group.

"Communal prompts" were used in which children in the communal groups were encouraged to hold hands and told they were a group that depended on each other to facilitate learning. Students were unified by social identities—school friends, a part of the school's culture—in which they depended on one another for learning.

In the individualistic, low-communal group, students worked and sat at their desks alone, quietly. "Individual prompts" were included in which researchers told students to work hard and that rewards were available if *individual* scores were improved. In addition, individual prompts reinforced autonomy and self-responsibility as opposed to group orientation. Results indicated that students in the high-communal group outperformed those in the individualistic group. Researchers explained that communalistic grouping has significant implications for mathematical achievement of African American students.

LEARNING STYLES BEGIN IN THE HOME

Why is the relationship between culture and academic engagement so meaningful? The answer is that the way in which we are raised as children, including the way we engage in our environments, creates a sort of map in our minds (Sternberg, 2003). Many African American children are raised in homes that are highly stimulated (Belgrave & Allison, 2014); music, movement, and bonding are key elements to creating their "maps."

African American parents may play music and sing to themselves, while children dance around the house; not only do children hear music from the radio or from their parents' mouths, but they also hear music from the television. In addition to music and movement, bonding with family members, friends, and fictive kin—including church family—is valued within this culture. Thus, children who are reared in these sorts of environments may respond automatically to syncopated music; their cognitive maps may steer them in the direction of activities that incorporate entertainment and music (verve), movement, and bonding (communalism). If these students do not identify these sorts of activities in their classrooms, they may create these experiences themselves (see Boykin, Tyler, & Miller, 2005). When students create these experiences in their classrooms, their teachers usually send them to the office; the reason is, the expressive behaviors these students present in the classrooms are often inconsistent with the class culture, which, in most cases, requires students to sit down, remain quiet, and work by themselves on assignments.

Children who are raised in homes that value communalism, movement, and verve are predisposed to high stimulation and bonding early in life. Because their minds have been molded by cultural characteristics that reflect movement, communalism, and verve, they may enter the classroom singing or humming to themselves; they may think of a song or beat and subconsciously play that beat on the desk or sing aloud during instructional time. Other children may have a strong desire to work with their neighbor or work in groups because they are used to working as a whole, communally.

AUTOMATIC PROCESSING OF INFORMATION

The statement "People act habitually" is true. The reason is our minds remember the behaviors we engage in most frequently. From engaging in behaviors over a prolonged period, our minds perform the behaviors for us, often without our conscious awareness. In fact, many of the things we do stem from subconscious processes; that is, many of the behaviors we demonstrate occur subconsciously (Sternberg, 2003).

Let's use an example of driving a car to understand better the way our subconscious minds operate. When you stop at a red light, what usually happens when the light turns green? Usually, you automatically release your foot from the brake, place it onto the gas pedal, and then accelerate. You remove your foot from the brake even without thinking about it. This happens even when your mind is preoccupied with thoughts. The reason is, you have removed your foot from the brake and placed it on the gas pedal in the presence of a red light for so long that your mind does it for you, without your conscious awareness. Because we are exposed to cultural characteristics early in life, and because we engage in these valued behaviors over a prolonged period, our minds produce the behaviors for us, often without our conscious knowing. This means that students who come from stimulating households may sing to themselves or tap on their desks in the classroom, without their knowing—and this does not necessarily mean they are off-task.

Cognitive learning styles are culturally determined (Hilliard, 1992; Watkins, 2002). For example, researchers have shown that many African American students have learning styles that are consistent with individuals of collectivist cultures (Shade, 1991, 1997; Varnum, Grossmann, Kitayama, & Nisbett, 2010).

But this does not mean that racial and cultural group members are monolithic—that they think, act, and display the same cognitive learning styles as members of their group simply because of phenotypic features, language, experiences, or national origin (Gutiérrez & Rogoff, 2003). In fact, in one study, White students from low-income backgrounds endorsed communalistic themes, and researchers used this finding to show that culture is learned based on cultural contact and is not determined by race (Boykin, Albury, et al., 2005).

Reportedly, White students in the previous study were exposed to Afrocultural characteristics outside of school and thus showed a preference toward communalism. These experiences show that we learn to value cultural characteristics through education and exposure; cultural values are not biologically determined.

Most African Americans display behaviors that reflect Afrocultural characteristics (Watkins, 2002; White & Parham, 1990). Others, however, depending on their degree of assimilation, may display behaviors that are completely dissimilar to Afrocultural backgrounds and values (Gutiérrez & Rogoff, 2003). For example, Oyserman et al. (2002) found that African Americans were more individualistic than European Americans in certain regards. Because of cultural contact with outside groups, some Blacks may function consistent with traditional Eurocentric ideologies and lifestyles, and many Whites may function consistent with the cultural system of Afrocentrism (Hilliard, 1992). Therefore, it would be a step backward if educators attributed learning styles to Black, White, or Brown students simply because of visible characteristics such as skin color.

The extent to which one functions according to traditional cultural systems or bicultural systems depends on the degree of exposure to such culture and the degree to which he or she values that culture (Hilliard, 1992). This holds true for the school system as well: It would be inaccurate to assume that children embrace Eurocentric learning styles simply because they are required to learn in an environment that focuses on traditional Eurocentric teaching styles. Moreover, pedagogy that resembles Eurocentric teaching styles may not be best practice even for Eurocentric American students (Belgrave & Allision, 2014; Hilliard, 1992), especially if they do not come from homes that value Eurocentric learning styles. In addition, pedagogy that resembles Afrocultural teaching styles may not be best practice for African American students (Belgrave & Allison, 2014).

An effective Tier 1 design would require educators to identify which of their students learn best by being placed in groups—cooperative learning—and which learn best by working independently. Research has shown that cooperative learning is an effective learning strategy among students and across race, class, gender, and culture (Haynes & Gebreyesus, 1992; Millis, 2009; Salend, 2001; Slavin, 1983), but does this mean that *all* students will prefer cooperative learning over working independent of a group? Some students may process information fast and learn new concepts relatively quickly compared to their same-aged peers; children who process information quickly may become frustrated when they have to work at a slower rate and wait for the group to catch up with their thinking. Although cooperative learning is best practice for most students, effective Tier 1 instruction would require educators to engage in research within their classrooms to create unique learning environments for all children.

Although it took years, I have identified my learning style, and it is consistent with the way my parents taught me as a child. My parents placed significant value on the family and neighbors, and church members were considered family. When we called someone in our church "Brother John" or "Sister Jones," it was not simply church jargon or religious practice, but rather, we actually considered them close relatives.

I can recall getting into a fight during my middle school years. When the teacher sent me to the office, the principal looked through my files to find a contact number for my parents. Because my mother and father were working and could not pick me up, the principal had to call the next contact person on the list: "Who is Sister Reed?!" my principal asked as he read the contact information and scratched his head. In response, I stated, "Oh, she is a close friend of the family." He erroneously believed that Sister Reed was a nun! Why my mother did not provide "Sister Reed's" full name is another discussion. Because our family placed great emphasis on family, bonding, and interpersonal relationships, I often desired strong bonds in the classroom and desired to work interdependently on assignments during instruction time. I was most engaged when provided these learning opportunities.

MISINTERPRETING AFROCENTRIC BEHAVIORS

During my graduate school experience, a couple of my professors identified me as a deceptive and sneaky student. I often found myself in my advisor's office, meeting with him and another faculty member because "my behaviors as a graduate student were inappropriate." I often found myself explaining why I did things. I recall saying, on several occasions, "I didn't mean to offend you," or "That's not what I meant." One of my professors became furious at me because I would constantly come into his office to discuss course content. Because I was so fascinated with learning the content and loved to get different perspectives, I would talk with each professor about the same content. Actually, from discussing the same content with three different professors and getting three different perspectives, I learned the content better than most of my graduate-level peers. In fact, although my GRE score was indeed the lowest in my cohort, I mentored many of my peers in the area of school psychology, psychology, and statistics—peers who had honorable GRE scores. I was able to process and retain my graduate-level course work because I had identified my learning style.

Not only did one of my professors become furious at me because I would go from one professor to the next with questions about some concept, but this professor also called me into his office because he thought I would benefit from "role-playing." This professor stated, "Okay, Dwayne, there is something you need to realize. How would you feel if someone were giving a presentation and you fell asleep . . . but instead of letting you sleep for that moment, the presenter said 'Alright, Dwayne, now is not the time to sleep'?" In response, I threw my hands in the air and shrugged my shoulders. At this point, my professor said, "You see, Dwayne, you still don't get it! I think we need to role-play so you will understand how you make people feel."

At this point, I said, "Look, if you want to share something with me or believe I may benefit from learning something, just tell me what's on your mind—I don't think role-playing is necessary." In response, my professor reminisced on a time when I gave a presentation in his class, and while giving my presentation, I called his name, in an attempt to wake him up. During my presentation, I explained that he should probably listen to what I had to say in order to give me the most appropriate grade. My classroom peers laughed in response to my comment. When he recalled this experience, during our office meeting, he told me that I was extremely rude and needed to learn better behaviors as a graduate student. In response to hearing this, I looked at him and shook my head.

Clearly, I brought to the graduate program cultural characteristics my professors were unfamiliar with. To be sure, I was not being deceptive and sneaky by meeting with all of my professors to discuss the same topic, and I was not trying to see which professor would provide the best interpretation of some concept. Rather, I was engaging in a learning style to which I was most familiar. I displayed a *field-dependent* learning style, and it was evident.

I learn best by using my entire environment, including the people within my environment. The more I pull from my environment, the more I learn and better process information. And I was not trying to embarrass my professor by jokingly telling him to wake up; saying "wake up" was my way of bringing entertainment into the classroom. When I said, "wake up," my peers laughed, I laughed, and the environment was less stressful. This was a good thing, considering we all were terrified to stand in front of the classroom to give presentations. Instead of understanding my learning style and why I did certain things, my professors identified me as a problem student. They interpreted my behaviors from their own cultural lenses.

I can recall explaining to my professors that I learn best by using my environment and that I was not trying to see which professor would provide the best interpretation of some concept; I explained that I was a field-dependent learner. I can recall telling my advisor, "I can only imagine what little children go through while in school who are field-dependent learners." Out of frustration, I went on: "If you, as a professor of school psychology, can't identify learning styles, why should we assume teachers can identify them?" At this point, I was really considered a troublemaker by my professors! I went on to say that many children who are misunderstood do not drop out of school but that they are pushed out by those who are in authority in the school system and by those who misunderstand their behaviors.

Meeting with my advisor was horrifying! I remember saying to myself, after leaving his office, "If we have another meeting to discuss how I act, I'm going to really tell him how I feel about him." Thankfully, I was not called into the office again to discuss my deceptiveness and sneakiness.

I remember breaking down in one of my professor's offices because I was so frustrated. My breaking point was in response to having to endure so much and being able to say so little. I took their verbal assaults without speaking out; I feared they would somehow interfere with my completing the program, and this was a torturing thought—after all, I had a wife and kid at home, and I was determined to graduate.

Interestingly, when I broke down, my professor recalled an article he and I had discussed: "Dwayne, what you are experiencing is consistent with your research. Remember the article you and I discussed last week that we found extremely interesting? It was the article that talked about how difficult college may present for students of color who bring to predominantly White institutions different cultural characteristics? You are definitely experiencing issues similar to what we read." He went on: "This is why multicultural training is needed. Dwayne, you clearly bring to the program communalistic characteristics, and I love it! But I believe the more communalistic you are, the more difficult it may be for you at this point—although I don't think you should change how you are. I know this has to be frustrating for you!"

When my professors wrote my letters of recommendation (the same professors who accused me of being deceptive), one characteristic they stressed was my social aptitude—my ability to work collaboratively with others. They explained that I had a unique way of engaging others, helping others, and appreciating others. Clearly, they spoke about my communalistic values.

CHILDREN OF COLOR ARE OFTEN MISUNDERSTOOD

I recalled my graduate experiences because I believe that children of color are misunderstood daily. The fact is, children of color aren't as rude as many teachers think. And behaviors such as moving around in the classroom and talking to neighbors while completing assignments should not always be viewed as disruptive behaviors. Because students learn differently and come from different backgrounds, educators should take time to identify what their students' behaviors actually mean.

Actually, most students try hard to please their teachers and other adults. I have noticed students try their best to please their teachers and to present themselves in a respectful manner. One youngster I worked with would lower his voice when he approached female educators he respected and would attempt to present as a polite young man. I can recall, on one occasion, when this young man approached a female educator in the building. He lowered his voice, smiled, and kind of leaned on one leg as he asked his question. When the female educator asked him a question, the young man did not say "yes," "no," or "yes, ma'am, no, ma'am." Instead, the young man replied by saying "yeah" and "naw."

It was clear to me that the youngster's presentation was as appropriate as he could display. But when he walked away, the female educator said, "See, that's what I'm talking about! These kids are so disrespectful! They don't say 'yes' or 'no,' but they say 'yeah' and 'naw'! And you know they would never say 'yes, ma'am.' They don't have it in them!" His behaviors did not reflect Afrocentric cultural characteristics, but the reality is, this young man probably was never required to say yes or no in response to a question; maybe he came from a community where youth believed articulating "yes" and "no" was lame—and because he responded by saying "yeah" and "naw" on numerous occasions, these responses came naturally.

Any serious RTI model would take these experiences into perspective. Earlier in this book, I stated that providing education is as socioemotional and sociocultural as it is cognitive (Bodrova & Leong, 2007). This means, how students feel about their teachers has a direct relationship with their level of academic engagement and performance in the classroom (Tucker et al., 2005), and this is true of students in general.

If students are unable to engage in behaviors that are valued within their homes and if educators constantly reprimand them for behaviors that resemble cultural responses to their environments, students may remain disengaged, even when research-based instruction and evidence-based interventions are implemented. As educators, it is important that we remain cognizant of the fact that research-based interventions alone may not engage unmotivated or avoidant learners; rather, how we deliver research-based interventions in the classroom, based on differentiated instruction, is what increases academic engagement.

CULTURE AND CULTURALLY BASED INTERVENTIONS

The RTI model encourages educators to refer to scientific strategies that have been shown effective prior to making educational decisions (Hierck & Weber, 2014). One problem, as it relates to culturally relevant pedagogy, is that many educators are unfamiliar with research as it pertains to engaging students of color (Delpit, 1995/2006; Howard, 2006). When I present to teachers and administrators, most audience members are unfamiliar with research on the effect of movement, verve, orality, and communalism on academic engagement. In addition, educators have been unfamiliar with research that shows that many children of color disengage in the classroom when they are required to learn in traditional Eurocentric classrooms—classrooms that place high emphases on individualism, competition, and bureaucratic orientations. Actually, the most engaging moments of my workshops surround discussions on culture and understanding characteristics that have been associated with African American culture. These experiences are most engaging because teachers usually have an "ah-ha" moment. They usually recall the times when their students congregate in their classrooms, create beats and songs, and ask to integrate music with instruction.

Educators may benefit from compiling culturally relevant interventions and referring to the references within this book. They may improve their instruction with children of color if they incorporate strategies that have been shown effective. One of the most difficult processes of RTI, as explained by many teachers I have trained, pertains to providing evidence-based interventions. Thus, a common question is, "From where do we get culturally relevant, evidence-based intervention strategies?" After presenting to a district on the effect of culture on academic engagement, educators wanted to know where they could find interventions that incorporate movement, communalism, and verve. Based on teacher feedback, it would be beneficial if schools compiled interventions that educators could refer to regarding culturally relevant pedagogy.

Educators who are interested in learning more about culture and culturally relevant interventions may benefit from reading *Creating the Opportunity to Learn,* by A. Wade Boykin and Pedro Noguera (2011). Although their book does not provide information on RTI, Boykin and Noguera report on an array of instructional strategies that teachers could implement in their classrooms to potentially increase academic engagement among students of color. These researchers discuss the importance of communalism, movement, and verve on academic achievement and provide caveats that educators must consider prior to incorporating culturally relevant instruction.

CHAPTER SUMMARY

Many RTI books and resources address skill-focused interventions, but very few shed light on the need to consider process-focused interventions. Skill-focused interventions are needed to increase skill, but if interventions are implemented in a manner that is not engaging, students will not apply themselves at a level that is needed to retain knowledge. Thus, process-focused interventions are just as important as skill-focused interventions. To increase performance among many culturally diverse students, educators must identify not only skill-focused interventions but also process-focused interventions surrounding culturally relevant experiences.

In the next chapter, I discuss the importance of entertaining and stimulating instruction for students who value African American cultural characteristics.

PART 2

Vignettes

"Entertainment?! Why Can't Our Children Just Sit Down and Learn?"

9

Tell me and I'll forget; show me and I'll remember; involve me and I'll understand.

—*Confucius*

I became interested in culture during the first year of my graduate schooling. An African American developmental psychology instructor had given me an array of articles and books on culture and its effect on academic engagement of Black children from low-income backgrounds. This instructor attended Howard University and studied with Dr. A. Wade Boykin, so this type of material was not new to him, although it was the first time I had read it. I was amazed at this material. I can recall staying up all night reading, waking up early morning thinking about the material, and reading more and more when I could find time. Not only was the material engaging for me, but also it was entertaining. Important questions surrounding this chapter include the following:

- Is it necessary to make education entertaining?
- What is perhaps the best way to prepare students of color for mainstream America?
- Is there a relationship between students who demonstrate Afrocultural characteristics and students who receive the most discipline referrals?

- Is it necessary to integrate Afrocultural characteristics in the classroom considering students may not be able to integrate such characteristics in mainstream America or at the corporate level?

WHY ENTERTAINMENT?

During my second year of graduate school, I was required to declare a thesis topic. Not only did I know the area of education I wanted to research, but I also had my topic and title: *The Effect of Cultural Characteristics in School on Academic Engagement.* When I declared this topic, I could not wait to share the news. I was ecstatic! I shared this topic with one of my graduate professors, who explained that he did not see the purpose of choosing such a topic. He explained that culture has very little to do with education and that I should focus on Ruby Payne's work and maybe research some of her material on poverty and children from impoverished backgrounds.

When I returned home, I discussed my topic with my wife over dinner. Although she was interested in the research, she explained that she had some concerns about the topic. After swallowing her food, she went in for the kill: "Entertainment?! Why can't our children just sit down and learn like other kids? And how come we have to make education entertaining? Everything doesn't have to be about music, dancing around the room, foot-working, and having fun! Our children need to sit their tails down somewhere and learn!" I could tell from her voice that although she wanted to support the idea, she had reservations.

As I listened to her, I understood her concerns. But I also understood that some children of color are extremely unmotivated and avoidant learners and that if we do not do something that will motivate them in their early years of education, then we will definitely lose them in high school. I then remembered the purpose of my study: If playing music and allowing these learners to dance around the room while memorizing math facts will increase academic engagement and math fact fluency, or if creating entertaining games that motivate children to engage in blending and segmenting words will improve fluency, then by all means, let's try it.

I also contemplated the research on field-independent and field-dependent learners. I thought, "If many children of color are field-dependent learners, then music, movement, and bonding with children in their classrooms may work as prompts and contextual clues they may use to memorize information better." Based on my feelings about the need to involve students in the learning process, I decided to move forward with the research, although I appreciated my professor's and my wife's concerns.

RTI requires teachers to be not only educators but also researchers. A few questions educators may want to research:

- How do we create a classroom that will facilitate engagement for children of color?
- How can we create a classroom that is learner friendly—one that incorporates pictures on the walls, pictures of not only White faces but also Black and Brown faces?
- What kinds of educational games can we play that include movement and dance in the classroom while learning?
- How do we create a classroom where students can lean and depend on each other to succeed academically, a classroom that discourages academic competition and individualism?

PREPARING CHILDREN OF COLOR FOR MAINSTREAM SOCIETY

Many African American educators have told me that Black children should seek to suppress their cultural characteristics while in school and learn to adopt the mainstream culture; their reasoning is these children will not be able to dance or listen to music in a college classroom or while working in corporate America.

My response to these statements is always the same: "Before we could talk about college or employment in corporate America, our children must become engaged at the primary and secondary levels. And if we do not connect them to the curriculum and teach them how to read, write, and compute numbers, they'll end up robbing someone's store, breaking into someone's home, in prison, or dead." There are not many options for students who are unable to read, write, and compute, and because opportunities are limited, they may engage in criminal activities to survive; they may resort to illegal ways to support themselves and their families.

All children must learn to become bicultural, and children of color are no exception; they must learn to function not only within their own communities but also within the school and within communities that are dissimilar from theirs. But one problem is this: Many children disengage because they are reprimanded for bringing to the classroom behaviors that are valued within their communities. They are reprimanded for creating rap songs and rapping them in class, creating beats on the desk, dancing, and talking with their peers.

It's true that children of color will not be able to dance around the room in college or play music or dance at the corporate level, but it may be intelligent to allow them to dance their way to academic success at the primary and secondary levels and, as they connect with the schooling process, teach them about the mainstream culture. After they experience success and realize the importance of education, educators could teach these children the importance of functioning in different cultures; this would be a good time to teach them that they will also need to learn to work independently and that music and expressive movement will be unacceptable in certain places. It will also be a good time to teach them that they must become competitive.

One example is teachers could create situations where children could be as expressive as they want; in this context, children could express themselves in song and dance. Educators could allow children to name the situation and explain why expressive movement and dance may be appropriate. In contrast to this situation, educators could create a situation where it would be inappropriate to express oneself through song and dance. It is imperative that children learn the need for variability within society and within their communities. But, first things first—educators must connect these students to the curriculum, and after these children become excited about education and learn that they are indeed intelligent, they will be open to learning how to function in different cultural settings. Not only will they be open to functioning in different cultural settings, but also they'll be willing to show their ability to do so.

One thing is true of most children of color: They are very expressive. When they become excited, they show it! They may jump out of their seats, laugh, hit their desks, give "their guys and girls" dap—a type of hand shaking gesture—and some may dash toward their teacher, full speed, with their hands in the air to provide a high five. Many African Americans are very emotional and animated, and their behaviors are acts of performances and dramatizations (White & Parham, 1990). A simple conversation may consist of overexaggerated hand and body movements, facial expressions, and daps; when conversing, they may interrupt each other to illustrate or emphasize some point, and this type of behavior demonstrates interest in the topic of discussion. It is not deemed inappropriate or rude.

MISINTERPRETING AFROCENTRIC VALUES

During my graduate school years, I attended a church in South Charleston, West Virginia. The organist at this church was a local middle school principal. Because many of the city's children of color attended the principal's school, I thought it would be a good idea to collect data on his students to complete my thesis. When I presented the thesis topic to the principal, he immediately told me that the research was needed in his school. At one point, before I could finish my sentence, the principal interrupted me. I could tell he was agitated; his face squirmed as he began to speak: "Listen, Brother Dwayne—This is how badly we need this research. Last week, 10 students were sent to my office. We had an assembly, right? And prior to the start of the assembly, all the students were sitting down quietly and were waiting patiently for everything to start. They were behaving themselves. Well, according to one of my teachers, music came on and, in response to the music, many of the students jumped out of their seats and began to dance and bounce around. She explained that their dancing was a sort of automatic response upon hearing the rhythmic music, and she sent all 10 to the office! She stated that they were disruptive and were unable to control themselves and thus should not be a part of the assembly."

Clearly, this experience presented a cultural clash. The teacher had expectations of her students that reflected traditional Eurocentric cultural characteristics. She expected them to sit down, remain in their seats, and remain silent—even while stimulating music played throughout the auditorium. These behaviors were the measures by which the teacher determined appropriate and inappropriate conduct. Contrarily, the students responded affectively to the rhythmic music that was projected throughout the auditorium.

These students did not premeditate being disruptive, for they had no idea that music was a part of the assembly. Rather, upon hearing the music, their minds produced expressive behaviors; their minds automatically demonstrated behaviors that are valued in their culture. Their dancing and bouncing to the music was the observable response of their minds being stimulated. Neurologically, their behaviors were consistent with how their minds were wired. Instead of considering expressive behaviors disruptive, educators may benefit from brainstorming ways they could use such positive energy to facilitate academic engagement among students of color.

ENTERTAINING, ENGAGING CLASSROOMS

Educators and researchers often create interventions and instructions, but students rarely have any say in how they would like to learn in the classroom. Are elementary, middle, and high school students capable of accurately determining what will motivate them to learn in the classroom? Stated differently, how much education and research experience must one have in order to determine if a particular instructional method would motivate them to engage academically?

An effective behavior modification system would encourage interventionists to interview a referred student to get a working understanding of him or her. Within the lists of questions, the interventionist would ask the student what motivates him or her to do well behaviorally and academically. Interventions are much more effective when the interventionist incorporates items and games into students' token economy system (G. Martin & Pear, 2007). Because such an approach has been effective, psychologists usually attempt to use as carrots those things that motivate students. But educators shouldn't wait for a behavior intervention plan or behavior modification system to ask what motivates their students to do well in the classroom. RTI is rooted in research-based practices, but instructions and interventions are often incorporated into the classroom without probing students to determine if they would enjoy the instructional method.

When students are part of a problem-solving team in which they contribute to solving their own issues, they are more prone to involving themselves in the process (G. Martin & Pear, 2007); they usually feel that their opinions are valued. In most cases, students may feel that they have to show educators that they themselves can live up to "their team's" expectations. Moreover, students are more willing to complete a task when educators provide them with options to choose from (G. Martin & Pear, 2007). In these instances, students feel respected and understand that they are a part of a team.

Educators often try their best to engage students at the Tier 1 level, but allowing students to choose how they want to be taught may be more effective than creating activities without their input. This does not mean that educators should allow children to pick course content, because, after all, teaching standard objectives is mandatory. But after standard objectives have been determined, research should be conducted on students within the classroom to determine how these standards should be taught.

Students often explain that their classrooms are boring. Some teachers spend countless hours brainstorming ways to engage their students only to find that, when they incorporate the long-thought-out strategies, the students fall asleep, draw on their desks, or bluntly say, "This stuff is boring me!" When students say their classes are boring, they usually refer to how instruction is provided in the classroom. From my experiences, when students said that class was boring, they explained that class was not as stimulating and entertaining as they liked. In other words, they rarely referred to the subject or content as being boring; rather, they referred to the manner in which they were required to learn the content.

Children and youth love to learn. This is not just my opinion, but rather, educational researchers have found this to be true (Adelman & Taylor, 2006). And a love for learning does not exist only in certain ethnic groups or races; all children, of every race and ethnicity, love to learn. Most children of color become disengaged because many do not become a part of the content they learn; many educators do not extend opportunities for them to role-play literature or incorporate entertaining games that will allow them to multiply numbers or divide objects. Students are often required to read from textbooks and answer questions at the end of each chapter. In many classrooms, young children are required to memorize sounds, but they themselves rarely become letters that talk. Allowing children to pick letters they would like to become enables them not only to memorize the letters and sounds but also exercise their working memory ability.

A strategy that teachers may benefit from is asking their students to evaluate their teaching methods and to explain what they liked and disliked throughout the quarter or semester. Educators may benefit from reincorporating these instructional methods the following quarter, based on their students' feedback. Educators may also benefit from having an outside observer collect baseline data on their class to determine the extent to which the instructional method engages the students academically. If the delivery model engages the students, then educators may benefit their students by continuing the method; if the delivery model leads to disengaging behaviors, then educators may benefit their students by tweaking the instructional method. Often, teachers incorporate instructional styles in their classrooms, and although their instructional methods are ineffective, based on student engagement levels, they continue to use those methods. Students provide qualitative research daily surrounding their teachers' instructional strategies, and as educators, it is critical that we consider their analyses.

Howard (2001) investigated African American students' perceptions of effective teaching in a cross-sectional study. Students were grouped into low, medium, and high achievement categories. The most common responses children gave regarding their ideas of effective teachers and instructions were (1) the importance of caring teachers, (2) the establishment of a community/family-type classroom environment, and (3) education as entertainment. It was concluded that students preferred pedagogy that was relevant to Afrocultural themes: the value of interconnectedness and interpersonal caring (communalism), compatibility of home instruction and school instruction (cultural continuation), and a stimulating, entertaining environment (verve).

MAKING STUDENTS A PART OF THE CURRICULUM

During my graduate school practicum, the school psychology, counseling, and education cohorts had the great opportunity to run a summer program. This particular program was no ordinary summer program; our goal was to teach middle school students by creating unique experiences for them, experiences that focused on making them a part of the curriculum as opposed to relying strictly on reading textbooks and discussing reading material in the whole group. I can recall thinking, "This would be a great opportunity to implement some of the research on cultural characteristics and academic engagement!" Thus, this experience, for me, was twofold: (1) to complete graduation requirements and (2) to see for myself the effect of Afrocentric cultural characteristics on academic engagement. This was an actively engaged program, so active that students might have appeared off-task because they were out of their seats, clapping, laughing, moving around, and interacting with each other.

All of my students who attended the program were required to complete summer school because they had failed one or more classes. They had to attend as a requirement in order to be promoted to the next grade. According to teacher reports, these students were extremely unmotivated, and some were "very aggressive." Many of the students entered the program on day 1 with aggressive attitudes; their behaviors reflected what their teachers had revealed. When they entered the classroom, they demonstrated flat affect; many put their heads on their desks and watched me from the corners of their eyes as I explained how entertaining the program would be.

A Culturally Relevant Approach to Teaching and Learning

Prior to starting instruction, I assessed my students informally. I asked questions to learn what my students enjoyed to do while at school, while at home, and within their communities. I also asked questions to see what my students believed they wanted to do when they graduated from high school. My students provided varied responses, but most indicated that they enjoyed music and beats. This assessment was a part of my lesson plan, in which my goal was to incorporate their interests with my instruction.

Prior to ending the day, I discussed the importance of science and what science means in our everyday lives. I explained that we would focus on science the first part of our days and asked them how they wanted to approach the science lessons. Students explained that they wanted to create beats to whatever they learned. This was perfect! I explained that the group could be a choir. I then asked who wanted to be the soloist, the choir director, and the drummer boy. I explained that their roles—soloist, drummer boy/girl, and choir director—would change daily. This would allow all students to fill a role.

Instead of giving them traditional homework on this day, the soloist, choir director, and drummer boy had to go home and work on their "skills." I recommended that the choir director stand in front of the mirror to practice directing the choir, the soloist had to practice singing while listening to the radio or television, and the drummer had to create at least three beats that he or she could use to keep the choir on rhythm while learning their science lesson.

From using their interests, my students went from staggering into the classroom with flat affect to running into the classroom and discussing with their peers how ready they were to sing in the choir. Students were eager to start the science lesson in which incorporating beats and singing a song related to the scientific method. I also printed out a "scientific method rap" that I had found online the night before. Students sang their songs, incorporated their beats, and rapped their way to learning the scientific method. At the end of the lesson, I divided the students into groups and recommended that they help each other memorize the method so they could recite the steps when asked. Students were able to explain the scientific steps in order, as well as how each step related to their lives and community experiences. As an engaging activity and way to measure their learning, students were given a passage in which they had to read and use the scientific method to solve a problem. For this passage, students where given the option of receiving a pair of Air Jordan tennis shoes from Champs shoe store or regular leather boots from Payless shoe store. The students were required to pick which would be more appropriate for the winter weather, a winter that would include days of zero degree weather. They were also required to make predictions about which would keep their feet most warm and use the scientific method to come up with a way of measuring this. The students became extremely excited about this as many completed their assignments standing up and often walked to their peers' desks to see what predictions they had made.

In addition to learning the scientific method, students were able to use bongos to create beats while learning the states and capitals. The drummer would start by clapping his hands, while saying "1–2–3–4—" After the drummer stated "4," he started his beat. Following the beat, the soloist sang something like, "What is the capital of West Virginia?" In response to the soloists' question, the choir answered by chanting, "Charles—ton, Charles—ton." This rhythm was used to learn all of the states and capitals. The students became even more engaged as professors who walked past their rooms stopped in to watch and clap along.

Now, I could imagine someone asking, as my wife once did, "Is all this necessary? Do students really need to create rap songs and sing in order to learn?" Well, the question should not be whether this type of instruction is necessary or whether students "need" to create rap songs and sing in order to learn. It is obvious that children of color can learn just about anything they want—if they are motivated to do so. But the question regarding incorporating such practices into the classroom should be, "Would children benefit from such stimulating instruction?" In other words, would children connect to the curriculum if they had these types of experiences in their classrooms?

Children of color who are considered motivated learners—those who come into the classroom on day 1 ready to engage themselves and learn—may not require such practices, although they also may benefit from the stimulation. However, unmotivated learners—those who do not possess intrinsic motivation for academic learning in their classrooms—may definitely benefit. These children may benefit because unmotivated learners usually become motivated when they find within their environments something they are interested in, something that motivates them to engage and participate during instructional engagement time. And if these children identify with cultural characteristics within their classrooms, then it is possible that they would become as actively engaged in school as they are within their communities. In fact, if children were as actively engaged in their classrooms as they are within their local churches, tests scores would increase, the achievement gap between Whites and non-Whites would close, and schools that find difficulty making adequate yearly progress would begin to show significant improvement in student achievement.

Implicit in these claims is that one of the major reasons children are not scoring high on standardized tests is not because they come from poverty and have not learned middle-class values. Rather, children are not engaged during instructional time. To pass any test, whether it is a standardized achievement test or a test of how to play tag during recess, someone must not only explain what will be on the test but also teach the basic concepts. More important, the learner must be motivated to learn what to do and how to play.

ENTERTAINING INSTRUCTION

Many educators have asked for feedback on what they could do to engage students academically. In most instances, I believe they wanted my opinion because they believed I would know how to motivate their students simply because I am a school psychologist. But my opinion may not engage their students, because in most cases, I have not asked their students what motivates them. In fact, when I would meet with teachers about their students, the first question I would ask was, "Have you asked him what would motivate or engage him?" To this question, educators usually said no.

Instead of getting the opinions of school psychologists on how to engage children of color, it would be most beneficial and educational for teachers to compile research on what children of color have to say about their classrooms. After compiling research on students' perceptions of the classroom, educators could collect data on students, by using questionnaires, to get their opinions of what will motivate them academically. If their responses are similar to the empirically based articles, then educators could refer to the reference sections of the articles to familiarize themselves with similar, evidence-based studies. From the articles in the reference sections, educators may come across culturally relevant interventions. This type of practice brings research into the classroom; finding what works by asking students and researching articles that focus on engagement are consistent with best practices.

I am a part of a group on Facebook in which group members discuss many issues, including education. Group members include lawyers, K–12 teachers, and professors. As I prepared the revisions of this book, I thought it might be interesting to get feedback from the professionals within this group about education, including how their children perceive "good teaching." To get their children's feedback, I sent the following post to the group: "Hello all! I am in the process of revising a book about improving instruction for African-American students and I would love to hear from your children. I would love to get their perspective on how we could make instruction in the classroom more engaging and entertaining." I asked the group members to ask their children how their teachers could make instruction more interesting. Their responses were consistent with research:

Ninth-grade student: "Teachers should make classes more interactive. Don't just lecture at students. Allow us to participate in or lead discussions and share ideas."

Ninth-grade student: "Connecting with students is very important to getting them more engaged. Get to know your students and their interests. Be creative, find out what motivates them, and incorporate their interests into the lessons, classwork, and homework."

Fourth-grade student: "I think teachers should listen to their students and stop making everyone do the same stuff."

Sixth-grade student: "Teachers should use more stuff like Scratch [a coding software program from MIT] in the classroom to make learning more interesting and more like the stuff I like."

Second-grade student: "She could be more skillful when saying three plus five equals eight. She can say it strong and exciting to make it fun." (Parents explained: "We interpreted her use of the word 'skillful' as meaning 'theatrical' or 'animated,' as that was the body language she displayed.")

In addition to providing her children's feedback, one parent commented: "Since they graduated from 8th grade, they don't even want me to mention the word 'school' . . . it's all about summer vacation now. But when I asked them to provide quotes for this project, they bolted up, turned off the Wii, and started spewing out responses before I could get my pen ready to write them down." Just asking them their opinion about this sparked something in them, which speaks well to the ninth-grade student's quote. The parent added, "Dwayne, I also found that when they were given a choice of homework assignments or projects, they were more eager to complete them sooner rather than later because they were able to choose what they wanted to do rather than being forced to do a project they didn't like. Kids have different strengths and talents and they work and learn differently, so naturally they will do a better job when they get to use their talents and work in their own way. Giving them a choice of assignments from a pre-established list provided by the teacher gives them a chance to select a project that best displays their strengths and talents. I think this works much better than the cookie-cutter, by-the-text book approach."

CHAPTER SUMMARY

Many African American students come from stimulating and engaging communities and backgrounds. Within these communities, many students listen to syncopated music, dance, bond, and show affection toward one another. Although many African American students are expressive and enjoy entertaining instruction, they often explain that their instruction is boring and mundane—and although they desire to work interdependently, move around in the classroom, and integrate music with instruction, many are required to work by themselves, remain in their seats, and are denied the opportunity to integrate music with instruction. For students who are field-dependent learners, integrating cultural values with instruction may present as contextual clues that students could use to increase engagement and learning in the classroom. Although this chapter talks about the importance of entertainment for many African American students, it is most critical that educators remain cognizant of variability among African American students in that just as some may desire movement and expressive activities, others may prefer to work in isolation and prefer more subtle activities.

In the next chapter, I provide additional information on engagement and explain why engagement is understood within the context of culture and cultural values. That is, although you and I may observe the same student in the same classroom, you may perceive the student as off-task, while I may perceive him as academically engaged. How we define *engagement* is rooted in cultural values.

What Does Academic Engagement Look Like for Many Children of Color? **10**

Anyone who tries to make a distinction between education and entertainment doesn't know the first thing about either.

—Marshall McLuhan

Academic engagement is highly correlated with school achievement and high school graduation rates (Adelman & Taylor, 2006). But an important question is, What is academic engagement? Educational researchers may respond to this question differently, based on their interpretations of engagement. Additional questions: Are students more prone to engage academically when activities reflect their cultural values? and Is it possible that children of color engage themselves in ways that are in stark contrast to how educators define academic engagement? Important questions surrounding this chapter include the following:

- What exactly is academic engagement?
- By whose standards do we define *engagement?*
- What does academic engagement look like for students who come from Afrocultural backgrounds?

CULTURAL VALUES ARE MEANINGFUL

Let's begin our discussion with one of the above questions: "Are students more prone to engage academically when activities reflect their cultural values?" Consider the following analogy prior to answering this question. When I presented my thesis topic to my graduate school advisor, he told me that he didn't see the relevance of studying the effect of culture on academic engagement; he explained that poverty had the single biggest influence on children's academic achievement. After listening to his understanding of the irrelevance of culture on academic engagement, I finally provided an analogy I thought he would appreciate: "Okay, consider this. If you invited me to a concert, I'd probably go. But whether I enjoy the concert would depend on the genre of the music. If the music was heavy metal, rock-n-roll, country, or hard-core rap, chances are, I would not enjoy myself, considering I don't usually listen to these genres.

If I were to go to the concert and the above music were playing, I would be present, but chances are, my mind would be elsewhere. And although the musicians would probably be singing or rapping their hearts out, and although the crowd would probably be bouncing to the music, I would be looking around at everyone, wondering what time the concert would be over. Essentially, I would be disengaged from the experience. On the other hand, if the genre were contemporary Christian music, jazz, or rhythm and blues, not only would I be present but also engaged—standing, rocking, singing, and throwing my hands in the air. I would be engaged in the experience, and my responses to the music would be automatic."

As I explained this analogy to my advisor, I attempted to show him that the extent to which I would have been engaged during the concert would have been based on how the music made me feel. I would have been engaged affectively. I explained that the music was analogous to culture. Because I have listened to gospel music, jazz, and rhythm and blues throughout my development, such music has become a part of me. In fact, when I hear music that I've listened to throughout my development, I may automatically nod my head to the music or tap my foot, and this usually happens subconsciously, without my conscious knowing. This does not mean that all people of color listen to the same genres of music I listen to, for I know African Americans who love country, rock-n-roll, and hard-core rap. I know other African Americans who do not care for Christian or jazz music. The point is, we are often more willing to engage in activities that reflect cultural values; in fact, our engagement might be automatic, based on the strength of the culturally relevant activity.

Music and the concert are, in the above example, analogous to instruction in the classroom. Many students in the classroom are either passively engaged or off-task because they do not connect with how instruction is presented and are not presented with activities that are related to their cultural values. Consequently, many of these students disrupt the classroom, frequently ask to go to the bathroom, or may fall asleep. At the high school level, students may skip class or come to class near the end of the period—all because they do not connect with what is going on during instructional time.

In the previous chapter, I explained my wife's concerns surrounding the effect of movement and activities in the classroom on academic engagement. Although she expressed her hesitation toward such instructional practices, she and I have created a very stimulating and engaging household environment; we have transmitted to our children cultural values such as the importance of music, movement, and expression in daily interactions. For example, family entertainment within my household often consists of encouraging our children to dance in the middle of the living room; we usually record their kinesthetic expression to music and then let them watch their expressive movements on some device. Periodically, I would grab my children by their hands and dance around the room with them. We engage in these stimulating behaviors so often that when my children would hear rhythmic music, they would "cut the rug," at the early age of 3 and 4 years—and they still break out in dance when they hear such music. In addition to exposure to music within our home, my children are exposed to music during community activities, including church functions and outdoor grilling.

If school psychologists and teachers were to observe my children's behaviors, without understanding what goes on in their homes, they would probably wonder if my children were diagnosed with ADHD; my children's movement-expressive behaviors would be clinically meaningful compared to their classroom peers who do not come from such stimulating backgrounds.

WHAT DOES ACADEMIC ENGAGEMENT LOOK LIKE FOR MANY CHILDREN WHO COME FROM AFROCENTRIC BACKGROUNDS?

What does academic engagement look like when demonstrated by children who come from Afrocultural backgrounds? To measure the extent to which children of color are academically engaged, evaluators must not only observe these students' behaviors in class but also understand why they may engage in particular behaviors.

I was involved in a problem-solving meeting in which the teacher's main concern was that her student, an African American male, was very disruptive and disrespectful. According to the teacher referral, this student would interrupt her during instructional time to ask a question, would often talk without raising his hand, talk to his peers about things unrelated to the assignment, and would blurt out answers. Prior to this meeting, the grade-level team implemented interventions with the hope to reduce his inappropriate behaviors. Their goal was to use behavior modification to reduce disruptive and blurting-out behaviors to a manageable level. Their intervention proved ineffective. The more they implemented behavior management interventions, the more this student blurted out and disrupted the classroom.

Because the teacher did not know what to do with his disruptive behaviors, she would send him to the office, provide timeouts, and, according to her, "ignore him when he wanted to answer a question." Now the question is, Was this student disruptive or academically engaged? Well, the answer depends on the cultural lens you use to analyze the student's behaviors. From a Eurocentric model, a model that values silence when someone else is speaking, raising one's hand prior to speaking, and strict adherence to rules and regulations, the student would benefit best from a self-contained classroom. But from an Afrocultural model, a model that values communal relations, emotional expressiveness, and call-response dialogues—communicative interactions between two or more persons whereby if one person is silent, he or she is considered bored and uninterested in the conversation—the student would be identified as on-task, motivated, and intrinsically driven.

Educators who desire to engage children of color academically must look beyond their own definitions of engagement. Blurting out an answer is actually an emotional response to the teacher's question; it is a response to some stimulus. And because some children who come from Afrocultural backgrounds are encouraged to express their emotions, often their expressiveness is habitual.

Why is this information significant? The purpose of reviewing this information is to allow teachers to take a closer look at what they might call disruptive behaviors and to consider behaviors demonstrated by many children of color in light of Afrocultural characteristics. Blurting out answers in class will no doubt become disruptive at some point, especially if a classroom full of children decided to talk at once. But in the midst of "blurting-out behaviors," it's important for educators to identify their students' academic motivation and desire to engage with the discussion at hand.

A CLOSER LOOK AT PROBLEM BEHAVIORS

Because response to intervention requires educators to use research to improve academic engagement and performance, educators may benefit from determining if their students' misbehaviors have cultural implications. We enter space with worldviews that make us who we are, and our perceptions of life often reflect cultural experiences (Belgrave & Allison, 2014; Diller, 2007). This is true of all people, not just people of color. Thus, when educators instruct in their classrooms, their instructions and the ways with which they create classroom rules coincide with cultural values of some sort. Likewise, when children enter the classroom, they bring with them rich cultural characteristics that are valued within their homes and communities. Unfortunately, many teachers identify these characteristics as deficits and attempt to reshape their students' thinking and behaviors. They attempt to shush them, discourage movement-expressive behaviors, and disallow dialogue while completing assignments.

Children who come from stimulating households, households that value movement expressiveness, communalism, and music, may indeed act differently from children who come from less stimulating households. Research on cultures has shown clearly that differences are not deficits (Diller, 2007), but it appears that this thought has not entered the school systems. More than 80% of behavioral referrals during my school psychology internship were due to students' "inability" to sit still in their seats, and these students were recommended for special education services. Educators believed that students demonstrated symptoms of ADHD and required an individualized education program (IEP).

Instead of identifying movement-expressive behaviors in the classroom as deficits or an inability to sit still, educators should seek to identify ways they could incorporate such behaviors into their classrooms. I was asked to instruct a self-contained classroom for 45 minutes because the self-contained teacher had an annual review meeting—IEP meeting—to attend. When I entered the room, I did not say anything for about 2 minutes; rather than going in and stopping what the students were doing, I took notes on the behaviors they demonstrated. Some students walked around the room, made beats on their desks, and rocked back and forth to the beats. Others made beats on their desks while completing math facts.

I noticed that some students would complete a few math facts, and once completed, they would look around the room, make a beat on their desk again, and then pick their pencils up to continue their assignment. I could have easily sent them to the office or provided a referral for pounding on their desks and talking to their neighbors—and I am sure the principal would have supported my decision. But I wanted to understand them and their behaviors and then try to identify academic engaging behaviors in the midst of what would be considered off-task, disruptive behaviors.

I noticed two students in the back of the room making beats with their mouths—they were beat boxing—and competing to see who could create the "coldest [best] beat." These students had a group of four watching and cheering them on. After taking notes on the class environment, I went to the students who were beat boxing and asked them what they were doing. These students admitted that they were making beats with their mouths and seeing who the best beat maker was. At this point, I got all of the students' attention: "Alright listen up. . . . Put your pencils down, stop talking, and stop making beats on the desk. I have something to say, and I need all of y'all's input. Do y'all see what John and Doe are doing back here? They think they can make beats! Listen—I would like to get the entire class involved to see which of these two can make the best beat. And if anyone of you thinks you can beat them, I'd like to see!"

I was stunned by the amazement in their eyes as they contemplated this opportunity. Before they were able to respond, I stated, "Listen, what assignments are y'all supposed to be doing at this point?" The students blurted out without raising their hands: "We're supposed to be completing this math worksheet." I then explained, "Okay, check this out. If y'all work at y'all's desks and complete this assignment, I will allow y'all to have a beat contest for the last 5 minutes I am in here. If y'all don't want to have a beat contest, then we could find something else to do, other than math facts." One student yelled, "I want to hang out of the window!" I think this student was serious, too. In response, I walked to his desk, put my hand on his shoulder, and said, "So you want to hang out of the window, huh? Okay, cool! Finish your math sheet, and when you finish working, you and I could discuss the danger in hanging out of the window. Do you want to jump out of the window while you are at it? Come here. . . . Look out this window. It's a long way down." At this point, the class laughed and said, "Mr. Williams, are you really going to let him hang out of the window?" I laughed with them and said I would discuss the danger in hanging and jumping out of windows when the students finished their assignments. The class laughed hysterically.

After this discussion, I walked around the room and praised and brought attention to students who began their math sheets. At the appropriate time, I allowed the students to put their desks in a circle—and they went at it! They made beats, laughed, dapped each other up, and asked me when I would be their teacher again. I did not have to send any of the students to the office because they desired to make beats and enjoy themselves in the classroom. Instead, I created an entertaining, communalistic learning environment.

I understand this was only 45 minutes and not a full day. And I know that these students probably cooperated because I presented something new and different to them. But the point is, as educators, we must observe our students and attempt to understand why they demonstrate certain behaviors. Instead of sending them to the office for making beats and moving around in their seats, we should seek to incorporate their interests into the classroom. This is no easy task, but who said teaching was easy? These students were willing to work with me because I was willing to work with them.

THE CHAOTIC CLASSROOM

When I observe a student in the classroom because of misbehavior, usually two or three other students demonstrate similar, if not worse, behaviors than the student in question. For example, I recall observing a student who was referred to the problem-solving team because of disruptive behaviors. During the observation, the teacher placed students into small groups and instructed them to review math facts with each other. The teacher had a group of three students that she worked with at the back of the room. As I observed the young man who was referred to the problem-solving team, a few of his group members got out of their seats and began playing basketball. They balled up their math worksheets and began to throw them into the classroom trashcan as if they were shooting jump shots from the perimeter.

As I watched the students shoot jump shots, more and more students joined them. The teacher intervened, but when she returned to her small group, the students continued their game. Eventually, a group of six students was playing basketball with their worksheets, while their peers laughed and encouraged them to continue. From watching these students, it was clear that they enjoyed basketball and enjoyed throwing objects into the trashcan. As the game became more intense, the teacher stopped the small group lesson and sent the six boys to the office. I'm sure they were written up for their behaviors; in fact, I would be surprised if they were not suspended for this.

These youngsters were definitely off-task and disruptive. But one question is, How can educators use such disruptive behaviors to engage students academically? The students were bored with sitting at their desks, looking at each other count with their fingers, so they decided to play ball. It was clear that these students desired entertainment. What I have noticed is, in most disruptive classrooms, only two to three students are disruptive, and the class feeds on their disruptive behaviors. I have also found that if the disruptive students are engaged, then usually, the entire class will become engaged because these students do not distract them.

One activity that could have engaged these ball players is calculating jump shots; that is, allowing the students to throw some sort of object, something like a sponge basketball, into a trashcan or bucket and allowing the students to add, subtract, divide, or multiply their shots made. This activity could have been entertaining if students were divided into groups of five and if the teacher allowed them to create team names for their groups. This sort of game would have allowed the students to support their team members (communalism), move around the room (movement expressiveness), and work cooperatively while learning math facts by playing basketball (verve) instead of counting on their fingers.

When I would recommend activities such as the basketball game to teachers, their main concern was they didn't want their classrooms to appear disruptive and out of control. In response, I would explain that noise resulting from academic engagement is always better than noise resulting from off-task behaviors.

Teachers could use these sorts of games at the Tier 1 level as prevention activities. Some students in the classroom perform poorly on standardized tests and curriculum-based measures because they have not learned basic skills in their classrooms. Some of these students haven't learned because they are often removed from the classroom in response to "disruptive behaviors," and because they are sent to the office and sent home so often, they are not exposed to instruction. They are not exposed to instruction, but we hope that 80% to 85% of our children will remain at the Tier 1 level, and we set goals of making adequate yearly progress across grade levels. These are unrealistic goals for schools that constantly send students home or remove them from the classroom. Actually, until we learn to engage children of color and children who demonstrate behavior problems in the classroom, it will be difficult to meet the Tier 1 percentage and nearly impossible to make adequate yearly progress across demographic areas.

It is impossible to be both academically engaged and academically disengaged at the same time; these behaviors are incompatible with each other. Many teachers focus on disruptive behaviors when their students demonstrate inappropriate behaviors in the classroom. These students usually display disruptive behaviors because the teacher has failed to engage them academically. In most cases, if teachers identify these students' interests and allow them to be leaders in the classroom, while incorporating their interests, these disruptive students will become engaged.

If we are expecting students of color to remain at the Tier 1 level, we must seek to engage them and incorporate activities they find entertaining.

Many children of color will remain at Tier 1 because they are intrinsically motivated and want to do well academically; unmotivated and avoidant learners will need games to prevent them from falling through the school's cracks and being left behind.

CHAPTER SUMMARY

We are more willing to participate in activities when they are interesting—when they move us behaviorally, cognitively, and affectively. We may engage in an activity that we do not enjoy, as an act of kindness, but our engagement level would usually be lower if we are uninterested in the activity, do not have a passion for the activity, and do not see how the activity is relevant to our lives. This is also true of our students in the classroom. Students come to the classroom with a wealth of interests, passions, gifts, and talents. And these passions were shaped throughout development and within the context of culture. Because engagement is defined within the context of culture, students may engage themselves in different ways; they may engage themselves in ways that are consistent with their cultural values. Students may prefer to talk with a peer while completing assignments, they may rock to a beat that resonates in their heads while writing, they may tap their feet while completing math facts—all while processing information at a deep level. If observed with traditional observation tools, these students may be identified as off-task if they did any of the above behaviors. The reason is many observational tools that psychologists use are insensitive to the cultural characteristics that are associated with African American culture.

In the next chapter, I discuss the relationship between motivation and engagement. I share my story of how motivated I became when I met an African professor at the university where I studied and learned that there was a student-instructor who was months away from becoming a psychologist. These were powerful moments in my life considering I had not met a Black psychologist and had not read about any Black psychologists while studying psychology during my undergraduate or graduate experiences. This experience affected me tremendously as a young African American student.

Motivation: The Key to Success   **11**

A people without the knowledge of their past history, origin, and culture is like a tree without roots.

—Marcus Garvey

What motivates students of color to do well academically? Some researchers have made the claim that if these students learn that their culture is rich and that their racial group members have contributed to history, then they will become empowered in the classroom (Ani, 1994; Asante, 1988; Hilliard, 1998; Richards, 1994; C. Williams, 1974). This was definitely true for me. Important questions surrounding this chapter include the following:

- What motivates children of color to engage in the classroom?
- Would students become motivated to pursue certain careers if they were exposed to people of color who worked in those professions?
- Are students of color often offended or embarrassed when African Americans are discussed in a negative light—do these experiences decrease motivation and engagement in the classroom?

WHERE ARE THE BLACK PSYCHOLOGISTS IN MOST PSYCHOLOGY TEXTBOOKS?

I studied psychology because I was fascinated with dreams, memory, intelligence (whatever that term means), and learning. My personal interests led me to graduate school to study school psychology and work with students who struggle emotionally and academically. Since my first year in undergraduate school up until my first few months of graduate school, I had no clue that there were prominent Black psychologists in the field. When I think back on this, I find it disturbing.

I recall reading the *History of Psychology* textbook and studying European psychologists and how they paved the way for modern-day psychologists. I recall studying this textbook and believing that the study of psychology began in 1879 with Wilhelm Wundt as the pioneering father. My instructors did not teach me that there were no Black psychologists but because we only studied European psychologists, their teaching was clear. They sent an implicit and subliminal message explaining that we did not talk about Black psychologists because there were none who contributed to the field.

It was not until November 2006 that I began to learn that there were many Black psychologists who contributed to the field of psychology. I accepted a position as a research assistant, for which I had to drive to the undergraduate campus to help with a character education study. The undergraduate campus was 40 minutes away from my home and approximately 48 miles or so away from the graduate campus.

Although my research assistant position lasted only 1 year, I met people and learned things that will stick with me probably for the rest of my life. The first person was an African professor. This professor pulled me into his office and told me how proud he was of me for studying psychology but that I must read books other than the ones required by my graduate professors; he explained that I must read literature about my people and get perspectives about people of color from people of color. As he told me these things, I was intrigued, but had no clue as to what he was talking about. This type of talk was foreign to me.

This particular professor motivated me like no other. I found myself walking to his office every time I was on the undergraduate campus, and he opened his door to me every time. He encouraged me to study the psychology of African tribes and to understand what psychology meant for Africans; he told me that it was most important for me to study the psychology of Black people, primarily African Americans. He explained, "After all, you are well informed about the psychology of Europeans and White people. It is about time that you start learning about your own people!"

I cannot express how powerful this professor's words were. It was clear that he read books and articles by leading researchers in the field of culture; he understood the power in understanding one's own culture and cultural contributions to society. It was evident that he believed, as Asante (1988) expressed, that when understanding ourselves as people and how we fit into the world, we must begin with our own culture. Similar to the professor I met, Asante explained that we must first start from where we are. He explained, "If you are Yoruba, begin with Yoruba history and mythology; if you are Kikuyu, begin with Kikuyu history and mythology; and if you are African-American, begin with African-American history and mythology" (Asante, 1998, p. 7).

Sometime after our discussion on Africans and Black Americans, the professor suggested that I meet an inspiring Black psychologist in the making—and this psychologist was an instructor at the university. He provided me the instructor's name and office phone number and told me that it might benefit me greatly if I connected with him. I did without hesitation. I took the phone number, dashed, literally, through the halls to my work office, and called him. When I called him the first time, he did not pick up, so I left a message. My excitement was comparable to meeting some celebrity. I was not excited about the person per se but about the possibility of meeting someone of color who was on his way to becoming a psychologist; the excitement was also in response to being able to learn about Black psychology and Black people's experiences from a psychological perspective.

As a Black psychology student, I experienced many things in the classroom that discouraged me and, at times, almost led me to discontinue my graduate studies. When I met this instructor, it became apparent that my experiences were not unique but were actually the norm for many Black men in predominantly White educational institutions.

My motivation to become a school psychologist and help children of color and children who come from impoverished backgrounds was strengthened from the interactions and dialogues I had with the instructor. He gave me a brief synopsis of why I should study Black psychology and the effect of culture on academic engagement. He did not spoon-feed me but instead gathered all of his articles on culture and Black people that he received during his tenure at Howard University, made copies of them, and placed them in a binder as a gift. He then gave me two books—*The Psychology of Blacks* (White & Parham, 1990) and *Other People's Children* (Delpit, 1995/2006). I now understand why he went out of his way to get me these materials. If he had not, who would have? In fact, if I had not met these two men during my graduate studies, it is possible that I would not have learned about the importance of culture on academic engagement.

I recall reading the articles on culture and academic engagement all throughout the night—literally, every night. I cannot put into words how motivated I became from reading material about Black psychologists and the contributions they made to social science. It was not until this time that I truly understood how identity is rooted in history. If these experiences have taught me anything, they have taught me that we must connect Black students with successful Black Americans; we must seek to understand what these children desire to become in life and expose them to Black people who have contributed to that particular field.

OKAY . . . AND YOUR POINT IS—

What do my experiences have to do with RTI? The answer is that inspiring children to do well could work as primary prevention. Children of all ethnicities and races enter school motivated to learn upon their first day of schooling (Adelman & Taylor, 2006). Their little minds are curious and their brains are like sponges. But sometime between second and third grade, children of color become disengaged and unmotivated in the class-room (Adelman & Taylor, 2006). Thus, research has shown that these children enter school motivated, but it has not shown why they disengage sometime around third grade.

Although there are many hypotheses as to why these children disengage—institutional racism, cultural discontinuity, lack of exposure to Black contributions to life, and so on—educators must engage in research to end this tendency in their classrooms. This does not mean that each teacher should seek to end this problem on a national level. What it does mean, however, is that they should seek to end this problem in their own classrooms. With that said, response to intervention at the Tier 1 level for children of color should be similar to Tier 1 for White students. That is, just as educators expose and connect students to curriculum that repre-sents their group members, children of color should be exposed to a curri-culum that represents their people. In other words, the curriculum should include not only accomplishments of European Americans but also African Americans—and Asian, Indian, and Latino Americans. Children of color should understand the accomplishments their group members have made to science and to the civilization of this great country.

Having a culturally rich curriculum does not mean simply talking about slavery and rehearsing how Europeans enslaved Africans, for this is indeed history, but it is a dehumanizing history. Children must know this history, but also educators must expose students to history that is inspiring and empowering.

A Depressing History

I can recall in the sixth grade, during Black history month, my teacher assigned a book for us to read about Black history. She assigned this book and recom-mended that we read the first chapter at home and return to school to express

(Continued)

(Continued)

our thoughts about the book. I recall her walking down the aisle and handing us our books. When I received my book, I was ecstatic—for there was a Black family on the cover of the book, playing in the field. When I cracked the book open at home, to my surprise, these Black people were not a happy family playing in some field, but rather, Black people preparing to pick cotton. When I came to this knowledge, my motivation to read this book ceased. I read it only because it was required. I did not want to come to school without having read it; I was the only Black kid in class, and I was sure people would look at me for some answer.

This book identified Black people as niggers, not as humans. The term *nigger*, from my recollection, was stated just about in every other paragraph—as if it was the topic of the book. Not only was I embarrassed to read it, but also I dreaded going to school the following day. I could not sleep that night because I thought about going to class and having to listen to my peers say "nigger" in their responses about the book. I even visualized my teacher using this term. I planned to skip school for this day, but knew what would happen if my parents found out.

When I realized skipping school would make things worse, I created a second plan, and this one would possibly come without a consequence. I walked to school early in the morning. I went early so that I could meet my teacher before school started. I beat her there and had to wait. When she arrived, I told her that I wanted to talk with her about the book. I explained that the book made me feel very uncomfortable and sad and that I did not want to read the book in class. I told her that I couldn't envision discussing the book's content among a group of White boys and girls. Her response was this: "Okay, Dwayne, then go to the library when we discuss it!" Her statement was like some sharp dagger that pierced my being. Her statement has stuck with me since that time, and I often share this story with teachers who read books that portray African Americans as inferior people.

I was taken back to this moment during my school psychology internship. I had to test a student for a specific learning disability and went to his class to get him. When I opened the door of the classroom, everyone in the room looked at me in silence. I smiled and asked the teacher what was going on. Before she could respond, a White student beat her to the punch: "We're reading a book about niggers and how Black people steal and rob people!" The teacher's mouth dropped as the little girl went on. Finally, the teacher interrupted her and said, "Well, we are reading this book, written by an African American woman. The class loved the book cover so I ordered it."

After listening to the teacher, I took the student I came to get and walked out of the room, leaving the door open. As I walked away from the room, one of the White students yelled, "Mr. Williams, you have to close the door. . . . Come back and close the door or we can't read our book!" When I heard this, I walked back and asked why the door had to be closed. This time, the teacher beat her students to the punch: "Well, I'm not sure how most people will take this book. So to be respectful of them, I just close the door." I looked around the room one last time only to see a group of Black children who looked both embarrassed and terrified. Although I went to the library when I encountered this experience as a kid, I saw myself in the Black children who looked at me when I entered their classroom; they looked as if they wanted me to take them by their hands and walk them out of the room. I was astounded to say the least and unsure how to handle this experience as an intern.

What type of effect do you believe these experiences have on children of color—for this type of information is disseminated at the Tier 1 level, and some teachers don't wait until February to share it.

It is clear that we have failed on a national level at engaging children of color. Because old practices have been ineffective for these children, educators must begin to shift their instruction as education shifts. The most oft-heard phrase about education is that "education is experiencing a paradigm shift." In fact, most RTI books explain this paradigm shift as moving away from simple teaching in the classroom to using data prior to making educational decisions. Education is definitely experiencing a paradigm shift, and this shift should move from traditional teaching to incorporating movement, communalism, and verve into the classroom at the Tier 1 level—and throughout tiers—to determine if these strategies will increase academic motivation among children of color.

CHAPTER SUMMARY

It is said that if you want to find out where you fit in the world, then you must start with your own people, and that, if you are African American, then you must begin with the contributions and achievements of African Americans. This idea is consistent with Marcus Garvey's statement: "A people without knowledge of their past history, origin, and culture, is like a people without roots." Finding out what motivates students is perhaps one of the most important components of any intervention. For me, meeting professionals of color who were professors of education and psychology—and discussing with them the need to study my own culture—was perhaps the most inspiring and motivating factor during my tenure as a graduate student.

Because I did not have the opportunity to learn from Black professors in undergraduate and graduate school, and because we never talked about the issues students of color face, I was grateful to meet professors who were invested in shedding light on these experiences. If it were not for my meeting the gentlemen that I met during my graduate school years, it is possible that I would not have had the inspiration and knowledge to write this book. When working with students of color, I often share my experiences of meeting these professors. In response, students often complain about not being exposed to the contributions of African Americans and that the only time they discuss "their people" is during discussions on slavery or when talking about Martin Luther King Jr.

In the next chapter, I discuss the law of reciprocity and the importance of making students feel appreciated and valued. I provide examples of students who disrespected their teachers because the students believed that they were disrespected. If students do not feel that you appreciate them and value their worth, it is possible that they will disengage, shut down during instructional time, and become blatantly disrespectful.

Respecting Children and Their Cultural Backgrounds

12

You demand respect and you'll get it. First of all, you give respect.

—*Mary J. Blige*

T he reciprocity principle is true, especially when it comes to respecting children in the school system and valuing their culture. The reciprocity principle has been studied extensively within the area of social psychology and states that we are usually kind to individuals who are kind to us—and are less kind to individuals who are less kind to us. Stated differently, we are more inclined to respect those who respect us. For example, the principle of *reciprocal liking*—which has also been studied extensively in social psychology—refers to liking those who show that they like us. To make this principle more personal, think for a moment about someone you began to like simply because that person treated you kindly and fairly. Now—think for a moment about someone who you believed treated you unkindly and unfairly. Did you develop positive feelings for that person you believe treated you unkindly and unfairly? Probably not.

It is critical that educators consider the reciprocity principle when providing instruction to students in the classroom and when moving them through tiers. If we show students that we care for them and that we desire their success, they will respect us and respond to our directives favorably. Conversely, if students believe that we are often disrespectful toward them, then they will be disrespectful toward us. This idea is consistent with the old adage that says, "If you want to have a friend, then you must be friendly." Likewise, if we want students to respect us, then we must be respectful.

Children show their respect in different ways. Often, because of how they were raised, some children may not verbalize their thankfulness or may not demonstrate in their behaviors how grateful they are, but on the inside, they care. The principle of reciprocity is true with regard to children in that, in most cases, children's acting-out behaviors and disrespect are often mirror images of how adults treat them, including teachers. In fact, many children act out because they desire kind treatment from their teachers but feel that they do not receive such treatment. Important questions surrounding this chapter include the following:

- How might the principle of reciprocity pertain to both negative and positive relationships within the classroom?
- Should adults respect children and youth? And if so, how should this respect look?

RESPECTING STUDENTS IN THE CLASSROOM

We are emotional beings in that we want to feel loved and want to know that people care about our well-being. These are basic needs. When these needs are not met, we become emotional wrecks. We begin to do things we would not otherwise do if our needs were met. When people do not feel loved or wanted, they usually attach themselves to people or detach themselves from people. In other instances, they may create chaos within their environments and communities; their behaviors usually reflect their thinking: "If I'm unhappy, I'll make sure others feel my pain!" This idea brings me to my next point.

Many of the children I work with—children of color who have been referred for special education services due to behavioral problems—express the same concern: "My teachers don't respect me!" I'm often amazed at how these children describe the relationship they believe they have with their teachers. They actually believe their teachers are out to get them—and their perceptions are reality, at least to them.

One day, as I was on my way to the restroom, prior to starting my morning, a teacher called my name; it appeared that she needed some help: "Mr. Williams! Good morning. I know the day has not started yet, but I really need your help. Can you please sit in a meeting with me in about 30 minutes? I have a young man that is extremely angry. If possible, can you please try to get through to him? He's been very disruptive and mad in my literature class."

I assured the teacher that I'd be present in the meeting, but I had no idea of the significance of her concerns. I thought that the meeting would be about some kid talking during instructional time, walking around the room, or making inappropriate jokes. When I entered the room where the meeting was held, the young man was sitting in a chair; he demonstrated flat affect. What was interesting was the way this young man looked at his teacher and me as we spoke to him. It was clear that this youngster was fed up, just as his teacher was.

For the first 10 minutes, the young man did not speak, although his teacher questioned him repeatedly. The teacher demanded an answer to her question: "Why did you walk out of the room without asking? Not only did you walk out of the room, but also you never came back. You just can't do what you want to do around here!" This teacher attempted to explain that she was liable if anything were to happen to him. As she spoke, he stared at her in silence. At some point, I interjected and explained that if he did not talk, we would not be able to understand how he was feeling. As I spoke, he looked at me, with flat affect, then grabbed his notebook and started writing. I thought he was going to write his thoughts and share them, but he didn't. He wrote something in his notebook, closed the notebook, and continued to stare at me.

His teacher asked the question again, at which time he spoke: "You were tweekin.' You overdid your job!" He responded angrily. The teacher asked the young man what he meant by tweekin' and went on to say, "I can't have you disrespect me. I'm 47 and you're only 13." In response, the young man said in a low tone, "Well, you disrespected me." The teacher attempted to get him to explain how she disrespected him, but initially, he did not answer. Finally, he stated, "Come on, you know what you did. Stop acting like you don't know what I'm talking about!"

Eventually, the teacher agreed to leave the room to see if he would talk with me without her present. After she left, the young man spoke freely: "This is the problem. She be trippin' on every little thing. I mean everything! I'm getting tired of this shit." I asked the young man why he walked out of the room and he stated, "All right, check this out, I came in the classroom after gym. I wasn't mad or nothing. Our room be burning up [hot]. I turned the fan on, and she just went off! I just looked at her and she was sittin' there screaming at me and stuff. She wasn't hot how I was; she wasn't sweatin' like I was! Man, I ask for the littlest thing in the class—to turn the damn fan on—and she got to tweekin.' When she started screaming at me because I turned the fan on, I just said, 'Man forget this shit!' and walked out." This young man went on to explain how he believes his teacher disrespects him every day but that she wants him to respect her in return.

This youngster did not care about consequences; he made this clear during our conversation: "I'm to the point to where I just don't care . . . and what can y'all do to me? Fail me? Suspend me? Kick me out? Y'all can't make me sit in

(Continued)

(Continued)

the classroom and be disrespected! If I want, I would walk out of this room right now . . . and y'all couldn't do a damn thing! In fact, I could walk out of this school building and y'all couldn't do nothing about it." He continued to vent: "Y'all ain't gone put y'all's hands on me. And I know that for sure! You know what, I could leave this school and not come back, but you know why I don't . . . because I want to learn. Y'all ain't making me sit down in class, or making me show up. I'm doing this because I want to. I control myself, y'all don't control me!"

It was clear that this young man's behaviors were motivated by power. He wanted to show that he had power over himself and his decisions and that no one could force him into doing anything. I interpreted his behaviors to mean that although the teacher could create rules and expectations in the classroom, she couldn't force him to abide by them. One question is, Why was this youngster so angry? I didn't know what his background was like. What I did know is he lived in a very rough neighborhood and I'm sure he had seen a lot of violence and chaos—in addition to feeling disrespected by his teacher. Whatever his background was like, it was clear that he was going to protect himself and not let anyone control him. Consistent with the principle of reciprocity, the young man was inclined to disrespect his teacher because he believed she disrespected him.

As we sat in silence, the young man would express himself periodically: "She ain't going to come at me wrong! I ain't no Rudy! She ain't going to come at me wrong! I'll just keep walking out of the room to avoid violence." As educators, we should realize that all behaviors are purposeful. In addition to power, his purpose for walking out of the classroom, was perhaps to avoid violence.

After moments of silence, I asked this young man what he wanted to do after he graduates from high school: "I want to design games. I love working with computers." I explained that he could begin working toward this goal now and that his best chance at achieving this goal was by doing well in school. In response, he stated, "Man, forget school! I'll drop out. If I gotta have teachers like her now, in high school, *and* in college—All right! My brother goes to college. He always tells me about how they act in the classroom. He said that they can get up and throw things in the trashcan when they want to. He tells me that they don't have to raise their hands to speak or get their teacher's permission prior to moving around. That's what I'm talking about! That stuff they do around here is for the birds!"

Clearly, this young man was speaking about the culture of his classroom in that he was fed up with his teacher's dependence on bureaucratic orientations—a core characteristic of Eurocentric culture that places value on strict rules and adherence to these rules. Examples of bureaucratic orientations include requiring students to raise their hands before speaking (if they don't raise their hands, then they will be penalized in one way or another), get permission to throw trash in the trashcan, and sit still at their desks. I could tell by this youngster's voice that he had had enough.

I found his comments about college interesting and that he thought he would be much more successful in college than middle school! His comments showed that his perception of his ability or inability to succeed at school was not based on his intelligence or skill set; rather, it was based on classroom culture. In other words, he believed that if he could come to class, be himself, and have fun in the process, he'd be successful.

FUNCTIONAL BEHAVIOR ANALYSIS—TEACHER ANTECEDENTS

When students demonstrate disruptive behaviors in the classroom over time, school psychologists usually conduct functional behavior analyses (FBAs) to understand better their behaviors. An FBA is a model in which school psychologists attempt to identify antecedents of the problem behavior and understand the consequence of the behavior. The antecedent of a behavior is anything that precedes the behavior, anything that may trigger the student's problem behavior. Consequences are things that motivate the student to continue demonstrating the problem behavior, for example, praise from peers, retaliation, the feeling that one possesses power over the classroom, power over one's teachers, and so on.

In the above vignette, the student walked out of the classroom (behavior) after the teacher yelled, "Turn off the fan!" (antecedent). The *consequence* of walking out of the classroom, or the thing that reinforced this behavior, was a feeling of power—the feeling that the teacher could control her classroom and fan but that the student had power over himself. To show his power, he walked out of the room and didn't come back. The consequence was also avoiding violence, as described by the student.

FBAs are helpful in understanding problem behaviors because an observer is able to see the behavior within the classroom; in other words, he or she is able, in most cases, to see what environmental factor(s) sets the kid off. In other instances, observers are able to see that the student demonstrated certain behaviors in the absence of classroom antecedents.

When most psychologists conduct FBAs, they usually identify the student or the student's peers as the antecedent. For example, if Johnny is the referred student, they may write something like the following: Johnny's peer kept making fun of Johnny's shoes (antecedent), and in response, Johnny got out of his seat and punched the student in the face (behavior). In other instances, school psychologists may identify the teacher's instructions as the antecedent: When Mrs. Doe directed her students to open their math books (antecedent), Johnny refused. When she asked Johnny to open his book (antecedent), he threw the math book across the room (behavior) and said, "I'm tired of this boring stuff!" (behavior).

Variables that are rarely considered when completing FBAs are cultural factors that function as antecedents to disruptive behavior in the classroom. For example, many children may act out because of how teachers manage their classrooms. Educators may not realize that they bring into their classrooms cultural characteristics, but it is impossible to have a classroom that is free of culture, for we create culture.

Because many children of color come from stimulating homes and communities, they may become bored when they are required to learn in less stimulating classrooms. And because we create culture, children of color may engage in their own cultural behaviors when they are bored instead of demonstrating behaviors that are consistent with the classroom culture. For example, educators may require their students to sit quietly at their desks and complete math sheets or listen to a lecture about history. These activities may appear boring to students who come from stimulating backgrounds. Children who come from lively homes may desire to learn in stimulating ways. They may desire to play games, move around the classroom, create raps or songs from their lit books, or simply learn in a group, with their friends (cooperative learning).

When these students are required to learn in a fashion that bores them, they may become disruptive. Many teachers explain that students usually disrupt the classroom to divert attention away from their reading or math deficits. This is true but not always the case. I have seen students who maintain "As" and students who score above the 25th percentile on curriculum-based measures demonstrate disruptive behaviors in response to their teacher's instructional practices. So my question is this: Should a student be made eligible for special education services and classified as emotionally disturbed simply because he gets frustrated with how he is taught in the classroom? Despite your answer, this is often how many students are referred and become eligible. These students are identified as not having the ability to control their emotions, and because their grades begin to drop in response to their boredom, many of the special education team members explain that the students' emotions are negatively affecting their educational achievement—or that their emotions are affecting their ability to learn.

In accordance with the response to intervention (RTI), best practices require educators to support their decisions with data. During eligibility meetings, teachers usually bring the student's track record and paper trail—the amount of times he was kicked out of the classroom because of "emotional outbursts," the amount of times the student refused to comply with classroom directives, the amount of times the student refused to raise his hand prior to speaking in class or getting out of his seat, the amount of times the student walked out of class, and the amount of times the student was suspended.

Students may be considered for special education services within the category of emotional disturbance (ED) when they are "unable to maintain a satisfactory relationship with their teachers or peers." In many cases, children are unable to maintain satisfactory relationships with their teachers because these students behave in the classroom similar to how they behave in their communities. They express themselves in a very lively and engaging manner; they are too "alive" for their classrooms and too stimulating for their less expressive teachers. Instead of getting the students' input on how to stimulate the classroom, most educators kick them out and send the students to the office. Emotional issues will always arise in students if teachers constantly kick them out of class. What always amazes me is that these same students are able to do well in other classrooms and are very creative in their communities.

Instead of identifying the students and their peers as antecedents to behavioral problems, teachers may benefit from identifying whether cultural factors in their classrooms are the causes to disruptive behaviors. They should seek to identify the extent to which their classroom rules clash with their students' cultural responses.

The manner in which educators speak to children of color may be the single greatest determinant of whether the student will become oppositional. In fact, this is true of people in general. Our behaviors usually mimic how people talk to us. For example, if a child is speaking loudly in the classroom, if the teacher yells at the student, the student will more than likely yell back. I have observed classrooms in which this has been the case. In one classroom, a student was talking to a peer in the classroom and instead of talking in a polite manner, the teacher yelled at the student. In response, the student yelled back: "I don't know who she think she yellin' at like that!" The student's response was enough to get her sent to the office and written up. The referral read, "Jane was very disrespectful to her peers and teacher during instructional time. She talked very loudly and when given the directive to talk in a quiet manner, she yelled at her teacher. This is not the first time this has happened. It appears that Jane has a difficult time controlling her anger."

CHAPTER SUMMARY

The principle of reciprocity states that we are more inclined to be kind to individuals who are kind to us—and *reciprocal liking* states that we are more inclined to like those who like us. The principle of reciprocity has significant implications for teaching and learning in the classroom. If students believe their teachers dislike them, then they may be more inclined to dislike their teachers. If students dislike their teachers, then they may refuse to engage during instructional time and become noncompliant.

Increasing engagement among students and setting the tone for lifelong learning begin with solid relationships and respecting students for who they are. Thus, if teachers and students do not establish relationships, and if students and teachers do not trust each other, then very little learning will take place in the classroom. RTI models rest on the foundation of relationships. When relationships are ruined, interventions won't work. It does not matter how many evidence-based interventions the school district purchases. If students and teachers do not invest in relationships and do not invest in celebrating cultural differences, then RTI will present as another ineffective model that is used to increase performance yet neglects the importance of relationships.

In the next chapter, I challenge readers to consider whether racism exists within their school buildings. It is common to assume, almost automatically, that racism does not occur within the school system. But research suggests otherwise.

Racism: Does It Exist in Today's School System? 13

Mother, mother, there's too many of you cryin.' Brother, brother, brother, there's far too many of you dyin.' You know we got to find a way—to bring some lovin' here today. Father, father, we don't need to escalate. War is not the answer, for only love can conquer. You, you know we got to find a way—to bring some lovin,' aw, here today. . . .

—*Marvin Gaye*

In his song "What's Goin' On," the late African American songwriter and musician Marvin Gaye spoke eloquently to the Black community and brought attention to the dehumanizing issues they were experiencing. He addressed mothers in song by acknowledging that there were too many of them crying. To the brothers, he lamented there are far too many of them dying. To the fathers, he reassured that they needed to not escalate—that war is not the answer, for only love conquers.

Marvin expressed his concerns in song during the 1970s, but today, many mothers are still crying, brothers dying, and fathers raging war against the system. I ask those who work within America's educational system the same questions Marvin asked during the 1970s: What's goin' on? What's happenin'? Marvin is not around today to pose questions, but I ask one that I believe would have been a concern of his: What's goin' on with our educators? Although we receive advanced training, we have been unsuccessful at educating children of color. And when I say children of color, I am referring to the majority of Hispanic and African American students.

One variable that may contribute to Black students' high level of disengagement in the classroom, and one that has been receiving more and more attention, is cultural racism (Lynn, 2006; Webb-Johnson, 2003; White & Parham, 1990). It appears that this concept exists within textbooks and on the web; it is rarely discussed within school systems, among educators, where such dialogue is needed most. Possible reasons why educators rarely discuss the concept of cultural racism:

- Some educators are not familiar with the concept.
- Many educators who have heard of such practices may believe it does not exist in their schools.
- Anything that pertains to "racism" is difficult to discuss.
- Some fear offending someone during a talk about racism.

Whatever the reason, a conversation surrounding culture and cultural racism is long overdue. It is always difficult discussing racism in any form, especially if someone is identifying you as the racist. But are those who operate America's schools culturally racist? Understanding the concept of cultural racism would allow you to debate this question more intelligently. Important questions surrounding this chapter include the following:

- What is cultural racism?
- What is individual and institutional racism?
- Do students of color believe racism exists within their schools?
- Is it important to address students' perception of racism in your schools?

DEFINITION OF CULTURAL RACISM

Cultural racism is the belief that the cultural ways of one group, including values, lifestyles, language/dialect, and worldviews, are superior to those of other cultural groups (Belgrave & Allison, 2014; Diller, 2007) and manifests in a society when a group has the power to determine what is appropriate, inappropriate, normal, and abnormal. Cultural racism exists when individuals from culturally diverse backgrounds are forced to value the cultural norms of a dominant culture, while being taught that their own culture is less important; often, this teaching—that their own culture is less important—is subliminal. In the classroom, subliminal messages may take the form of ignoring the values of culturally diverse students, while forcing students to learn and behave consistent with Eurocentric values. An example of cultural racism is the tendency to assume that classical music is superior to rap (Belgrave & Allison, 2014) and more meaningful than rhythm and blues (R&B).

Throughout this book, I have differentiated between characteristics associated with traditional African American culture and traditional European American culture, with the latter values being more prominent in school systems. To illustrate cultural racism that is prevalent in America, I often refer to Wijeyesinghe, Griffin, and Love's (1997) argument, in which they explain that "cultural racism takes the form of practices that attribute value and normality to White people and Whiteness, and devalue, stereotype, and label people of color as 'other,' different, less than, or render them invisible" (p. 93).

INDIVIDUAL AND INSTITUTIONAL

Cultural racism can occur at two different levels—at the (1) individual and (2) institutional level. At the *individual* level, cultural racism is consistent with ethnocentrism and occurs when people believe their cultural patterns are more meaningful and rich than the values of other cultural groups, and believe that their values lead to success compared to the values of others. At the *institutional level,* cultural racism occurs when institutions are run, whether implicitly or explicitly, by the beliefs that the cultural ethos of one group is superior and more meaningful or relevant than the cultural ethos of another group (Diller, 2007). The most common reason for supporting Eurocentric values in America's schools, by most Black and White educators, is that they lead to success. Educators often say that children will do well academically if they

- learn to stop moving around so much in class,
- raise their hands prior to leaving their seats,
- learn to compete against their peers, and
- worry about their own education and stop worrying about their peers' success.

When cultural racism occurs at the institutional level, it often manifests because of the organization's policies, rules, and expectations—not because individuals within the organization are culturally racist (Belgrave & Allison, 2014). For example, I have met with teachers who have explained that they desire to incorporate music within their lessons, but because of their district's policies, they are prohibited from doing so. Thus, according to the above definitions, many educators may demonstrate cultural racism, but as stated, this does not necessarily mean that they are culturally racist; educators who demonstrate such behaviors may do so because they follow the rules and regulations of their school's culture.

In a society that embraces Eurocentric values over other cultural patterns, it appears that it would be most intelligent to learn to behave consistent with Eurocentric ideologies. In fact, this is often the most common argument that is debated when I present during seminars; educators across race explain that Black students need to embrace and identify with Eurocentric values. Educators have also stated that these students must learn to suppress their own cultural values, especially if their cultural values are leading to negative attention from teachers. Although such beliefs are common among educators, research shows that African American students who embrace their own culture and racial identity tend to achieve at high levels, whereas African American students who score high on Eurocentric values and cultures tend to achieve at lower levels (Spencer et al., 2001). It is well documented that racial identity and achievement, including grade point average (GPA) scores, are correlated, in that when African American students embrace their cultural and racial heritage, they tend to excel academically (Adelabu, 2008; Kerpelman, Eryigit, & Stephens, 2008).

Kindergarten Orientation

My son turned 5 just in time to start kindergarten the 2011–2012 school year. My wife and I went to my son's kindergarten preparation day—a meeting his school held for incoming kindergartners and parents. This preparation meeting was filled with people. It was a diverse crowd. I was excited about hearing what the school was doing for incoming kindergarten students, considering students are expected to read a certain number of words per minute by the middle and end of their first-grade year.

It was clear that the school incorporated an RTI model. Educators did not discuss the model, but their language made it evident: "Our goal is to prepare our children for their next years. We are now instructing by using a model in which we screen our children and provide interventions to children who score low." I couldn't control my smile as they indirectly discussed RTI. I was excited. After all, I believe in the RTI model if it is culturally relevant. I was, however, able to control my smile within 5 minutes of the discussion. The principal began to explain that their desire is to have all students do well in the classroom based on their model. She went on to say that we as parents could help in the process: "Our rules are straightforward. We teach our children to remain attentive at their desks, keep their mouths closed when people are talking to them, and their bodies still." She provided examples as she demonstrated these rules. To illustrate her point, she forced her lips closed tightly, expanded her eyes, and threw her arms down to her side, in a robotic fashion.

I looked around the room as she spoke, only to see people of all races and ethnicities taking notes. I mean these parents attempted to write down everything the principal stated, and some asked the principal to repeat herself, as they missed a rule or two. It was clear by their taking notes that they desired for their children to do well—and their children probably would, if their little minds are not used to entertaining, lively environments. The principal encouraged the parents to start their children on some trial—to teach them how to be quiet and still when people are speaking to them. As the principal spoke, I thought about children who come from stimulating backgrounds and how these regulations will more likely lead them to the principal's office instead of to educational success. As I sat there, I couldn't help but think that, for some children, this model—sit still, don't move, remain silent model—will become a recipe for disaster!

Thus, in America, educators teach students to value certain values both explicitly and implicitly, and students of color learn, often subliminally, that their ways of life are not only unappreciated but also "bad." Often, when students engage in behaviors that reflect their culture—such as communal behaviors, movement-expressive behaviors, and call-response behaviors—or engage in behaviors that are inconsistent with the Eurocentric model taught in their school, they are usually reprimanded; when such behaviors are repeated, over time, some students are referred for specialized services because they are "unable" to control their emotions, unable to sit still in their seats, and struggle with establishing and maintaining relationships with teachers. In my experiences, students almost always became oppositional and disrespectful to teachers when they experience cultural clashes in the classroom.

Most educators learn to value Eurocentric cultural characteristics from the time they enter kindergarten to the time they enter the classroom to teach. When they enter the classroom to teach, they almost automatically create rules that are consistent with Eurocentric values. They may identify their rules as appropriate and normal for any structured community or classroom; although it is not always obvious, there is a hidden culture embedded in these rules, and that culture is consistent with Eurocentrism.

Educators also learn this culture from the textbooks they read throughout their undergraduate and graduate experiences. Prior to current initiatives, educators were taught that a well-managed classroom is where students remain in their seats, while silently looking at the chalk-board or listening to some lecture (Moe, 2001). Educators identified this type of classroom as a structured and controlled environment.

Prior to classroom walkthroughs, I've heard educators state, in the staff lounge during lunch, that they were preparing for their evaluation. They all would repeat common phrases: "I hope my students don't make a fool of me—I hope they sit at their desks quietly and listen to my lesson; I hope they act like they have some sense." If the latter phrase were reversed, it would state, "If my kids don't sit at their desks quietly or listen to the lesson, they lack sense."

What is interesting is many African American educators, who come from Afrocultural backgrounds, demonstrate culturally racist behaviors against their own culture. Even more, they tend to overengage in Eurocentric ideals compared to White and Black educators who come from Eurocentric backgrounds. The late Carter G. Woodson, in his book, *The Mis-education of the Negro,* explains why this happens. He explained that people of color enter predominantly White institutions as Black men and Black women but leave as well-trained White people (Woodson, 2006). He pointed to race, but it is clear that he also referred to culture, as he explained that some Black people who come from traditional Afrocultural backgrounds begin to think and act similar to the values and ideals of the system that taught them. The system reflects the hidden Eurocentric culture.

Other researchers have made similar observations. In their book, *The Psychology of Blacks,* White and Parham (1990) discussed African Americans who attempt to deny any identification with Black culture; they explained that these African Americans deem the cultural behaviors of Eurocentrism superior to those of Afrocentrism. Hare (1965) described these African Americans as Black Anglo Saxons, and Frazier (1962) described them as Black Bourgeoisies. It has been reported that although these Black people deny cultural connections to Black culture, they are often observed snapping their fingers, bobbing their heads, tapping their feet, and, essentially, moving their bodies rhythmically to syncopated music.

In his book, *Kill Them Before They Grow,* Michael Porter (1997) posed a very thought-provoking question to African Americans: "How do you act in the presence of White people?" (p. 9). This is a powerful question in that I see many African American educators change their tone of voice and behaviors when speaking and interacting with their White colleagues in the school building or when speaking with White parents during parent-teacher conferences or during special education team meetings. These educators often overarticulate their words and alter their voices to the point it is difficult to understand them.

DOES RACISM ACTUALLY
EXIST IN THE SCHOOL SYSTEM?

Response-to-intervention initiatives require educators to incorporate culturally relevant instruction in the classroom, and consistent with data-based decision making, educators must make a concerted effort to identify why Black and Brown children perform the poorest in their schools. The most common variables involved when discussing these students' poor performance are (1) skin color, (2) culture, (3) parents, (4) teachers, and, of course, (5) students. Notice that I did not state poverty. Although students who come from impoverished backgrounds deal with a host of inequalities, students of color—across class—experience similar issues surrounding underachievement compared to their White counterparts. Researchers have debated why students of color, across class, lag behind their White counterparts, and although many reasons have surfaced, racism is a common belief among scholars (Howard & Reynolds, 2008).

Students of color who assimilate to school, college, or Eurocentric culture may have an easier time navigating their way through the system compared to students who bring with them Afrocultural values. However, this does not mean that they do not experience issues with race. For example, in a study that examined the effect of ethnic bodily movement styles on teacher perception, researchers investigated whether the stroll (type of walk associated with African American male adolescents) affects teachers' perceptions of (1) achievement, (2) aggression, and (3) need for special education services (Neal, McCray, Webb-Johnson, & Bridgest, 2003). One hundred thirty-six middle school teachers in a suburban school district took part in the study. Researchers used questionnaires and videotapes as instruments. From the videotapes, teachers observed Black and White boys walk from their lockers to their classroom desks. Both students walked in an upright position from their lockers, and after this walking pattern, both Black and White students *strolled* from their lockers.

The upright position is a walking style that exemplifies a steady stride, in which arms and legs swing in unison, according to walking motion. During this type of walk, the position of the head remains forward. White males have been associated with this style of movement. Strolling is identified as a walking style that is an interplay of swaggered movement expressiveness, a slightly tilted head, and an exaggerated knee bend. Teachers were asked to report the walking style that best represented intelligence, aggression, and need for special education services.

Results indicated that teachers perceived the walk that has been associated with Black males as an indication of lower intelligence, aggression, and needing special services compared to students who walked in a style similar to White males. However, African American students were perceived as more intelligent and less aggressive than White students who engaged in African American cultural movements. Researchers explained that, based on this study, White males who are perceived as "acting Black" may be perceived more negatively than Black males (Neal et al., 2003). These scholars explained that cultural information should be considered in detail prior to referring students of color for special education services. This, they argue, is especially true when referrals are made based on the perception of maladaptive behaviors.

Earlier in this chapter, I explained that race is a variable that should be examined when questioning why children of color perform poorly in the classroom. The reason is clear: There are disproportionate numbers of Black and Brown children who receive specialized services in the classroom across the country (Mid-Atlantic Equity Center, 2009). The one variable that shows consistency with the emotional disturbance eligibility is skin color, although other variables come close in the lineup. I'll predict that the real issue is not simply skin color but also, as Neal et al. (2003) have observed, skin color paired with Afrocultural expressions, demonstrated in a predominantly Eurocentric community.

Neal et al. (2003) examined teacher perceptions, and the variable used was walking patterns, but in the classroom, walking patterns may be likened to other cultural expressions such as constantly making beats on the desk, singing to oneself while working, rapping lyrics to oneself, moving around in one's seat, getting up without permission, talking to peers during "in-seat work," and engaging in patterns of call-response behaviors during instructional time.

STUDENT PERCEPTION OF RACISM IN THE CLASSROOM

Many White educators have told me that historical factors such as slavery and racism do not affect the achievement of students of color. They explained how far removed children of color are from the days when slavery was constituted. Although many educators hold these opinions, one of the most common reasons African American students give to explain how their teachers treat them reflects racism: "I hate to say it, but she act like she don't like Black people! All you have to do is come in here and see how she treats us as compared to the White students." This is a response of a third-grade African American male student. Most educators and people call this type of phrase "pulling the race card." Similar to the third grader's feedback, the perception of many students of color I have counseled is not about the *here and now* but is rooted in history.

WHAT IS THE HERE AND NOW?

Many graduate training counseling programs explain that it is best practice to focus on the here and now when counseling students. Focusing on the here and now simply means focusing on issues that are currently happening in one's life and how that individual feels about those issues. For example, the question is always, "Okay, I understand what happened to you years ago, but how does that experience make you feel now, and what can we do about it today?"

Focusing on the here and now is an attempt to get students not only to identify issues but also to talk about how those issues are currently affecting them. One thing that should be understood when working with many children of color is that their perceptions of life are deeply rooted in history: racism, prejudice attitudes, and stereotyping behaviors. Stated simply, many believe that racism still exists; many believe that Black people are often prejudged and stereotyped in negative ways. It's important to state that children do not create these perceptions on their own. Rather, they create these beliefs and attitudes from history and current interactions with people.

Often, when students talk about racism or stereotyping, educators dismiss the student's accusation. Other teachers sit down with the student and ask, "Now do you really think I don't like Black people?" Regardless of what the child says during these interactions, the fact is, educators may make students feel as if they dislike people of color or that they show favoritism in their classrooms. It is interesting to note that many children of color state that they believe their teachers show favoritism in the classroom and that they believe teachers have negative attitudes toward people of color. This is alarming considering that this perception is not held by one student but rather by many.

Since many students of color hold these perceptions, school systems must create programs that address perceived racism. Perceived racism refers to the students' perception of racism in their schools. In addition, school systems must have an ongoing dialogue about race and culture within their schools. Although problem-solving coaches meet to identify problems, analyze data, and implement interventions to correct problems, coaches rarely focus on the problem of perceived racism, which again refers to behaviors teachers demonstrate—behaviors students might perceive as racist.

IDENTIFYING PERCEIVED RACISM IN YOUR SCHOOL

One way to identify the problem of perceived racism is to have students complete a questionnaire that measures their feelings of racism within their respective school buildings. Following this measure, educators could analyze the data and discuss how students feel concerning this issue. It would be interesting to compare subgroups and see what the relationship is among students who believe racism is high in their schools and those students' academic performance, including academic engagement, grades, test scores, and behavioral referrals.

I would predict that students who perceive some of their teachers as racist will perform poorly in the classroom. My reasoning is consistent with research in that there is usually a correlation between achievement and teacher-student relationships (Tucker et al., 2005). For example, when teachers establish strong relationships with students, students usually perform well in the classroom; when teachers have poor relationships with students, students usually become academically disengaged.

Educators, including support staff, focus on the here and now, but the perception of many students of color is rooted in history. And the solution to this problem is not focusing on students' "misperceptions about racism" but rather seeking to understand why they believe some teachers treat them differently and what these interactions look like. In many cases, students focus on the here and now; they tell support staff and administrators they trust that they believe some educators treat them differently because of their skin color. Although students do not directly state that these perceptions make them angry, their behaviors in the classroom and reason for referral tell the story. A problem-solving model that focuses on perceived racism follows.

PROBLEM-SOLVING MODEL TO IDENTIFY PERCEIVED RACISM IN THE SCHOOL SYSTEM

I. Identify the problem

   a. Have students complete a questionnaire that measures perceived racism in the school system.

II. Analyze the data

   b. Analyze the students' responses to the questionnaire; consider the feedback from subgroups, including students who receive the most referrals and students who disengage in the classroom.

III. Implement intervention

   c. Offer a building-wide workshop on institutional racism and cultural racism based on student feedback from questionnaire.

   d. Provide opportunities to engage in book clubs about race relations and the effect of the student-teacher relationship on performance.

IV. Determine the effectiveness to that intervention

e. After continual workshops and dialogues on perceived institutional and cultural racism, readminister the perceived racism questionnaire and compare students' responses that were given prior to the workshops and book clubs (baseline data) to their responses that were provided following the workshops and book clubs (intervention data). This information will show if the students' perceptions have changed regarding perceived racism.

Administrators have told me that they have tried to have discussions surrounding perceived racism in schools with building staff, but the discussions were usually terminated prematurely because people became offended. The outcome: Students of color continued to suffer. From my experiences with working with teachers and administrators on perceived racism within schools, it appears that districts will try all types of interventions to see if the behaviors of African American students will "improve" but rarely follow through with interventions and professional development that surround institutional and cultural racism.

In addition to identifying what students think about racism in their schools, it may be beneficial to school improvement to identify parents' perceptions of institutional and cultural racism in schools and to compare student and parent reports. It's important to collect data on how parents perceive racism in their children's schools because student perception of racism in schools may mirror parent perception of racism.

With most behavioral rating scales, it is best practice to allow not only students to complete a scale to identify their own perceptions of their behaviors and emotions but also parents and multiple teachers to complete a scale to report on their perceptions of the students' behaviors. The purpose of having many raters report on the same student is to compare how others might perceive the same child and to see if the raters identify similar behavioral or emotional problems in different settings. The same should be true for solving the problem with perceived racism: Students, parents, educators, support staff, and administrators should all complete a questionnaire that measures their perception of institutional and cultural racism in their schools, and these data should be compared.

THE MAKING OF SCHOOL CULTURE

Refusing to incorporate cultural characteristics in the American school system began during the 1600s (Pai, 1990) and is now the fate of many students of color (Boykin, Albury, et al., 2005; Boykin, Tyler, & Miller, 2005).

Before education became state property, it was run partly by parents. It was from their pockets that schools were financed, including public education. In rural communities, such decisions as which textbooks to use, how to arrange lesson plans, and when schools should begin and end were determined by parents (Moe, 2001).

The years between 1830 and 1840 brought changes to the ways in which schools were run, changes that are responsible, in part, for designing the organization and school culture of today. This was a time of economic growth, increased transportation, and immigration. The coming of individuals to America from Europe expanded the population pervasively. Protestant ministers were worried about the newcomers and perceived their behaviors as sinful. They were afraid that parents from the urban poor would spread their sinful vices to their children. To combat the vices of parents, reformers called upon the school to indoctrinate a particular belief system. In other words, the school was to instill particular cultural characteristics and values within children who attended. This would be done by spreading republican morals and promoting bureaucratization. As such, control was snatched from the hands of parents and handed over to state authorities (Moe, 2001). From this time forward, school culture has been demonstrative of White middle-class values and ethos.

The development of a bureaucratic system was a strategic way of forcing immigrant students to conform to Anglo values, to reject their own ways of life, and to conform to a White middle-class culture (Patterson, Hale, & Stressman, 2007). During the process of assimilation, immigrant children were coerced to neglect their native tongues and to adopt the preferred school language.

School-based bureaucracy is a hierarchical construction of power that regulates and controls. In the desire to control and enforce, this system has been charged with lacking the ability to respond to the multicultural needs of students. Instead of acquiring a responsive approach to the needs of students, students are expected to conform to the establishment of the school (Patterson et al., 2007). The American school culture is a materialistic system that reflects individual autonomy, competition, and bureaucracy (Boykin, Albury, et al., 2005; Boykin, Tyler, & Miller, 2005). This system deems cognitive processes more relevant than affective processes.

Mainstream characteristics that prevail in school systems have been identified as a "hidden curriculum." That is, classrooms within the American education system do not exist in isolation of a particular culture. Rather, hidden deeply within the curriculum is a cultural socialization pedagogy that exists and subliminally affects the minds of students (Boykin, Albury, et al., 2005; Boykin, Tyler, & Miller, 2005).

One potential cause of academic disengagement of students of color is forced assimilation. Pressuring a child to act like someone other than himself or herself interrupts learning (Neal et al., 2003). Others have argued that the way in which teachers normalize classroom behavior preferences inhibits the cultural skills of African American students (Boykin, Albury, et al., 2005; Boykin, Tyler, & Miller, 2005). Because African American students have demonstrated academic ability and competence when Afrocultural themes are incorporated into their learning environments, normalizing behavioral preferences that exclude Black ethos can be damaging to students of color.

If students of color assimilate to mainstream ideals, they may not be adversely affected by Eurocentric themes that dominate the classroom. But, for African American students who bring to the classroom characteristics that emphasize Afrocultural customs and thus have not shown evidence of assimilation, opposing values may collide (Boykin, Albury, et al., 2005; Boykin, Tyler, & Miller, 2005). These researchers concluded that experiences that are salient within communities that do not typify the school setting should be incorporated into the classroom to balance cultural characteristics. Without such balance, students experience cultural dissonance.

Osborne (1997) investigated whether school culture is responsible for the negative achievement of minority students, namely, African American and Hispanic American students. This was a qualitative study in which data were initially collected on 24,599 eighth graders. The first analysis was based on the assertion that African Americans' self-esteem is higher than European Americans,' although African Americans perform more poorly in the classroom. Hispanic Americans' academic performance and self-esteem were compared to the former two groups.

It was found that European Americans had the highest grades and GPAs. African American students showed the highest self-esteem across all levels, but their GPAs and grades dropped lower and lower as they advanced from 8th grade to 12th grade. Hispanics reported the lowest self-esteem, and their grades dropped with their self-esteem. African American boys disidentified with school more strongly than any other subgroup. Researchers concluded that disidentification of African American and Hispanic American students was due to cultural and language barriers.

In a study in which researchers were asked to investigate the potential causes of academic failures and high dropout rates, and to improve the school's achievement status, researchers examined the effect of school culture on disengaging behaviors. Researchers decided to shed a light on the school culture as opposed to automatically attributing the cause to poor parenting and other deficit and child-pathological models (Patterson et al., 2007). It was found that the school culture was in stark contrast to the student population it served; the majority members were Hispanic Americans (although African Americans were also represented in the study), educated within a Eurocentric culture. In addition, reports from teachers about their understanding of why students drop out reflected deficit thinking which assume inherent deficiencies within racial minorities and low-income families.

As explained by the researchers, this style of thinking made it almost impossible for educators and administrators to consider debilitating factors such as school culture. Because of their thinking, educators absolved themselves totally, while placing the blame and burden on students, parents, and communities.

INSTITUTIONAL RACISM AND ACADEMIC DISENGAGEMENT

Lynn (2006) argues, of all factors that may contribute to the disengaging behaviors of African American students, institutional racism is one variable that is rarely examined; race is rarely scrutinized because it is often viewed synonymously with culture. As Lynn posits, when race and culture are viewed synonymously, it is difficult, if not impossible, to understand the exact role race plays in the poor performance of African American students.

Does race matter in identifying poor performance in school? Yes, race matters when analyzing the disengaging behaviors of African American students because, since the 17th century, it has been used by Europeans as a strategic marker, a way of classifying and designating false perceptions of superiority and inferiority among ethnic groups. While designating their group superior to others, Europeans painted false perceptions of their worth in relation to others. From this practice, two things have occurred: (1) racism and (2) the belief that persons should learn, emulate, and conform to Eurocentric values. Race matters because, although it was used to classify and designate during the 17th century, these same ideals—ethnocentric principles—have been communicated across generations and now serve as the foundation of school culture (Lynn, 2006).

To understand race relations, scholars have referred to critical race theory (CRT) (Hassell, Barkley, & Koehler, 2009). This theory seeks to analyze, interpret, and counter racism as it exists in society and school settings. Using CRT, researchers and scholars have come to an agreement—education in America is racialized. That is, the school culture and educational pedagogy are normalized in such a way that advances the superiority of White people through historical teachings, apparent contributions, and achievements (Lynn, 2006).

For some students of color, schooling has been a barrier to overcome in that time spent in classrooms is tailored to further solidify the dominance and unequal rights of Whites, while subordinating the heritage, culture, language, and values of Black and Brown people. Such subordination is visible when understanding how history is taught. Given that Africans were not brought to America to be educated but were brought as labor supplies, their history, as it is taught in schools, is one of slavery, oppression, injustice, domination, and misery (Lynn, 2006).

This history is one of defamation; the subliminal message to Black children in the classroom: "Your ancestors were de-Africanized, acculturated in a way that they were forced to not only ignore but also to reject their culture, history, and ethos. Your ancestors were taught to value what was Eurocentric and to forget about that which was Afrocentric. Although your people were emancipated, they were forced to bury their identities and culture and act, talk, walk, and think like White people. Your people were forced to make Eurocentric values—European culture—their own. And now, it is your turn to reject your culture, your way of life, and conform to these same values."

Within the purview of stratifying groups, the school system and culture have been charged with excluding education that pertains to African and African American contributions and achievements. This, researchers believe, is an act of racism and may contribute greatly to academic withdrawal. If the history of their people were included in mainstream education, a history that is rich in achievements and accomplishments, as opposed to a history of bondage and inferiority, Black and Brown students might acquire a sense of belonging and become more empowered than they are by simply hearing about achievements of White people (McWhorter, 2003).

In addition to excluding information that pertains to certain ethnic groups, school systems disseminate historical knowledge that is inaccurate (White & Parham, 1990). Such inaccurate information is believed to be motivated by White supremacist ideals. For instance, African American children are taught that Hippocrates was the first physician, Pythagorus was the originator of an algebraic formula, and that Columbus discovered America (White & Parham, 1990). However, "all should know by now that the first physician on the planet was Mhotep, an ancient African Egyptian, Pythagoras borrowed his algebraic formula from the ancient Egyptians, and Columbus was lost" (White & Parham, 1990, p. 90).

White and Parham (1990) referred to psychology to describe how information in the classroom is taught, but not from a historical perspective. These researchers explained that although psychology has been around for thousands of years, its origination is credited to Wilhelm Wundt in 1879. These researchers explain that it should be known that psychology was borrowed from Africa and "popularized" in Europe and then America. White and Parham blame the school system for explicitly erasing the rich, historical connections to ancient Africa.

McWhorter (2003) argues for a more immediate approach to Black history, the dissemination of the accomplishments of Black people since the early 1900s. Such a history would include, among other information, Chicago's Bronzeville (also called "Black Metropolis"), which was a location of Black-owned entrepreneurialism. It has been postulated that focusing on these and other achievements may be more inspiring to children of color rather than immersing them in a history of chains and shackles.

In providing information that excludes the contributions of other ethnic groups, while crowning early European thinkers, Lynn (2006) has described the school system as a politicized institution that advances White supremacy, a system that subliminally and negatively affects students of color. White and Parham (1990) explained that the school system must be scrutinized and considered when understanding the difficulties of engaging students of color in the classroom. If racism is a critical factor within the school culture, according to self-system theories of engagement, motivation to participate in academics will be low (Valeski & Stipek, 2001).

HAS RACISM BEEN SILENCED WITHIN THE SCHOOL SYSTEM?

Racism, since the *Brown v. Board of Education* decision, has been silenced (Schultz, Buck, & Niesz, 2006). For example, researchers investigated the presence of racism in a multicultural school setting and found that it was alive and well but disguised by the facade of equality and the presence of multiculturalism.

To break the silence about race and racism, researchers arranged a forum in which a group of eighth-grade students were encouraged to verbalize and write about their experiences with race at school (Schultz et al., 2006). It was noted that the discussion of race in this particular school was very minimal, in the form of discussing Dr. Martin Luther King Jr. or Rosa Parks. Rarely were there discussions of race and racism in the context of personalized experiences at school.

In the study, there was a consensus among writers that described harmony within the school. But such harmony was a consequence of getting rid of all the Black kids who were "prone to violence." One teacher explained that because of the way bussing is organized, the Black kids they receive are from "good" or "well-maintained" residential areas as opposed to poor communities that are poverty stricken. However, she explained that one particular bus brings in children from the city and that if the bus stopped coming, for whatever reason, it would not be missed. Based on these explanations, researchers concluded, the extent to which the school was perceived as conflict free and academically successful was based on quietly excluding those believed to be undesirable and successfully silencing racism.

Initially, students were hesitant to write about racialized experiences because they did not want to contradict the school's unofficial motto, "We all get along." Because students were hesitant to write about their racial experiences at school, researchers recommended that students write a "fictional play," a play that represented their experiences with race within the school context. In the fictitious writing, Black children were treated more poorly than White children, and although both races engaged in negative, disruptive behaviors, Black characters were reprimanded more often and more harshly than Whites.

Black characters felt they did not receive civil rights at school relative to White characters, and White characters believed discussions of Blacks receiving civil rights were unnecessary. Even more, White characters believed Blacks insisted on discussing civil rights, which, to the White characters, was a boring and overly discussed topic. Researchers suggest teachers discuss racism with students within the context of school culture to understand racialized schooling experiences and needs of those who are non-White (Shultz et al., 2006).

Given the fashion in which the school culture is designed, including cultural discontinuity of non-White students and racialized behaviors, it has been postulated that, in order for African American children to succeed in school settings, they must adopt cultural characteristics that are consistent with Eurocentric views (Ogbu, 1985). Such adoption will align African American students with the values of school culture, mainstream values, which in turn will have an indirect impact on the many educators who disregard multicultural relevance. They will perceive students of color as more worthy and, thus, set aspirations as high for them as they do for children who resemble themselves. However, it has been documented that African Americans do not have to take on Eurocentric characteristics to perform well in that they do well when they embrace their own culture (Spencer et al., 2001).

Others suggest that forcing students to commit to other cultural ethos and values, while excluding their own, is damaging (Delpit, 1995/2006). Instead of coercing Eurocentric characteristics, educators should "teach" children of color the rules of power that are valued and regulated by mainstream ideals, rules that are needed to succeed in America, while incorporating culturally relevant knowledge and characteristics. By doing this, all children will be equipped and will have the power to succeed, while retaining cultural and ethnic pride (Delpit, 1995/2006).

Although an abundance of research and theories has explained the influence of Afrocultural characteristics on minority students, it would be a disservice to simply prescribe learning styles and behavioral preferences based on perceived "ethnic" or "cultural" membership (Gutiérrez & Rogoff, 2003). Because culture does not reside within the bodies, minds, or souls of individuals but is instead "lived" out by persons based on "predisposed" engagements and cultural activities (Gutiérrez & Rogoff, 2003), students are erroneously stereotyped when categorizations and assumptions are made based on the historical reference of group identification and group membership. Such practices are responsible for equating culture with race, ethnicity, language, and national origin (Gutiérrez & Rogoff, 2003).

Although race and ethnicity are constant over one's lifetime, culture has a tendency to change. That is, a child with Black skin and phenotypic traits that characterize Blackness may be more receptive to Eurocentric culture than Afrocultural characteristics, and his perception and interests may reflect experiences and engagements that are more consistent with Eurocentric values and ideals. Because this is true, students should be treated as individuals, even if they share the same ethnic background.

> What's the deal, what's the deal, man, what's happenin' . . . what's happenin' brother . . . I want to know, I want to know what's happenin' . . . Hey, man I just don't understand what's goin' on. What's the deal, what's the deal man . . . what's happenin'?
>
> —*Marvin Gaye*

CHAPTER SUMMARY

Cultural racism is a term that is rarely discussed among educators in the school system. It is the belief that the cultural ways of one group, including values, lifestyles, language/dialect, and worldviews, are superior to those of other cultural groups. Eurocentric cultural characteristics dominate the teaching practices in America's school system in that students are required to learn consistent with Eurocentric teaching styles and are expected to adhere to rules and norms that are consistent with Eurocentric values. When students deviate from these cultural norms or demonstrate behaviors that are valued within their own culture, they are often provided negative consequences. Although it would be intelligent for students to become bicultural—and learn to function within the context of school and Eurocentric culture—it is important that teachers create opportunities for students to engage in culturally relevant activities.

In the next chapter, I discuss the importance of parental involvement and explain why partnering with parents makes for the most effective RTI models.

Getting Parents to Buy Into Your RTI Model   **14**

I'm confident that, with some education, kids will do just fine. It's up to parents and educators to help them become aware.

—Jim Boyce

Any effective RTI model will have, at the forefront, a plan to engage parents in the process. Engaging parents in the RTI model is critical and helps educators make sound educational decisions. Most RTI models require educators to implement rounds and rounds of interventions prior to making educational decisions. At most eligibility meetings, at least one person questions whether the referred child actually has a learning disability or if the child hasn't had the appropriate interventions. Most often, this person is the parent. Parents trust the decisions of the eligibility team when they themselves understand the eligibility process. One meeting on one day is not enough time for parents to understand the process of how an RTI model works. Thus, it is critical that schools host events that provide parents with information on how RTI works and why RTI is their model of choice for preventing academic deficits, intervening when students show signs of failure, and identifying students who might require specialized services. Important questions surrounding this chapter include the following:

- Why is it critical that parents buy into the RTI model?
- What information do parents have about their children that is critical when considering why students are not responding well to interventions?

- Do parents of color devalue their children's education?
- Why do some parents miss parent-teacher conference and individualized education program (IEP) meetings?

There is no support like parental support. Although we rarely admit it, parents understand their children better than any educator in the school does. We like to believe that we know children better than their parents because children sit in our classrooms all day and may engage in behaviors that might shock their parents. But parents have the most relevant information about children, information that sheds light on why a child may not learn at grade level or why a child may have emotional issues. This information comes from prenatal care, early childhood, environment factors, and a wealth of other background information. One of our goals as team members should be to work cooperatively and collaboratively with parents so that they gain trust in our ability to provide services for their children; when they trust us, they will believe that confidentiality truly exists and will begin to share things about their lives and their children's early development that may pinpoint learning difficulties and negative behaviors. In fact, educators engage in qualitative research when they gather information from parents about a student's early development and community life, and we should look at it in this light.

PARENTS KNOW BEST

Often, educators go online in an attempt to find symptoms that fit their students' behaviors. I have had teachers describe their students' maladaptive behaviors to me and ask me why I think the students act the way they do. When teachers ask me this question, I provide the same answer to them all: "The best person to ask these questions would be the parent." The reason is, I could go into the classroom and observe how off-task and disruptive a child is, but an observation will not tell us why a kid acts the way he does—nor will an IQ, achievement, personality, socioemotional, or adaptive test.

These measures will let us know how the student reasoned; whether the student performed above, at, or below grade level; whether the child is believed to have personality or socioemotional issues; or whether the child is able to function independently in some environment. These tests will not tell us why a child is reasoning the way he or she is. Some may say, "Well, IQ or neurological tests will provide this information," but this is not exactly true either. However, although it is important to get to the root of an educational problem, the most important factor is improving academic and behavioral deficits. And parents are valuable players in these areas only if they trust their schools and their children's teachers.

CONNECTING WITH PARENTS OF COLOR

When I would talk with educators about students who were referred for special education services, I would get a common response: "Their parents just don't care!" These statements are contrary to any RTI model. The reason is we as educators have very limited information about parents, their perception of education, and their beliefs about schooling their children. The only time it would be appropriate to conclude that parents don't care about their children's education is when the parents actually state this. Educators often make predictions about parents based on status variables and limited data (see Payne, 2001).

Educators usually believe parents don't care about their children's education because many parents are unable to attend IEP, parent-teacher conferences, and other school-related meetings. But we must realize that it is inappropriate to make cause-effect predictions about parents just because we can't get in contact with them regarding school-related issues or because they do not show up on meeting days. And it is prejudicial to make cause-effect conclusions based on socioeconomic factors (Sattler, 2008).

Parents of color care tremendously about the educational success of their children (Delpit, 1995/2006; Fogle & Jones, 2006; Jeynes, 2003, 2007; Kozol, 1991; Lopez, 2011; Polakow, 1993; Schorr & Schorr, 1998). Parents of color have many reasons why they may not be able to attend school-related activities, including meetings; their children's education is only one of life's variables they juggle. Educators usually interrupt me when I share this idea with them. They usually state, "But education should be the primary goal of any family unit!" When educators make this statement, I usually ask them what would be most important for them—attending a school meeting for 30 to 45 minutes or missing the meeting (to keep your job) so that you could provide shelter, running water, and food for your children in a declining economy.

I shared this issue because many parents of color who come from low-income backgrounds are performers. They usually have a laundry list of things they juggle—and I have worked with many who have been laid off because they constantly missed work to attend some school meeting concerning their child's "inability to sit still in his seat" or overall "misbehaviors."

BRONFENBRENNER'S ECOLOGICAL MODEL

Educators must understand the juggling acts that many low-income parents perform. The more variables parents have to juggle—because of limited resources, single parent, and so on—the more stress and socioemotional problems their children may experience at school. Bronfenbrenner's (1977) ecological model best explains this point.

Bronfenbrenner's (1977) ecological model sheds light on four different, yet overlapping, systems that affect children's development and thinking. In his work, Bronfenbrenner shows that it is almost impossible to understand maladaptive behaviors, socioemotional problems, and academic underachievement without first taking a close look at social, political, and economic conditions that impose on the developing child. Bronfenbrenner's model looks *outside* the child for reasons that may explain "abnormal" behavior, instead of looking *within* the child.

Historically, educators have looked within the child to explain maladaptive behaviors and academic underachievement; they believed that when children experienced learning difficulties, they usually had neurological problems (learning disability) that warranted special education services. Bronfenbrenner's work shows that we as educators must take a closer look at systems to understand why children demonstrate certain behaviors instead of automatically attributing academic and behavioral problems to neurological deficits. He explains that ecological systems are partly responsible for developing the child's perceptions of life, and we know that children usually behave consistent with their perceptions, whether their perceptions are accurate or inaccurate.

Microsystem

The microsystem is the first system in Bronfenbrenner's ecological model and comprises experiences, institutions, and influences that have a direct effect on a child's development, cognition, and worldview. This first system includes *experiences* with

- one's culture—behaviors that are valued within their homes;
- community life—behaviors that take place within their neighborhoods;
- discrimination—unfavorable treatment by individuals or groups because of race, class, gender, or appearance;
- racism—persons who are believed to be inferior by individuals or groups because of skin color; and
- stereotyping—individuals who are grouped and labeled based on race, class, or gender.

Institutions that comprise the microsystem include

- family,
- school,
- church,
- pediatric services,
- social services, and
- daycare centers.

Bronfenbrenner explained that personal *experiences* and *institutions* within the microsystem affect the developing child and *influence* his or her worldview about life.

When institutions within the microsystem interact, these systems create the second layer of Bronfenbrenner's ecological model. He called this layer the *mesosystem.* The mesosystem includes interactions among parents, children, and members of organizations. Examples include parents, children, and teachers; parents, children, and daycare providers; parents, children, pediatricians, and schools; and parents, children, church members, and schools. Essentially, members of institutions and parents meet to make decisions about the child.

Let's take, for example, parents, teachers, children, and pediatricians. A teacher may refer a child for an evaluation because the child can't sit still in his or her seat, won't raise his or her hand without asking permission, and is failing miserably academically. If the parent signs a consent form to allow the child to be evaluated, he or she would fill out behavioral rating scales concerning the child's behaviors at home. The parent would eventually take these rating scales (along with rating scales from other teachers) to the child's pediatrician, who would complete an interview, review the rating scales, and determine if the child's impulsivity is because of some disorder, such as ADHD.

After meeting with the child's pediatrician, if the child is diagnosed with ADHD, he or she may receive services or accommodations within the school setting; if the child is not diagnosed with ADHD, he or she may not receive special services or accommodations within the school setting. Essentially, members that make up the mesosystem work together to make decisions concerning the child.

Exosystem

The exosystem is the third layer of Bronfenbrenner's ecological model. This system includes institutions or persons that do not affect the developing child directly but may affect her or him indirectly. Children may not have knowledge of institutions or people that comprise the exosystem. Children may never come in direct contact with those who operate in this particular system, but they definitely experience the effect of people who operate it. Examples of this system include the legal system, public assistance, and government/educational lawmakers. Employers also comprise this system: Supervisors or managers may require parents to work long hours or commit to some committee on their jobs, which means children may be home alone for extended hours.

Macrosystem

The macrosystem is Bronfenbrenner's fourth and final layer in the ecology system. This system contains values, rules, ethos, and customs. The macrosystem affects children in that they have to conform to rules, customs, and ethos of the mainstream culture; the culture that reflects the macrosystem usually conflicts with beliefs and cultural values of children of color. See Trawick-Smith (2006) for a review of Bronfenbrenner's model.

Educational researchers identify Bronfenbrenner's model as culturally sensitive in that educators should not evaluate children of color in isolation of social, historical, and economical factors that may impede on their learning and achievement. Sociohistorical factors include the historical roots of slavery, Jim Crow laws and oppression, factors within their immediate environment, and experiences students may face because of a declining economy and their parents' inability to secure employment. In addition, educators should consider Bronfenbrenner's model to understand why some parents of color may not be as involved in their students' education; in other words, instead of criticizing parents for not attending school events, IEP meetings, and teacher conferences, teachers should seek to understand how systems may interfere with how involved parents will be within the school system. A good example is having to work multiple jobs to care for children and being required by supervisors to work additional hours throughout the week.

PARENTS' ROLE IN THE RTI MODEL

I often provide workshops for school districts, in which administrators would invite parents and community leaders to the school to learn about RTI. In these workshops, I do not go into detail about RTI; rather, I provide an overview of RTI by showing parents and community leaders how students were educated prior to using RTI as a model. I compare education with the discrepancy model and show how, with RTI, students do not have to wait to receive effective supports. One of the main goals of these workshops is to show parents and community leaders how they could use RTI principles within their homes (parents) and community organizations (community leaders). What role should parents play in the RTI process? Although there may be an array of responses to this question, a key role is to provide additional support within the home and community. Parents should have knowledge of RTI and how it works. They should understand that when students do not respond well to instruction, then teachers will provide them with more time to learn the content, in smaller groups. In addition, parents should have a solid knowledge of why students are moved through tiers and provided with additional supports.

It is my opinion that teachers and coaches should not bog parents down with a lot of jargon surrounding RTI. When I train parents, I explain that parents should focus on the concept of *more time*—that is, providing their children with more time on homework and skills that have not been mastered within the classroom. If parents are unable to provide this time, because they work or have other duties within the home, they should work to connect their child with someone within the community. Teachers could provide parents with evidence-based strategies to use within the home, such as repeated and buddy reading, peer mentoring, and so on. All districts that are implementing RTI would benefit from having workshops for their community leaders and parents to show them how they could incorporate principles of RTI within their organizations and homes. Without the support of parents and community leaders, we will never truly know if a student is achieving at his or her greatest potential. We would never truly know how that student would have performed if he or she had those supports. Parents and community leaders are the game changers in any RTI model.

CHAPTER SUMMARY

Parent participation is critical to ensure effective RTI practices. Because RTI practices could become overbearing for parents who are not as familiar with the model, it is important that educators do not bog parents down with RTI jargon. It is important that parents understand the basic components of the RTI model and learn the importance of "more time." When parents create opportunities for students within their homes to work on homework, they provide more time, apart from school, to practice. Because many parents are unable to provide supports within their homes—because of multiple jobs and so on—it is important that parents and educators work together to identify community resources that are available to assist students with tutoring and mentoring services. If students do not have the opportunity to learn outside of school—especially students who struggle academically—they will more than likely qualify for specialized services. Thus, it is critical that parents and educators identify strategies that could assist students with "more time" to learn content within the community.

In the next chapter, I discuss how schools could collaborate with community organizations to increase the effectiveness of their RTI model.

Using Community Resources: A School–Church RTI Approach

15

It takes a village to raise a child.

—African proverb

Educating children is challenging. An array of factors affects academic engagement and achievement, including parental, dietary, community, socioemotional, cognitive, cultural, and the student-teacher relationship—and the list goes on. Because a number of variables play into ensuring academic success for all children, community agencies and leaders must assist schools with the process of improving achievement. Important questions surrounding this chapter include the following:

- How might local churches assist local schools with creating sustainable RTI models?
- What role could community leaders play in providing Tier 2 and 3 supports within their organizations?
- What are Tier 2 and 3 evidence-based strategies that community leaders could use within their organizations to increase performance among students in the classroom?

CHURCH INVOLVEMENT

During my internship, the high school I worked at did an amazing job at reaching out to local churches to solicit their help with improving performance among students of color. Many of the Black educators at this school attended local churches, and because they understood the importance of the church within the Black community, many of these educators gained permission from various pastors to discuss education within their local churches. These educators and pastors "opened the doors of the church" to discuss education with parents at least twice a month. Those in attendance included parents, students, grandparents, aunts, uncles, clergy professionals, and educators.

During these sessions, attendees did not have Bible study and elders did not preach or teach about Jesus Christ. Actually, the only mention of Christ was during the opening prayer—directly before our session—and during the closing prayer, in which attendees ended their session.

Instead of controlling the sessions and teaching biblical principles, the elders listened to and attempted to understand what was going on in their communities and local schools; they questioned how they might assist schools with the challenge of engaging students of color and closing achievement gaps.

During these sessions, educators talked on a plethora of topics, including the importance of establishing a relationship with principals and teachers, academic engagement, graduation requirements, and financial aid for college. I assisted with discussing the purpose of RTI and how parents and community leaders might assist schools in establishing these models. These sessions were informative, and parents were extremely receptive.

I can't stress enough the importance of the church within the Black community. In fact, from my experiences, many African American parents were more receptive to recommendations from their pastors than to recommendations from their children's educators. This was especially true regarding recommendations surrounding special education decisions. I should add, however, that my mention of the church within the Black community does not mean all Black persons value church and spiritual leadership.

MEETING WITH LOCAL PASTORS AND ELDERS

Because local church pastors are influential within the Black community, educators and service providers should schedule meetings with these community leaders to discuss closing the academic achievement gap between White students and children of color; educators should meet with these spiritual leaders to determine how these leaders and their parishioners might assist the school in improving performance among children of color. This does not mean showing local leaders student test scores, for this is a breach of confidentiality.

The school and the church are similar in that they provide an array of services. For example, the school is filled with educators who are trained in specialized areas of knowledge, including math, science, reading development, and English; in addition, students have access to school psychologists, counselors, and social workers. Students have access to these services at the taxpayers' expense. All students have to do is show up for school and take advantage of these services.

The church is full with men and women who desire for children to succeed within their communities and schools. Parishioners come from varying backgrounds and are skilled in many areas. Churches have youth groups; students convene to learn how to live productive lives as citizens. Many young men live in single-parent homes. Although research speaks to the vital role of fathers within the homes, children and youth do not have control over whether their father will stick around or even support them. And it goes without saying that schools do not have this control either. To this end, youngsters who attend church are surrounded by positive men: pastors, elders, deacons, youth ministers, and other clergy and lay professionals. This information is extremely important, as we know that, in most cases, the success of young males is based on having positive men in their lives; if young men have positive mentors in their lives, then they have a great chance at success as adults, regardless of whether these youngsters' fathers are around or not. This means, instead of complaining about children who do not have positive relationships with their fathers, educators should work to attach these youngsters with positive men—and the church is filled with such men.

An important question is, How can community and church leaders assist local schools? African American students who attend local schools usually attend local churches. Children of color would benefit greatly if educators, including social workers, guidance counselors, and school psychologists, would work cooperatively and collaboratively with clergy professionals to provide services for students. An equally important question is, How might this look?

COMMUNITY ROLE IN RTI

When I speak with community leaders about the RTI model, a common question is, How could we help? Community organizations could help schools create sustainable models by providing opportunities for students to increase skills outside of school. The basic premise of RTI is that most students who struggle do not need extraordinary supports. Rather, they need more time to practice the skill they have not learned. Thus, the concept of "Tier 2" and "Tier 3" refers to additional time, in smaller groups. When students engage in evidence-based practices outside of school, practices that have been shown to increase targeted areas, students receive Tier 2 and Tier 3 support—depending on the amount of students within the afterschool learning group. To this end, clergy professionals could assist schools in that they could offer tutoring and mentoring services within their churches. In fact, many churches offer these services. Students who struggle in school need additional time on tasks and more services that are intensive. Best practices within an RTI model requires intensive services for students who do not respond to general education instruction. Schools and churches could collaborate to provide students who are performing poorly in the classroom with intensive services after school at their local churches, in addition to services provided in school. This means that through training, churches could work as Tier 2 and Tier 3 intervention service providers in that they could work collaboratively with teachers on improving some skill deficit.

Time is not only precious but also limited; this is especially true for educating students during school hours. Because students come to the classroom with varying needs, general education teachers often do not have enough time within school hours to provide intensive interventions for students who need them most. Because this is true, many students are pulled out of their classrooms to receive services; depending on when pull-out services are implemented, students may miss portions of Tier 1 instruction. One unintentional consequence of pulling students out of the classroom is that many students find it difficult to grasp the knowledge they missed. This is especially true of students who process information slowly and those who have poor working memory skills.

THE SCHOOL-CHURCH RTI MODEL

Schools and churches could work collaboratively by creating what I'll call a *school-church RTI model.* With this model, schools could provide services consistent with the RTI model. Prior to or during the problem-solving process, educators could brainstorm with parents about persons within the community who might assist the problem-solving team with implementing interventions within the community. These may include church leaders, the YMCA, Boys Club, fraternity and sorority members, and other community organizations and leaders. After this conversation, parents could sign consent to have these leaders attend the problem-solving meeting, and together, the team could create an action plan dedicated to improving the student's performance. This idea is consistent with Bronfenbrenner's (1977) ecological model and includes the support of people who are most meaningful in the student's life. Brainstorming about community leaders who might assist the problem-solving team should take place when educators identify students who have already received Tier 1 interventions but are not responding to them.

Tier 2 and Tier 3 Interventions at the Church Level

Tier 2 interventions at the church level could consist of clergy professionals implementing some intervention the team had previously agreed upon. Let's use as an example improving reading fluency. Research has shown that repeated reading builds reading fluency for beginning readers (Daly, Chafouleas, & Skinner, 2005). At the church level, clergy professionals could create reading stations within their churches for students to practice reading the same book repeatedly for a certain amount of time. Ideally, this book would incorporate sight words that are at the student's instructional level. This would be considered an intensive service because not only would the student have had 90 minutes of reading instruction in the classroom and pull-in or pull-out services during school, but also she or he would have these services available at the church level within a small group. The following strategies could be used within the churches, strategies that are evidence based:

- *Making Words*—provide students with manipulatives such as letters, tiles, and magnets, and show them how to make new words or help them spell their site words.
- *Partner Reading*—students partner with another student and take turns reading paragraphs or pages. For example, a student might read the first paragraph and the other student read the next paragraph, or the student might read a page and the other student the next page.
- *Taped Reading*—students read along while listening to a tape recording of the passage.
- Allow students to become authors and write stories; allow students to count how many words they write within their stories and challenge them to write more and more words "per book."

The above strategies have been shown to increase reading, writing, and comprehension. Teachers could also recommend strategies they use at the

Tier 1 level. Community leaders could use these Tier 1 instructional strategies as Tier 2 and 3 supports, based on the amount of students placed within the learning group. When groups consist of two to five students, Tier 1 instruction works as Tier 2 supports; when teachers are working directly with individual students, one on one, Tier 1 instruction works as Tier 3 supports (Alber-Morgan, 2010).

As mentioned, the church-level services could work as Tier 2 or Tier 3 interventions, depending on the time, intervention, and amount of students per group, and this would be in addition to the services offered at school.

Clergy professionals could include African American cultural characteristics within their learning environment by incorporating movement, dance, music, bonding, and overall entertainment during intervention time. Consultation is most important with this type of model. Educators, including school psychologists, would have to train clergy professionals on the RTI model and the purpose of the model. Despite how difficult this may sound, it can be done.

One thing that hinders achievement with students is teacher perceptions of how difficult some process may be. Because of their perceptions of the difficulty level of some intervention, many teachers refuse to buy into the model, and other teachers may procrastinate or drag their feet because of their beliefs. Educators and clergy professionals, I want you to know this: The school-church RTI model can definitely be done if teachers and clergy leaders work collaboratively.

Students may buy into this model if they perceive it as entertaining as opposed to simply learning. This means that clergy workers might collect offerings from their parishioners for this type of service. Offerings could be used for purchasing snacks for the students; offerings could also be used for entertaining outings and games for those who attend the sessions. I remember we would have *lock-ins* or *shut-ins* at my church when I was a kid. During lock-ins, children would spend the night at the church and learn about the Bible, watch movies, play games, eat food, and see who would be the first and last person to fall asleep. Churches could have similar lock-in sessions but incorporate academic instruction, interventions, and social emotional learning training.

Determining the Effectiveness of the School-Church RTI Model

Simply incorporating these interventions at the church level is not enough. Rather, at some point, educators and clergy would have to determine if their interventions are working. I would recommend that educators stick to their school's problem-solving model, which in most cases might resemble the four-step model.

1. Identify the problem.

2. Analyze the data.

3. Implement an intervention.

4. Determine the effectiveness of the intervention.

Notice that in the above problem-solving model, educators would have already completed Step 1 and perhaps Step 2. Clergy professionals might be most resourceful at Step 3, by working collaboratively with schools on implementing research-based interventions within their settings after school. Consistent with the team's decision that took place during the problem-solving meeting, educators could determine the effectiveness of their interventions by assessing the skill(s) the intervention worked to improve. Based on progress monitoring data, educators would work with clergy professionals on whether they should continue or replace the intervention.

One important factor in this model is praise. When students achieve the slightest growth, they should receive praise. Clergy professionals could call on students during church services and praise them in front of the church. This would be even more powerful if the students' teachers were present—clapping and cheering along with family and friends!

Such a model may be extremely powerful in that it would provide both educators and parents with information about the student's responsiveness to intervention not only within school but also outside of school. For example, I've been a part of problem-solving meetings in which teachers recommended a full case study. Although teachers recommended a full case study, parents believed that their child did not receive enough support prior to testing.

In other cases, students would qualify for services with a specific learning disability (SLD), but parents would believe that their child did not have a learning disability; rather, these parents believed that their child did not have the right support from teachers. And in many cases surrounding this issue, the parents were right. In one instance, at an eligibility meeting, an irate parent stated, verbatim: "My son ain't got no damn LD. Y'all just ain't teaching his ass the right way!" She really put the team on the spot. In her defense, the team came to the meeting without any progress monitoring data, but the parent was not having it. She constantly said, "Show me what y'all have done to help him!"

In review, the *church-school RTI model* would consist of consulting with clergy professionals about the importance of RTI and explaining the process. The only role clergy professionals would have in the problem-solving model is assisting with Step 3 by implementing interventions and activities to improve skill deficits. This type of model does not have to be solely church related but could also extend to any organization. I used the church because the church plays a critical role in the Black community.

CHAPTER SUMMARY

It takes a village to teach all students. The underlying notion of RTI is that most students who struggle academically do not have learning disabilities. Rather, they just need more time to learn, in smaller groups. They need instruction that is appropriate for them, including instruction that is aligned with their learning styles. One problem surrounding RTI is *time*. Often, there is not enough time during the school hours to provide the amount of additional support to those students who need it most. And when these students leave the school building, they may not have the supports needed to learn skills. Since the church is one of the most prestigious organizations within the Black community, and because the church provides an array of resources, educators and administrators may increase performance among their students if they partner with clergy professionals. Local churches provide tutoring services, as well as have mentoring programs and "youth groups" that could be aligned with school related practices. With the support of educators, churches could create programs that reinforce school-church collaboration.

If a student is receiving Tier 2 supports, he or she will remain at Tier 2, move on to Tier 3, or return to Tier 1. The determining factor of which direction the student would move is based on the amount of time he or she has to learn and the effectiveness of instruction. If the student is provided additional time in school, has additional time within his or her community, and connects with the curricula, chances are that he or she will return to Tier 1. If the student disengages because he or she believes instruction is boring and does not practice reading within his or her community, chances are that he or she will move to Tier 3 and eventually qualify for special education services. The student would qualify not because of some disability but rather because he or she did not practice, which is another way of saying that the student was not provided *appropriate* opportunities to learn.

PART 3

Application

Tying It All Together

Having knowledge of African American cultural values means nothing if educators are unable to integrate such values in the classroom with instruction and within their RTI models. In the chapters that follow, I show examples of how educators might integrate instruction with cultural values discussed within this book. Since educators are required to provide instruction aligned to their state standards, I discuss cultural values within the context of Common Core State Standards (CCSS), considering many states have adopted the standards. This book does not endorse the use of the CCSS but provides examples of how culturally relevant instruction, RTI, and the standards should be aligned. Readers should consider the chapters that follow as examples of how they might be able to align culturally relevant instruction, RTI, and their own state standards, regardless of whether their states have adopted CCSS or not.

Teachers have emailed me and expressed that they feel overwhelmed with having to consider RTI, the CCSS, teacher evaluation systems, and now "culturally relevant RTI." We discuss cultural characteristics within the context of standards because RTI and the CCSS actually align in that the standards do not dictate how teachers should teach in the classroom (Common Core State Standards Initiative, 2010). Rather, the standards explain what students should know by the end of the year. RTI components allow educators methods of determining if students are learning what is expected of them—and culturally relevant instruction is one way to enhance engagement while teaching standards, whether these are the CCSS or other state standards. Teachers should not perceive RTI and standards as fragmented practices. It might be helpful to perceive RTI as a set of procedures of teaching and measuring what we want students to learn and responding, proactively, when we find that students have not learned the content—whether learning objectives are standards or not. We should consider culturally relevant instruction as a method of using the interests, passions, and values of the students to increase engagement and academic motivation.

In the following chapters, I provide examples of how RTI and standards align. I also show how integrating cultural values with instruction may improve teacher evaluation ratings. Following a discussion on how to align communalism, movement, orality, and verve with standards, I dedicate the last chapter to tying all of the information discussed in this book into an RTI model. As mentioned, integrating cultural characteristics is a means to teaching the standards. Let's consider how educators could integrate communalistic activities and other African American cultural values with instruction—aligned to standards.

Peer-Mediated Learning: An Emphasis on Communalism

16

Some of the most important influences on whether students learn have to do with their peers.

—*Julian Betts*

If you have opened this book and directed your attention to this page, while ignoring all other chapters, trust me when I say that you have missed out on valuable information. I understand that we all want interventions *like right now!* but if you rely on this chapter and the chapters that follow to meet a goal, you will identify some good strategies but will have missed out on valuable information that will assist you with working effectively with the students similar to whom I describe in this book. This chapter ties together components that have been discussed within the previous chapters. To gain the most from this chapter, it is imperative that you start your reading at the introduction section and consider the examples and case studies that are provided throughout this book.

THE IMPORTANCE OF CORRECT RESPONSES

Two of the most important goals as educators are to (1) engage students in the classroom and to (2) increase academic performance among all students. Often, much emphasis is placed on academic engagement in the classroom in that research shows that when students are engaged during instructional time, they often do not display disruptive behaviors (Adelman & Taylor, 2006; G. Martin & Pear, 2007), but even when students are actively engaged, if they do not produce *correct* responses during whole-group discussion or during independent seatwork, engagement and motivation will be short-lived (Mitchem, Young, West, & Benyo, 2001; S. J. Wood, Murdock, Cronin, Dawson, & Kirby, 1998), and disruptive behaviors may resurface. Effective teaching requires skill and talent; simply having knowledge of content and being able to disseminate information in the classroom is often not enough to engage—and maintain engagement—among many students of color. An important question to engaging and maintaining engagement is, "How do I create opportunities for my students to produce correct responses during whole- and small-group instruction?"

Engaging students at the Tier 1 level, paired with creating opportunities for students to provide correct responses, is essential to enhancing and maintaining academic motivation in the classroom. Because engagement and correct responses are key to improving academic motivation, this chapter includes evidence-based strategies that have been shown to boost class-wide engagement and enhance correct responses among students through peer-mediated instruction.

I begin with class-wide, peer-mediated strategies because it is often difficult for teachers to isolate and work only with a few struggling students in a classroom. Rather than providing interventions for a few students only, it is much more effective to integrate class-wide strategies that will target all students who have similar deficits. In addition, peer-to-peer interactions and communal learning within the classroom are deemed much more effective than teacher-directed interactions (Daiute & Dalton, 1993; Vygotsky, 1978; Yilmaz, 2008).

PEER-MEDIATED INSTRUCTION

Peer-mediated instruction is a strategy that allows students to work together to achieve goals. When I train teachers on cultural awareness and communalistic behaviors, I often recommend that they pay particular attention to how students of color enjoy working and bonding with each other throughout the school day. Unfortunately, this bonding process often leads to referrals to the principal or dean's office; educators often identify these behaviors as disruptive in the classroom. I recommend that teachers stand in the hallways during passing periods to identify bonding behaviors, as well as observe students during lunch periods and during PE. Students are most communal during these times in that they usually are not provided consequences for engaging in such actions.

Peer-mediated instruction allows students to engage in communalistic behaviors in the classroom without receiving negative consequences.

With peer-mediated instruction, teachers allow students to support each other by working interdependently. In addition, teachers encourage students to practice a given task, provide each other (or their groups) with immediate feedback, and recommend that students support each other in the learning process (Rathvon, 2008).

Evidence-Based Support Surrounding Peer-Mediated Learning

Allison and Rhem (2007)

Gersten et al. (2007)

Maheady, Harper, and Mallette (2001)

McMaster, Fuchs, and Fuchs (2006)

CLASS-WIDE PEER TUTORING (CWPT)—A PEER-MEDIATED APPROACH

Class-wide peer tutoring (CWPT) is a peer-mediated evidence-based strategy that has been shown to increase engagement and performance among students, including students with learning and other disabilities. CWPT is a strategy that I particularly value in that I remember desiring this strategy in the classroom during my early education. During my elementary through high school years, I performed poorly in school. When teachers singled me out to answer a question, I would become embarrassed because I could not answer the simplest questions. I could not answer the question because I rarely completed homework at home—I rarely practiced, and it showed in my responses. In fact, I could count on one hand the amount of times I remember studying throughout my K–12 education. Consequently, I had no academic confidence in the classroom. I enjoyed instruction most when it was class-wide or when we were allowed to work interdependently. So what is CWPT, and how is this strategy related to African American cultural values discussed throughout this book?

Strategy 1: Peer-Mediated Learning and Communal Opportunities

Greenwood and colleagues developed CWPT to increase achievement among urban, low-income students who were identified as at risk for academic failure (Rathvon, 2008). The main purpose of CWPT is to create opportunities for additional practice for all students within the classroom. CWPT has been shown to increase academic productivity and provides ample learning practice opportunities for students, "frequent opportunities to respond, immediate correction, frequent assessment, and public posting of performance" (Rathvon, 2008, p. 142). When students help each other succeed, bond while practicing, care about each other's success, and assist each other to achieve shared goals, they engage in communalistic behaviors. CWPT is an example of working together communally, sharing, and leaning on peers to master content and skills in the classroom.

How to Use This Strategy

Rathvon (2008) explains, "In CWPT, students practice basic academic skills four times a week, with each student serving as tutor and tutee during a 30-minute tutoring period. On Fridays, students are tested on the material presented during the week and are pretested on the material for the upcoming week" (p. 145). This strategy often includes both competitive and collaborative approaches. Because research shows that many students of color prefer to work collaboratively, rather than competitively, I recommend that teachers create cooperative and collaborative opportunities to ensure that all students master the content. When students master the content, competitive games and activities can be integrated, based on the feedback and preference of students.

Baseline Data

To identify how effective CWPT is, educators could provide preassessment of the material that will be assessed on Friday (see above paragraph). Teachers could create authentic assessments, assess the knowledge of their students, and obtain baseline data of their students' knowledge. After implementing CWPT throughout the week, educators could reassess students to determine if the CWPT strategy was effective at improving performance. This is a process of comparing baseline and intervention data (pre-and-post data). CWPT has been used to increase engagement and performance in many academic areas, including reading and spelling (Alber-Morgan, 2010; Daly et al., 2005).

A Review of CWPT and Characteristics Associated With African American Culture

Communalism: This practice involves bonding, sharing, and working interdependently.

Movement expressiveness: Teachers should encourage students to use their entire environments to learn and practice the content instead of requiring them to work at their desks independently. Students should be encouraged to use their bodies—act out content and create songs, rhymes, and themes to practice rehearsing the content.

Verve: Teachers should provide opportunities for students to engage in varied activities, work with their friends, and learn from all stimuli within the classroom.

Strategy 2: Communal/Cooperative Learning—A Peer-Mediated Approach

Cooperative learning is a peer-mediated instructional strategy in which students are placed in groups; while in groups, students work collaboratively to achieve common goals (Alber-Morgan, 2010). Cooperative learning has been an effective instructional strategy at increasing engagement and performance for students across race, class, gender, and culture (Millis, 2009; Salend, 2001). Many educators are familiar with and integrate cooperative learning opportunities within their classrooms but may not associate the technique with culturally relevant instruction for African American students.

It is important to note that cooperative learning in and of itself is not a culturally relevant strategy. Simply grouping students and encouraging them to work interdependently is not synonymous with communalistic learning—which is a valued learning style among many students of color (Belgrave & Allison, 2014). Although these two learning/instructional groups have much in common, communal learning groups emphasize harmony, affection, connectedness, sharing, and community (Seiler & Elmesky, 2007); emphasis is on harmony, bonding, and affection rather than simply working collaboratively. Communal and cooperative learning groups are contrasted with individual learning—in which students are required to work by themselves—and competitive learning—in which students compete against one another to earn the best grade.

In a study that comprised African American and European American students, it was found that African American students preferred communal learning groups over individualistic and competitive groups; moreover, African American students who were placed within the communal groups—in which there was an emphasis on harmony, bonding, and sharing over individual and competitive learning—outperformed all other students within the study (Albury, 1998).

Evidence-Based Support Surrounding Communal/Cooperative Learning

Seiler and Elmesky (2007)

R. T. Cunningham and Boykin (2004)

Wilson-Jones and Caston (2004)

Researchers have documented the effect of communal and cooperative learning among African American students, and educators have used these strategies to increase engagement and performance across subjects.

Effective cooperative learning strategies include literacy circles and jigsaw activities (Alber-Morgan, 2010). Because there is evidence that African American students may perform best within communal learning groups, educators should work to provide these opportunities for students at the Tier 1 level. Educators should provide these experiences for students who embrace communal learning styles prior to moving them through tiers. When determining special education eligibility, team members should determine if students were required to work in isolation when moved through tiers or if students were afforded opportunities to work collaboratively and communally with other peers in the general education classroom.

Strategy 3: Response Cards—A Peer-Mediated Approach

The use of response cards in the classroom is an evidence-based strategy that has been shown to increase engagement, achievement, and on-task behaviors (Heward, 1994; Randolph, 2007). In addition, this strategy has been shown to assist students with providing correct responses during whole- and small-group instruction. With response cards, teachers provide dry erase boards, notecards, or "preprinted response cards (such as signs with the answers printed on them)" to increase participation during instructional time (Alber-Morgan, 2010, p. 29). Using response cards allows students to respond to questions simultaneously by holding up their response signs. Alber-Morgan (2010) provides a list of interventions that teachers could use with response cards:

Phonemic awareness: Teachers could introduce words to students and encourage them to write the initial, medial, and final sounds.

Alphabetic principle (relationship between sounds and symbols associated with sounds): Teachers could write words on the board and model how to pronounce each sound; after watching their teachers model the behavior, students could write the word on their response card and practice pronouncing the sounds.

Vocabulary: Teachers could provide definitions to students from a list of vocabulary words or words from a reading, science, or history book. In response, students could write the term and provide the definition on their response board.

Reading comprehension: Teachers could ask questions about a book or topic and have students provide their understanding of the book or topic. With this exercise, Alber-Morgan (2010) recommends teachers ask a series of questions about a topic and have students write "yes" or "no" on their response boards or "true" or "false" (p. 29).

Math: Teachers could present math facts verbally and have students write the problems on their boards; students could work together to identify the correct response. Once they have the correct response, they could raise their hands or show their cards/boards.

To increase engagement, educators could divide the class into small communal or cooperative learning groups. Students could identify a name for their group and a mascot. With each group, students could take turns acting as the expert student and assist each other with solving problems. When response cards are paired with CWPT, students are provided ample opportunities to practice and are able to receive immediate feedback from their peers. Students become much more engaged when response cards are paired with interactive activities, music, and dance (Alber-Morgan, 2010).

A Review of Cultural Characteristics
Associated With Using Response Cards

Communalism: working interdependently, sharing, bonding, and showing affection

Movement expressiveness: allowing students to move around (compared to staying in their desks), allowing students to move their bodies to engage in the learning process

Orality: allowing students to sing or rap the words from response cards, call-response interactions

Verve: incorporating interactive games and activities, creating variability within instruction

Assisting Teachers With Implementing Tier 1 Interventions

Fidelity to the agreed-upon plan is arguably the most important aspect of any response-to-intervention (RTI) model. If teachers do not follow the plan—if they fail to progress monitor or fail to provide enough time for students to learn the skill—then the intervention may not be effective. Usually when interventions are not effective, team members explain that something is wrong with the students; consequently, students are moved through tiers and eventually are referred for specialized services without evaluating fidelity to the plan and evaluating the intervention effectiveness.

One of the greatest concerns that I have as a school psychologist is that teachers are often left on their own to figure out how to increase engagement and participation in their classrooms. When they are provided assistance, the assistance usually focuses on some behavior modification strategy that targets one or two students in the classroom. Although the interventions provided may be effective for these one or two students, teachers do not have time to focus their time only on these students. The reason is clear in that some teachers have 30-plus students to engage and instruct. Because of this, many teachers have explained that they often do not implement strategies that are provided by school psychologists and/or grade-level teams. They explained that when they focus on one or two students, other students become disengaged. To this point, Rathvon (2008) explains that interventions and instructional strategies should address the entire class, and these interventions should be easy to deliver. Because research explains that peer-mediated instruction has been shown to increase time on task and decrease behavior problems in the classroom, teachers are encouraged to provide instruction within the context of CWPT, cooperative/communal groups, and choral responding. Not only have these strategies been effective across race, class, and gender, but also they align with communalism, movement expressiveness, orality, and verve. Educators are encouraged to use these class-wide strategies when presenting materials across subjects.

CHAPTER SUMMARY

Many educators explain that they have heard of culturally relevant strategies but are unsure how these strategies should look in the class-room. Although educators make these comments, some actually implement culturally relevant strategies without their conscious knowing. For example, communalism has been identified as a valued characteristic within the African American culture. There are many evidence-based strategies that teachers use daily that could lead to communalistic approaches to teaching and learning, including *class-wide peer tutoring* (CWPT) and *cooperative learning.* It is important to note, however, that if students do not work together to achieve the same goal, if they are not interested in the success of each other, and if they do not show care and positive regard toward each other while working in peer-mediated learn-ing groups, then such groups do not reflect communalistic learning. Communalism refers to value placed on bonding, sharing, group identity, and working interdependently. If students are not bonding, sharing, and working interdependently, with the goal of helping all achieve, then such groups should not be considered communalistic.

In the next chapter, I provide culturally relevant approaches to improve reading, writing, and spelling skills. I explain the importance of teaching these skills at the Tier 1 level.

Culturally Relevant Reading and Writing Instruction

17

There is an art of reading, as well as an art of thinking, and an art of writing.

—*Clarence Day*

In this chapter, I will share evidence-based instructional strategies that educators could implement at the Tier 1 level to teach reading, writing, and spelling skills. One of the most common questions among educators surrounding culturally relevant instruction is, "How do these strategies look within the classroom?" In response, I explain that most educators have implemented some sort of culturally relevant instruction some time in their career, although they may not have associated the strategy with African American culture. For example, many primary-level teachers integrate song, dance, and other movement-expressive activities with instruction to engage students at the Tier 1 level and throughout tiers. When teachers read books at the elementary level, they often disguise their voices, become animated, and allow students to move around while learning. Song, dance, and kinesthetic movement-expressive activities are used to teach days of the week, numbers, letters, and shapes, although this is not always the case.

Other teachers may rely less on song, dance, and expressive movements during instructional time. Educators who do not integrate movement-expressive activities—or other characteristics associated with African American culture—in their classrooms could do so by slightly tweaking the way they deliver instruction in the classroom.

Let's take a look at a few Tier 1 evidence-based reading and writing strategies and discuss how these strategies pertain to the four characteristics associated with African American culture. From viewing the following instructional strategies, you will notice that culturally relevant instruction is often common practice within the classroom; however, culturally relevant teachers are intentional about integrating these characteristics rather than implementing them in a haphazard fashion. When considering culturally relevant instruction, remember that, throughout this book, I compare skill-focused and process-focused strategies—and explain that culturally relevant practices are all about differentiating instruction by *content, process,* and *product.* Thus, educators could provide content that speaks directly to African American culture (content focused); they could also integrate communalism, movement expressiveness, orality, and/or verve with the standards and with content (process focused). That is, they could identify an effective reading or writing strategy and combine communalism, movement, orality, or verve with the strategy. Therefore, process-focused, culturally relevant instruction includes integrating communalism, movement expressiveness, orality, and verve across academic subjects.

During the elementary school years, teachers work with students to crack the alphabetic code (Tompkins, 2006). To do this, they use a variety of reading strategies to increase basic reading skills. For the purpose of identifying culturally relevant instruction aligned with African American cultural values, I spent some time reviewing Gail E. Tompkins's (2006) book, *Literacy for the 21st Century: A Balanced Approach.* I was inspired by this book when I first read it in graduate school, and so I decided to review it to identify evidence-based, culturally relevant strategies. The book includes reading and writing activities from a variety of evidence-based studies; activities within this book are common practices within elementary and middle schools, practices that are aligned with African American culture.

USING POETRY TO TEACH
READING AND WRITING SKILLS

Research shows that the use of poetry is a good way to teach reading and writing. Poetry is fun, incorporates rhyme, and is engaging in the classroom. Tompkins (2006) says, "Poetry surrounds us; children chant jump-rope rhymes on the playground and dance in response to songs and their lyrics" (p. 276). Tompkins's response is certainly evident in many inner-city neighborhoods where students are often observed creating stimulating and interactive games that include rhyme, such as double-dutch and single-dutch jump rope. In addition to engaging in jump roping activities, students engage in many games within their communities and neighborhoods, including tag and freeze tag. As I wrote the last sentence, this chant came to my memory:

My momma and your momma were hanging the clothes

My momma punched your momma right in the nose

What color was the blood?

This is a very negative chant, but as a kid, it was a common phrase that was used prior to playing tag within the housing projects where I lived. We used this phrase to determine who would chase and attempt to "tag" all other players. No one wanted to be the "chaser"—the person who had to chase everyone around the park. Although this example is negative and I would not recommend using this with students nowadays, the chant is literary—but we, the children within my community, had no idea our phrase had literary meaning. No one made this connection for us. Another strategy we used to identify the chaser or the person who would be "it" was to have all participants put their foot in a circle. Someone would chant, "Bubble gum, bubble gum in a *dish*, How many pieces do you wish?" Someone (the counter) would touch each foot based on the rhythm of the song. The person who had to "wish" how many pieces was required to state a number, for example, four pieces of gum. From this, the counter would count the feet in the circle the amount of times mentioned—in this case, four. The fourth person could take his or her foot out of the circle and was exempt from being "it." If we had known that our phrase was literary, we probably would have connected with literature more quickly than we did.

Strategy 1: Rhymed Verse

Example: Tompkins (2006) provides the following example (p. 279):

"I see a funny little goat

Wearing a blue sailor's coat

Sitting in an old motorboat"

Purpose: The purpose of rhymed verses is to allow students to identify rhyming words in reading passages and to practice writing words that are similar in spelling. Students learn word families by identifying rhyme words that have similar ending sounds but different beginning sounds. In the above example, *goat, coat,* and *motorboat* rhyme.

Traditional Teaching: Although rhyme verse activities lend themselves to the characteristics of orality (oral expression; call-response type interaction) and movement expressiveness (rhythmic), these activities could present as boring if students are required to sit at their desks alone and are reprimanded for incorrect responses or for attempting to work with a student for such activities. Students may become bored if these activities are mundane and predictable (the opposite of verve).

Culturally Relevant Rhyme Verse Activity: At the Tier 1 level, allow students to get out of their seats to practice rhyme schemes. Students could stand by a peer's desk or all students could stand in a circle. Prior to presenting the instruction, explain to students that "we are like a big family working to reach the same goal!" Allow students to become a band, choir, or R&B group—and allow them to name their group. While practicing the rhyme scheme, allow students to "move" or "dance" as they please. Explain to students that "we are about to have some fun! We are about to dance, step, stomp, move around, and learn strategies that will help us read better." If there is a student that is very hyper and/or likes to be the center of attention, work with that student to create a rhyme verse and allow her or him to perform the verse in front of the class. Assign roles for the students—allow students to be the director, drummer boy or girl, organist, and/or choir soloist.

Review of Cultural Characteristics
Within the Above Examples

Communalism: emphasis placed on family, bonding, group identity, sharing, helping, and working interdependently

Movement expressiveness: emphasis placed on movement, dance, rhythm, and song

Orality: emphasis placed on oral expression, call-response interactions

Verve: variability—with hand clapping, stepping/stomping to rhymes—stimulating, entertaining; integration of song and dance

Note: Notice how activities that integrate communalism, movement expressiveness, and orality create "vervistic environments"—environments that are entertaining, fun, interactive, and engaging. Also notice that, in the above example, teachers are encouraging students to work interdependently to meet a common goal rather than encouraging students to compete against one another (competition) or work in isolation (individualism); in addition, students are not punished for interacting, talking, and bonding during activities.

When I used this activity to work with my children in the home, I asked this question: "Do you all know what rapping is?" In response, my daughter said, "I do, I do—rapping is making songs that rhyme!" From her response, we have created a "rapper's desk" in our home, where my daughter and son create stories, songs, and rap verses that rhyme, and a performance stage (the living room), where they use a toy microphone to perform their art in front of the audience (my wife and me—and extended family). My children become extremely engaged with the use of poetry to learn reading and writing skills to the extent that they have created binders of "rap lyrics," songs, and stories that integrate their site words, social studies words, and "word sorts."

CULTURALLY RELEVANT WRITING AND SPELLING ACTIVITY

Not only do primary-level teachers engage in reading instruction that is consistent with communalism, movement, orality, and verve, but they also engage students in spelling and writing activities that reflect these characteristics. Students at the primary level read books and engage in interactive writing to compose sentences that reflect sight words and vocabulary.

Strategy 1: Chanting and Clapping to Learn High-Frequency Words—Use of Word Wall

Example: Tompkins (2006) provides the following scenario:

Ms. Williams has her students sit on the floor near the word wall to introduce and post the words on the wall. She uses a cookie sheet and large magnetic letters to introduce each new word. She explains that two of the new words—"house" and "soon"—are from *A House for Hermit Crab* [the story they are currently reading in class]. She scrambles the letters at the bottom of the cookie sheet and slowly builds the new words at the top of the sheet as students guess the word. She begins with *h,* adds the *ou,* and several children call out "house." Ms. Williams continues adding letters, and when they are all in place, a chorus of voices, says, "house." Then Kari places the new word card in the H square of the word wall, and students chant and clap as they say

(Continued)

(Continued)

the word and spell it. Ms. Williams begins, "House, house, h-o-u-s-e," and students echo her chant. Then she calls on Enrique to begin the chant, and students echo him. Then Ms. Williams repeats the procedure with the three remaining words. The next day, Ms. Williams and her students use interactive writing to compose sentences using each of the new words they write.

The hermit crab has a good shell for a house. He likes it but soon he will move.

"You're too small for me," he says. "I have to move, but I will always be your friend." (p. 152)

From the above example with Ms. Williams's instruction, can you identify any of the four core characteristics that have been associated with African American culture? Let's consider this question.

Communalism: Ms. Williams created a family-type environment. Students worked together to meet a common goal in that they were not competing against one another but helping each other achieve success; students worked interdependently rather than independently—in which all students used each other and the teacher to identify the words to chant.

Movement expressiveness: Students learned the words in a rhythmic fashion as they chanted and clapped throughout the learning experience.

Orality: Students engaged in "call-response" interaction as they chanted and echoed each other and echoed the teacher. When stating the sounds of the words, they did not simply state a letter; rather, it was expressive. Students did not have to raise their hands to speak, and when students spoke freely or chanted, they were not reprimanded.

Verve: Ms. Williams created an engaging environment. Students moved, chanted, bonded, and interacted with each other. Instruction was not mundane but rather varied, as the students echoed Ms. Williams's chants and eventually echoed each other's chants.

Tier 1 Instruction

Ms. Williams's instruction lends itself well to the four core characteristics associated with African American culture. This type of instruction must take place at the Tier 1 level. Students who are perceived as hyper and off-task should be chosen to lead chants and create words from books and other assigned readings. Students should be encouraged to dance, stomp, step, and perform as they state their words. In addition, these students should receive enormous amounts of praise from their peers and teachers. In the above example, Ms. Williams also engaged her students by having them write the letters they chanted. Culturally relevant writing instruction would include allowing students to write in groups and "share the pen" in which each group member contributes to the writing by sharing the same pen—by writing and passing the pen to a neighboring peer—to write their thoughts.

CULTURALLY RELEVANT USE OF WORD WALLS

Students learn high-frequency words during the primary grade levels. These words are usually placed on word walls within the classroom. P. M. Cunningham (2000) recommends the following when using word walls:

1. Introduce the word or words within context.

2. Have students chant and clap the spelling of the words (similar to the scenario with Ms. Williams in the above example).

3. Have students practice reading and spelling the words in a word workstation.

4. Have students apply the words they are learning in reading and writing activities.

The instruction, as recommended by Cunningham (2000), places emphases on *orality* (chanting/call-response interactions), *communalism* (bonding, interdependency), *movement expressiveness* (clapping, rhythmic instruction), and *verve* (varied instruction, entertainment).

The above examples of reading, writing, and spelling activities integrate cultural characteristics associated with African American culture. Let's now take a look at a few evidence-based reading instructional strategies and identify how we could tweak the strategies to make them culturally relevant for students who embrace communalism, movement expressiveness, orality, and verve.

EVIDENCE-BASED INSTRUCTION

Choral responding: instructing the entire class to respond simultaneously to a question posed by the teacher. Student responses should be short, consisting of one to three words (Alber-Morgan, 2010).

Purpose of strategy: to increase active engagement among all students.

How to Make Choral Responding Culturally Relevant

At the Tier 1 level, teachers should make choral responding as lively and entertaining as possible. Alber-Morgan (2010) explains that choral responding is most effective when teachers present this strategy at a "lively pace" (p. 29). To increase the movement-expressive theme, teachers could encourage students to use their entire body to respond, including their hands, in a rhythmic fashion. Students should be allowed to stand up while responding or allowed to stand next to a peer in the classroom.

When choral responding is presented to students as described above, not only does it integrate movement expressiveness but also it reflects *communalism* (as students and teachers bond through active instruction), *orality* (as students engage in call-response interactions), and *verve* (as instruction is varied, entertaining, and fun).

CHAPTER SUMMARY

Research shows that providing instruction by use of poetry, singing, chanting, rhyming, and dancing is effective for all students at the elementary level to teach reading, writing, and spelling. Teachers often use such strategies to increase engagement among students in their classrooms by these methods and thus provide instruction that integrates communalism, movement expressiveness, orality, and verve—although they may not be familiar with the research on these characteristics. Although singing, dancing, chanting, and using poetry might be related to culturally relevant themes, it is important for teachers to know the research on culturally relevant instruction so that they could provide such instruction intentionally—with identified goals—in a matter-of-fact manner.

In the next chapter, I explain why educators must not *reserve* culturally relevant strategies for when students underachieve or disengage in the classroom. Rather, they must use such strategies at the Tier 1 level to increase academic engagement and to prevent off-task behaviors from occurring. In addition, I explain the importance of communalistic approaches to teaching and learning across tiers.

Communalism and Instruction at the Tier 1 Level   **18**

A teacher gives, a teacher shares, but most of all, a teacher cares.

—*Rita Ghatourey*

A common question that teachers and administrators ask is, At what tier should we present culturally relevant instruction? During seminars, teachers explained that they have attempted culturally relevant instruction when students have been identified as unmotivated and disengaged. To be sure, culturally relevant interactions and instruction should be a part of Tier 1 instruction and should begin the day students enter the school building.

The purpose of providing solid instruction at the Tier 1 level is to prevent disengagement and academic problems. Thus, educators are encouraged to provide the most powerful instruction available to connect students to the curriculum. Providing culturally relevant instruction at Tier 2 and Tier 3 makes sense, considering the goal of interventions at these levels is to get students to return to Tier 1, but our goal is to prevent them from needing Tier 2 and 3 supports. Based on my experiences with working with students of color at the high school level, communalistic classrooms may be the most effective process-focused instructional strategy compared to other characteristics.

WE ARE FAMILY

Communalism refers to the preference for bonding, sharing, group identity, and interdependence. Building communalistic classrooms and environments requires that teachers spend the entire school year establishing and maintaining solid relationships with students and allowing students to establish bonds with their peers. The bonding process that is inherent in communalism should extend throughout the year, but it is vital that educators are intentional about creating communalistic classrooms during the first few weeks of school. At the middle and high school levels, it is vital that teachers create this bonding process at the start of each quarter or semester and emphasize relationship building throughout the semester. Examples of being intentional about creating communalistic classrooms and school environments include making and reinforcing comments such as the following:

- "We are like a big family reaching common goals!"
- "We are one!"
- "We will help each other achieve goals!"
- "Helping each other achieve is one of our primary goals in this class!"
- "You will succeed because you have the help of everyone in this class!"
- "You all are like brothers and sisters—you need one another!"
- "I am so excited about being able to help you on today!"

Educators should not only make these statements daily but also should demonstrate behaviors that are commensurate with their statements. Educators should reinforce this family theme through teacher-student interaction when providing instruction and directives, disciplining students, praising students, and talking with students one on one. This family concept must become one of the most important themes in the classroom; it must become a top priority. In addition to providing these statements, educators should provide praise, reinforcement, and rewards when students engage in behaviors that are communalistic—behaviors that reflect bonding, sharing, and working interdependently to achieve goals. Educators should also integrate this theme within their school's positive behavioral interventions and supports (PBIS) models, models that provide proactive strategies to increase positive behaviors among students throughout the school building.

COMMUNALISTIC BEHAVIORS ARE OFTEN DISCOURAGED IN THE CLASSROOM

Students who come from communalistic backgrounds often create bonds in the classroom with others and enjoy helping their peers achieve. I often share with teachers a story one of my colleagues told me. When I asked my colleague how his son—whom I will call Brian—was doing in school, he explained that Brian was doing well academically but that he had been getting on "red" lately. The color red was a part of Brian's school's discipline system; students who got into trouble throughout the day would end the day on red, which indicated that students demonstrated a range of inappropriate behaviors.

My colleague began to shake his head in frustration as he told me how Brian was doing in school: "Man, Dwayne, I received a letter from his teacher stating that Brian's main problem is that he tries to help students in class in that instead of helping students with their work, he is expected to remain in his seat; he is required to focus on his own assignments." My colleague went on: "You see, Brian's teacher does not realize that he really enjoys helping his peers learn; he enjoys helping other people—he even tries to help me do things around the house. He is above average with his math and reading, so he finishes his assignments before most other students, and when he is done, he tries to help his friends who struggle with math."

My colleague explained that he encourages Brian to help others achieve, which was in stark contrast to the rules and norms established in Brian's classroom. After receiving negative reports from Brian's teacher, my colleague scheduled a parent-teacher meeting to better understand Brian's "misbehaviors." From the meeting, my colleague learned that Brian was often placed on red for offering help to peers and helping when others needed assistance. Clearly, my colleague described a cultural clash within the classroom, a clash between *communalism*—which was a household norm—and *individualism*—which was a classroom norm.

Brian, in the above example, came from a cultural background that places value on communalism. I provided this example to show that students often demonstrate behaviors that are valued within their cultures, and if classroom norms or the school culture does not embrace these characteristics, students will be identified as noncompliant, oppositional, and defiant. Students at the elementary level will continue to receive "reds" throughout the week. The problem with receiving reds and being reprimanded in the classroom for engaging in valued behaviors is students will eventually disengage and shut down during instructional time. In addition, it is possible that they will harness negative feelings toward their teachers. Over time, they may become unmotivated and avoidant learners, and it may be difficult to create solid relationships under these conditions.

TEACHER-STUDENT RELATIONSHIP QUALITY (TSRQ)

Communalism is at the heart and soul of creating relationships. Prior to implementing any instructional lesson or considering any standard, teachers must assess their relationships with their students. This idea is consistent with the old adage: *People don't care how much you know until they know how much you care.* This statement definitely applies to students in the classroom, particularly to African American students.

Research on teacher-student relationship quality (TSRQ) shows that when students believe their teachers care about them, students perform better academically and respond positively to directives. Iruka et al. (2010) found that the performance of many Black students was consistent with how students interpreted the quality of their relationship with teachers. In a similar study, Black students who agreed with statements such as "Most of my teachers care about me," "My teachers praise my effort," and "Discipline is fair" performed well in math, English, history, and science (Stewart, 2008).

Often, when I speak with students who have been sent to the dean's office, I ask them this important question: "How do you feel about your teacher?" Common responses that many African American males provide are, "She has favorites in the classroom and I am not one of them," "She treats me differently compared to other students," and "She acts like she does not like Black students."

I was a part of a meeting that included a student, his parent, and the student's teacher. The meeting was scheduled because the student often demonstrated inappropriate behaviors in the classroom. When asked why he demonstrated such behaviors in the classroom, the student stated, "Because . . . why should I respect her when she doesn't respect me?" In this meeting, the teacher provided a list of inappropriate behaviors the student demonstrated within the course of 2 weeks. In response to her list of behaviors, the student explained, "I was not the only one doing that. In fact we [he and his class peers] were all doing that in your class! You just singled me out." In response to his statement, the teacher explained, "Okay—even if everyone else was doing these things, I am most concerned about your behaviors; we are talking about you right now, not them!" Based on this response, the student expressed a few swear words and said, "See, Mr. Williams, this is the stuff I was telling you about. When other students do stuff, she ignores them, but when I do the same things, she kicks me out of class and says she is only concerned about what I do. Ya'll are going to have to put me in another class or we are going to keep having this same issue throughout the year." He then stormed out of the office and slammed the door. After the student slammed the door, the teacher turned to the parent and said, "You see, this is what I deal with daily. He has a difficult time controlling his emotions when I provide directives." Unfortunately, the teacher did not consider the student's feedback and how her behaviors made him feel.

It is true that the young man in the above example demonstrated inappropriate behaviors by swearing and slamming the door on his way out. But the cause of the inappropriate behaviors is what is most important when identifying how to improve the young man's actions in the future. His perception of his teacher was negative. In terms of teacher-student relationship quality, he felt that she did not respect or care about him; he also felt that she was unfair and that she was not empathetic.

When students have these sorts of problems in their classrooms—problems similar to the student in the above example—they are often referred to social emotional groups, and interventions are considered to correct their "inappropriate" and "noncompliant" behaviors. The best intervention in this situation surrounds improving the quality of relationship between the young man and his teacher. Research is replete with studies that show the relationship between (1) how students of color perceive their teachers and (2) student engagement (Byrnes & Miller, 2007; Hamre & Pianta, 2001, 2005).

COMMUNALISM AND CONVENTIONS OF STANDARD ENGLISH

Let us now take a look at how we could integrate communalism with instruction. Since most states have adopted the Common Core State Standards (CCSS), I will discuss instruction within the context of the standards. Let's begin by looking at the conventions of Standard English (language). One of these conventions is

Demonstrate command of the conventions of Standard English grammar usage when writing or speaking.

Many educators teach grammar by criticizing how their students speak (Delpit & Dowdy, 2002). In a classroom I once observed, when a student of color verbalized a response to a question, the teacher focused on the student's Black Vernacular English (BVE) rather than focusing on whether the student provided the correct answer. In most cases, when students of color responded, their responses were correct, but the teacher would say, "Okay, did you hear what you just said? That is not how you say that. That is incorrect grammar; it is poor English!"

When considering teaching the commands of Standard English grammar usage, an important question is, "How do I teach grammar without offending or speaking negatively about my students' speaking style?" This question is extremely important and relevant in creating bonds and relationships with students. When teachers speak negatively about the ways their students speak and deem their students' vernacular as "bad English," students may begin to harbor negative feelings about their teachers.

In a research project, in which middle school, inner-city students were interviewed about their attitudes toward their teachers, one young girl expressed frustration at her teacher's overcorrecting instructional style of teaching: "Mrs. _____ always be interrupting to make you 'talk correct' and stuff. She be butting into your conversations when you not even talking to her! She need to mind her own business" (as cited Perry & Delpit, 1998, p. 19). Based on this young girl's response, Lisa Delpit—one of the authors of the book *The Real Ebonics Debate* (Perry & Delpit, 1998)—stated, "Clearly, this student will be unlikely to either follow the teacher's directives or want to imitate her speech style" (p. 18). In addition to Delpit's statement, it is unlikely that this student would perceive this teacher's classroom as communalistic.

When teachers explain that their students' ways of speaking are "bad," they are not only speaking negatively about their students' ways of speaking, but in many cases, they also speak negatively about their students' parents,' relatives,' and community leaders' language (Perry & Delpit, 1998). This is particularly true of students who value and speak BVE. If students are constantly corrected when speaking or reading in front of their peers, they may refuse to speak during instructional time and refuse to read aloud in class in fear of speaking incorrectly or speaking *badly.*

When teaching the standards of grammar, one of the best ways to integrate communalism is by embracing the manner in which students speak. Instead of criticizing their language, teachers must embrace their students' vernacular and show how their ways of speaking differ from Standard English. It is vital that teachers make the classroom a safe learning environment so that students of color do not become afraid to speak or engage during instructional time because of how they form words and create sentences. It is vital that they do not feel ostracized because of their vernacular.

Perhaps the only thing worse than not knowing how to read is being made to feel that you do not know how to talk. When students are made to feel that they do not know how to speak or that their way of speaking is inappropriate, many silence themselves; they become less engaged during instructional time, and although they may know the answer to a question, they may not verbalize it (Perry & Delpit, 1998).

NURTURING INSTRUCTION

Integrating communalism with teaching the conventions of English requires what I will call *nurturing instruction*. Teachers must nurture their students during the process of teaching grammar; they must focus their instructional time on teaching grammar, while being careful not to make students feel inadequate about their speaking. Teachers must be careful not to criticize BVE but learn to embrace it. From my experiences with working with unmotivated students, they become more willing to speak and learn within the confines of the classroom when instruction is nurturing. They are more engaged and become more vulnerable with their use of language. This means they will speak even when they know they are not yet proficient at using Standard English and grammar. When educators teach using a nurturing style, students may become more prone to bonding in the classroom and more receptive to receiving feedback from their teachers.

Integrating communalism with the standards of language and conventional English focuses on the "process" of delivering instruction. Educators have often asked how they could create communalistic classrooms or how to integrate communalism with instruction. Put simply, communalism represents the manner in which teachers create an atmosphere of trust and respect. It is a process of creating a classroom where students feel that they belong and that they fit in. When students believe they are inferior because of their vernacular or because of academic skill deficits, it is possible that they will feel as if they do not belong.

Questions surrounding communalistic classrooms include the following: "How do I make all of my students feel welcome?" "What must I do to show my students that I care about them as young people, not just as students?" "How do I make students who have learning disabilities feel that they can indeed learn in my class; how do I make them feel safe?" "Do my classroom rules clash with my students' cultural values?" These questions are consistent with psychologist Abraham Maslow's hierarchy of needs. According to Maslow, in order for individuals to perform at their highest potential, they must feel safe, they must feel that they belong, and they must establish positive self-esteem, among other needs (Viney & King, 2003).

Teachers create a safe learning environment for all students by creating classrooms where students can learn at their highest potential without being judged, criticized, and humiliated because of inappropriate responses or because they might use nonstandard English. Students must trust that when they speak, their vernacular will not be used as an example of how *not* to speak. Teachers could make students feel that they belong and help them find an academic identity within the classroom by explaining that all students fail at some point and that failing is a part of learning. Teachers could create a place of bonding by providing positive feedback and praise for effort instead of focusing on incorrect responses only. From providing nurturing instruction, students will eventually feel positive regard from their teachers, feel that they can express themselves and engage without criticism, and, from engaging over time, may develop positive self-esteem about their abilities in the classroom. When teachers create an environment where students feel that they are safe, feel that they belong, and feel that they can grow and build esteem, they are able to thrive academically. I used a literacy example in this chapter, but educators should provide nurturing instruction with all subjects throughout the school day. Building relationships and affirming students are key.

ADDITIONAL ACTIVITIES THAT PROMOTE COMMUNALISM

Because communalism speaks to caring, helping, and leaning on others for support, educators should create opportunities for students to collaborate on activities as much as possible. The following are additional examples of activities that promote communalism.

- *Reading theaters:* Students act as characters in a poem or story and act out the script
- *Listening to music:* This details the importance of bonding with others and discussing how students could create that type of classroom environment (an example of this is the song "We Are One," by Frankie Beverly and Maze).
- *Language experience approach to reading and writing:* Children tell their stories about their lives and languages and the teacher/students dictate the experiences. Students and teachers acknowledge and praise each other's experiences; experiences and stories are then used as reading materials. The stories are compared to other materials read throughout the school year (Ashton-Warner, 1965; Stauffer, 1970).

- *Interactive writing* (Tompkins, 2004): Students and teachers "share the pen" as they write. This activity would be interesting if students and teachers shared the pen to write lyrics and songs with vocabulary and chapter concepts.

Teachers could modify these activities based on grade level (primary, secondary levels) and skill levels. Essentially, activities that reinforce team building, caring, respect, and working interdependently could create a communalistic environment, if such activities are engaged over time.

Integrating communalism when considering the standards requires that teachers establish a nurturing environment and nurturing instruction. It is a process of creating a family-type classroom, where students and educators promote interdependence, sharing, and bonding. The CCSS speak to *what* students should know; culturally relevant instruction speaks to *how* instruction should be delivered in the classroom. It is important that when teachers align instructional lessons with the CCSS, they ask the following questions: How can I reinforce community, sharing, and bonding with this activity? How do I reinforce communalistic behaviors? When instruction is provided in a communalistic manner, teachers should praise their students for working interdependently and for working as a family. In the chapters that follow, I introduce activities that researchers and teachers have used to teach Standard English and grammar. As you will see, the activities not only integrate communalism but also include characteristics such as movement expressiveness, orality, and verve. Remember, communalistic activities have been shown to engage students of color at the Tier 1 level—and throughout tiers.

CHAPTER SUMMARY

Teachers have shared with me that they often attempt to identify culturally relevant strategies to use when students of color do not respond to Tier 1 instruction. Although it is important to integrate culturally relevant strategies at the Tier 2 and Tier 3 levels, it is most important to integrate such practices at the Tier 1 level to prevent academic disengagement. One of the most powerful characteristics, from my experiences with working with students, is communalism. When students learn in communalistic environments, they are able to work interdependently, interact with their peers while working, and engage in family-oriented activities during instructional time. Such instruction should occur at the Tier 1 level to increase engagement and learning.

In the next chapter, I discuss activities that integrate movement-expressive activities educators could integrate at the Tier 1 level and across tiers.

Movement and Instruction at the Tier 1 Level

19

The one thing that can solve all of our problems is dancing.

—*James Brown*

In a previous chapter, I explained that I worked with a student who was moved through tiers and struggled to connect with the instruction in the classroom. When I met with the student, I asked him what would motivate him to engage in the classroom and complete his work. His response: "All ya'll have to do is let me listen to my music." This young man explained that it was not his intent to be disrespectful, but that if he could listen to his music while working, then everything would be all good. When I asked him if he shared his thoughts with his teacher, he said, "Yes, but she won't let me!"

If music engages and enhances learning for students in the classroom, then integrating music with instruction might be an effective *process-focused* intervention. In addition, if students perform at their highest potential when their instruction is paired with music, then instructing in the absence of music, for these students, might be considered inappropriate instruction. This chapter focuses on integrating music and movement with instruction to enhance engagement and academic motivation.

MOVEMENT AND MUSIC WITHIN AFRICAN AMERICAN CULTURE

Although culture changes over time, Lawrence Levine, the late American historian, explained that the love for music within African American culture has gone unchanged. Levine's observation surrounding the importance of music within African American culture reflects movement expressiveness. The following quote sheds a light on why *music* is a construct of movement expressiveness when defined within African American culture.

> Movement is defined as the interwoven mosaic of movement expressiveness, dance, percussiveness, rhythm, and syncopated [rhythmic] music. For those persons for whom this cultural theme is relevant, movement and music, taken separately or coordinated, are ways of engaging life itself and are vital to one's psychological health. Also conveyed in the movement theme is a rhythmic orientation toward life that is manifested in speech patterns or physical activity. (Boykin, Tyler, & Miller, 2005, p. 531)

Movement encompasses many features and is not restricted to simply moving around, physically, within one's environment. Movement reflects a kinesthetic, bodily motion, but the characteristic also speaks to emotion and internal harmony. Emotions that are attached to movement expressions may not be as readily noticeable compared to the physical gestures of movement (although it is possible to identify emotions by documenting behavioral responses such as facial expression, tapping of the feet, and overall bodily arousal emitted from music). Although movement-expressive behaviors are valued by many African American students, this characteristic is usually deemed inappropriate in the classroom, and students who demonstrate expressive behaviors throughout the day often place themselves at risk for being referred for special education services compared to students who do not demonstrate such behaviors (D. D. Williams, 2013).

Throughout this book, I have expressed the detriment of believing that all Black students are receptive to and value characteristics that have been associated with African American culture. To reiterate this point, I would like to redirect your attention to an important sentence in the above definition: "For those persons for whom this cultural theme is relevant, movement and music, taken separately or coordinated, are ways of engaging life itself and are vital to one's psychological health." This portion of the definition explains that for some African American students, music and expression are used to engage life and are vital to their psychological health; for others within the African American community, music is not a valued characteristic and does not engage them in life to the extent that it engages those who value music and expression. We do not know which students are receptive to movement and music until we invest in learning about their backgrounds and cultural values.

MOVEMENT-EXPRESSIVE BEHAVIORS OFTEN CLASH WITH CLASSROOM NORMS

During a conversation I had with my daughter's teacher about reading performance (during her early years of schooling), my daughter's teacher stated, "I should also make you aware that she moves a lot while reading. She moves and is very active as compared to most other students in the classroom. What are your thoughts on this?" In response to this question, I explained that, as early as 2 years old, I would play movement-expressive games with my daughter to teach letter naming. I would also allow my daughter and son to become *letters that spoke*, in which they would make letter-sounds and act as if they were a part of the alphabet. They would become their letters of choice, dance within the learning environment, and create sounds to produce words. In addition, we would learn with music playing in the background.

Our learning environment was very stimulating and engaging, so engaging that my children wanted to play the letter games all day—even when playing outdoors and when visiting relatives; they taught their cousins and friends how to play the letter games. They rarely ever got tired of playing. Because my daughter is used to learning in stimulating ways, sitting on the floor in a circle with other students to read may become less engaging for her, which is what was taking place during reading time in her classroom.

RESEARCH ON MOVEMENT EXPRESSIVENESS

The importance of movement and music within the African American community is well documented. A plethora of studies shows that instruction, paired with the presence of music and the opportunity to move, enhances performance among African American students (Allen & Boykin, 1991; Boykin & Bailey, 2000; Boykin & Cunningham, 2001). Instead of providing an array of evidence-based examples on movement expressiveness and engagement among African American students, I will provide a brief synopsis of a study and additional references where the study's results were replicated. The following should work as an example of how to incorporate movement at the primary level; educators could modify the example for older students and for different classes.

Allen and Boykin (1991) provided one of the first studies that showed the impact of movement and music on the performance of African American students. In this study, first- and second-grade students were required to recall a set of picture pairs, or sets or pictures, in which their memory was assessed. In this study, researchers created two conditions. In the first condition, which was called low-movement expression (LME), researchers provided the picture pairs to students in a traditional instructional method. Students sat at their desks and worked alone; music was not included within this condition. In the second condition, which was called high-movement expression (HME), researchers provided the picture pairs in a rhythmic fashion; they played syncopated music in the background. In this condition, students were allowed to clap their hands and move to the beat of the tune.

The results showed that White students performed better within the LME condition and Black students performed better in the HME condition (Allen & Boykin, 1991). The results of this study have been replicated and that, when incorporated with instruction, music and movement have been shown to increase both engagement and performance among African American students (Boykin & Bailey, 2001; Boykin & Cunningham, 2001).

In the above studies, Black students performed better when the setting allowed for movement-expressive behaviors and when music was a part of the learning experience. White students performed better while sitting in seats, quietly, and working on tasks without the presence of music. But this does not mean that all White students in the classroom will prefer to sit in their desks quietly while learning. Similarly, it does not mean that all Black students in the classroom will learn best when movement and music are tied to instruction.

The above studies show that it is critical that educators differentiate their instruction, considering students have different learning styles and learn differently under certain conditions. Not all students are going to learn under the same conditions. Moreover, not all Black students will learn under the same conditions as the Black students did who were included in the above studies. Similar to the Black students in the studies, many White students might perform better when movement and syncopated music are paired with instruction; this has certainly been the case with the students I have worked with, especially White male students. The point is race does not determine how students will respond to instruction. The culture in which the student was reared might determine how the students respond to instruction, but this is not always the case either, for students demonstrate behaviors for a variety of reasons. It is inappropriate to believe that culture explains all behaviors (Boykin & Noguera, 2011).

MOVEMENT-EXPRESSIVE INSTRUCTION AND THE COMMON CORE STATE STANDARDS

Now that you are familiar with the effect movement and music have had on the engagement levels of many African American students, an important question is, "How do I take this information and align it with the Common Core State Standards (CCSS)—or how do I align it with my state's standards?" Let's consider these questions. Remember, the cultural characteristic, *movement expressiveness*, not only incorporates movement-expressive behaviors but also emphasizes music and rhythm. It reflects movement that is animated and stimulating, and gestures such as coordinated expression and kinesthetic motion (Boykin, Albury, et al., 2005; Boykin, Tyler, & Miller, 2005).

Although there are a number of standards for different subjects, it is important that educators keep in mind that standards have themes and are closely connected. For example, the following statement is taken from the Common Core State Standards Initiative (2010), under the heading "An Integrated Model of Literacy":

> Although the Standards are divided into Reading, Writing, Speaking and Listening, and language strands for conceptual clarity, the processes of communication are closely connected, as reflected throughout this document. For example, Writing standard 9 requires that students be able to write about what they read. Likewise, Speaking and Listening standard 4 sets the expectation that students will share findings from their research. (p. 4)

MOVEMENT-EXPRESSIVE ACTIVITIES AND K–5 STANDARDS

Standards for students within kindergarten through fifth grade comprise expectations for "reading, writing, speaking, listening, and language applicable to a range of subjects, including but not limited to ELA" (Common Core State Standards Initiative, 2010, p. 4).

When integrating movement-expressive activities with instruction, it would be helpful for educators to identify reading, writing, speaking, listening, and language activities that include rhythmic behaviors, animated gestures, and stimulating, interactive learning. In addition to creating an entertaining classroom environment, research has shown that students are more engaged when animated content is presented—that is, content that reflects expressive behaviors and activities that take place within a story—compared to content that is less expressive (Allen & Boykin, 1991; Boykin & Bailey, 2001; Boykin & Cunningham, 2001).

Movement and Reading Standards for Literature

K–5 Literature Expectations

One of the most reassuring notions surrounding the standards is that they "focus on results rather than means" (Common Core State Standards Initiative, 2010, p. 4). The Common Core State Standards Initiative (2010) manual interprets the latter phrase this way: "By emphasizing required achievement, the Standards leave room for teachers, curriculum developers, and states to determine how those goals should be addressed" (p. 4). The manual goes on to explain, "Teachers are thus free to provide students with whatever tools and knowledge their professional judgment and experience identify as most helpful for meeting the goals set out in the Standards" (p. 4).

Standards for kindergarten include assisting students with identifying key details within text. One of the best ways to integrate movement-expressive activities with reading is by allowing students to perform or role-play the instructional content. Acting or role-playing a theme from a book chapter or novel allows students to observe their peers act out the content and become expressive. It also allows students to become playful and creative, which increases entertainment and engagement in the classroom.

I'll use an example that could take place at the elementary grade levels. Prior to reading a book, teachers could show students the book cover; they could allow them to guess what the book is about and act out what they believe the main idea is. The teacher could demonstrate this activity by asking a student to assist with the demonstration. The teacher could hold the student's hand, walk around the room, and explain that holding the student's hand while walking is an expression of caring—and that he believes the book is all about caring for others. The teacher could allow students to connect with a partner and allow them to act out what they believe the book is about. After reading the book and identifying key ideas as a whole class, students could then act out the main ideas from the book through dance, play, collaboration, and gestures. Educators could modify this activity and incorporate it when teaching older students.

These examples not only incorporate movement but also create communalistic environments—bonding, connecting, and working interdependently to learn key ideas. Activities such as these increase entertainment and affection, and they break up the monotony in the classroom. The big idea about this sort of instruction is that it involves movement, play, entertainment, performance, and bonding—which taps into all four core characteristics that have been associated with African American culture: communalism, movement expressiveness, orality, and verve.

In fifth grade, students will learn to "quote accurately from a text when explaining what the text says explicitly and when drawing inferences from the text" (Common Core State Standards Initiative, 2010, p. 12). To integrate movement expressiveness with this expectation, educators could show videos of Dr. Martin Luther King Jr. or other famous speakers and point out the way these great leaders stood and postured when they presented. They could then allow students to become the great leader by standing up and using similar gestures and postures that were used by the speaker to explain the text. It is important to note that, although it would be wonderful to allow students to imitate African American leaders and actors, students should imitate who they desire to imitate, regardless of race. For some students at the elementary level, their model might be Spiderman, Superman, or Wolverine. Jim Carey or Adam Sandler might be the model-actors for older students. Chris Brown, Music Soulchild, Jay-Z, Kanye West, or Kendrick Lamar might be model-entertainers for students who are passionate about music and dance. Students could also personify their favorite actors or actresses and explain how the content would look if their text was converted into a movie.

Grade 6–12 Literature Expectations

Expectations for sixth-grade reading: "Cite textual evidence to support analysis of what the text says explicitly as well as inferences drawn from the text" (Common Core State Standards Initiative, 2010, p. 36).

An example of an activity that incorporates movement-expressive behaviors for 6th- to 12th-grade students is allowing the classroom to become a performance arts studio. Educators could give students the option to act and perform while citing evidence from the book; educators could allow students to work in small groups to create a scene or 60-second performance. Similar to the above example, students could personify their favorite actor or actress while reciting evidence from the text and inferring based on their knowledge of the reading. Students could also ad-lib while performing to make the lesson more entertaining and unpredictable.

The examples included in this chapter provide brief examples and strategies that integrate movement-expressive activities with literacy. As mentioned throughout the CCSS initiative manual, teachers have complete autonomy to create the type of lesson they believe will be most engaging for their students. Activities in this chapter emphasize movement—including allowing students to perform, act, and recite their literature and content. It is important that educators allow their students to pick whom they would like to personify—although students may portray their favorite actresses or actors, they might also desire to portray politicians, clergy professionals, or relatives.

As stated in the Common Core State Standards Initiative (2010) manual, standards speak to what students are expected to know by the end of the year. Teachers are free to use their professional judgment and creativity to help students learn what is expected. Because research is replete with studies that show the effectiveness of using music and movement to engage African American students, integrating these characteristics with instruction would be considered culturally relevant, best practice, and appropriate instruction.

CULTURALLY RELEVANT ACTIVITIES AT THE PRIMARY AND SECONDARY LEVELS

Educators often integrate activities that incorporate communalism, movement expressiveness, orality, and verve at the elementary level. For example, in the early grades, teachers incorporate entertaining games, listen to music, use rhyme to teach letters and concepts, dance, and enjoy their time in the classroom (Tompkins, 2006). Sometime after the primary levels, teachers rely less on entertaining games and focus more on lectures and individual work. Following are additional activities that are culturally relevant for students surrounding literacy and writing at the primary and secondary levels.

Writing and Talking Projects (Tompkins, 2006):

- Allow students to give a readers' theater presentation of a book.
- Allow students to write a script and present a play about a book, as well as integrate personal and cultural experiences with the book theme.
- Allow students to dress as a character from the book and answer questions from classmates.
- Write and present a rap about book chapters, themes, and concepts.
- Use creative music in the classroom such as "Rap Facts" to allow students to engage their working memories and fact fluency skills.
- Begin instruction with a popular, appropriate rap or R&B song and tailor instruction around the song.

- Allow students to "publish" their lyrics.
- Allow students to collaborate to perform a concept—rap or sing book content to the class; allow students to video record their performance and critique it.
- Allow students to videotape a commercial for a book in a culturally relevant way—using music, rap, dance, and drama.

The above activities are a few examples of culturally relevant activities that integrate communalism, movement expressiveness, orality, and verve. Remember, communalism and verve are created through engaging, caring interactions. From working together, students learn to value each other, bond with each other, and assist each other. Educators could align activities similar to the ones above to teach standards.

CHAPTER SUMMARY

Movement has been identified as a core construct of African American culture. Students who embrace movement may desire expressive activities while learning. These students may desire to listen to music while working, may tap their pencils in a rhythmic fashion while thinking deeply about some concept, may tap their feet to a beat while listening to instruction, and/or may engage in dance-related movements throughout the school day. A. Wade Boykin and colleagues have conducted an array of studies on the effect of movement on academic engagement among African American students.

In the next chapter, I discuss orality at the Tier 1 level and explain how educators could integrate activities that are related to orality with instruction. In addition, I discuss how educators could align orality instruction with the standards.

Orality and Tier 1 Instruction

20

If you talk to a man in a language he understands, that goes to his head. If you talk to him in his language, that goes to his heart.

—*Nelson Mandela*

In the book *The Skin That We Speak,* the late psychologist Asa Hilliard spoke to the importance of understanding language within the context of culture. He explained, "Children all over the world learn to speak the language of their cultural group at about the age of two" (Delpit and Dowdy, 2002, p. 89). Hilliard expressed an important sentiment: Language is a hallmark of culture. Not only do children learn their parents' language at an early age, but also children learn key expressions of language by imitating their cultural group members. Orality is a hallmark feature when considering language within the context of African American culture. Orality is not simply a process of speaking or relaying a message, but more important, it is performance based and includes an emotional component that engages both speakers and listeners (Belgrave & Allison, 2014). Because orality is a core characteristic within African American culture, the focus of this chapter is on integrating orality with instruction—and aligning such instruction with the standards.

THE SPOKEN WORD

Orality, as a core characteristic of African American culture, has been defined by Boykin, Tyler, and Miller (2005):

> Orality refers to the special importance attached to knowledge gained and passed by word of mouth. It implies a special receptiveness to the spoken word and a reliance on oral expression to carry meaning and feeling. There is often a reliance on the call and response mode of communication, whereas to be quiet and wait one's turn to speak often implies a lack of interest in what the other person is saying. Also captured within this notion of orality is the idea that speaking is construed as a performance and not merely as a vehicle for communicating information. (p. 532)

Orality, as described by Boykin, Tyler, and Miller (2005), is clearly apparent in the communicative interactions among most African American people in general and African American students in particular. The rich expression of orality is most prevalent within predominantly African American churches. It is not uncommon for pastors and ministers to preach and teach the Gospel of Christ with extreme fervor during Sunday morning services. Ministers do not simply express their thoughts when relaying the Gospel. Rather, their messages are impactful, lively, and stimulating. Their words stir emotions. While the minister *calls* (speaks), congregants usually *respond* by saying, "Amen!" "Preach it!" or "C'mon, now!" Others might say, "You betta preach that word!"

The interplay between the preacher's call and the congregant's response creates an atmosphere of verve as members become excited about the word of God, move from their pews into the aisles, and, occasionally, shout and rejoice as the Spirit leads them. The expressions of words take on a special meaning of their own, and congregants not only listen and process the spoken word but, more important, *feel* the experience; they are moved emotionally, and such emotion is difficult to restrain. In describing his experience with Sunday morning church services, music, and love, B. B. King summed this orality experience up perfectly:

> Archie Fair is the nearest thing I know to God on earth. He talks like his words have already been written out in a book. Each word carries weight; each sentence carries good meaning. His sermon is like music and his music—both the song from his mouth and the sound of his guitar—thrills me until I wanna get up and dance.

He says one thing and the congregation says it back, back and forth, back and forth, until we're rocking together in a rhythm that won't stop. His voice is low and rough and his guitar is high and sweet; they seem to sing to each other, conversing in some heavenly language I need to learn. (King & Ritz, 1996, p. 16)

The phrase "He says one thing and the congregation says it back, back and forth, back and forth, until we're rocking together in a rhythm that won't stop" (p. 16) is the essence of orality. To be sure, there are no rules to such dialogue. Speakers are not required to remain silent until given the signal to speak. Rather, speaking is natural and generated through emotions, and respondents illicit feedback based on how they feel.

In his autobiography, King explained that he was not the brightest student academically; he stuttered when he spoke, he was an introvert, and he struggled with managing emotions. In today's system, most educators would explain that King's profile—stuttering, poor academic skills, emotional deficits—warranted an individualized education program (IEP). But for King, he learned, processed information, and expressed himself not through an IEP but through orality, within the context of music (King & Ritz, 1996). King's autobiography is significant because it shows that cultural characteristics truly mediate learning, and if students find learning difficult, then educators must work diligently to identify innate gifts, talents, and abilities to assist students with identifying career choices that align with their strengths.

It is vital that educators understand the value of the spoken word within African American culture; it is also vital that educators understand emotions that are generated from spoken words and that, in most cases, speaking, for many African American students, is performance based, rather than simply conveying a message. I have heard many educators, during problem-solving meetings, state that their students are overly animated when they speak and interact with their peers. In addition, African American males have been described as hyper and aggressive in their interactions. Educators have identified these behaviors as disruptive and inappropriate for the classroom environment. Such behaviors from students (emotional responses) and negative perceptions about those responses from teachers create cultural clashes in the classroom.

If educators are to integrate the expression of orality with instruction and align their lessons with standards, it might be helpful for them to first identify orality as culturally relevant to many African American students and use expression as a tool to engage students academically.

ORALITY AND THE CCSS

Now that we have defined orality, let's discuss how educators could connect orality-based activities with instruction, aligned with the Common Core State Standards (CCSS). For many African American males, integrating orality with instruction is simply a process of allowing them to create music or poetry from their literature. This has definitely been true with the students of color I have worked with. One simple intervention I have used with many African American students who were usually disengaged and off-task in the classroom was to integrate their interest in music with instruction. When students had the option to create lyrics from their lessons, they became much more interested and motivated to engage academically. This was true for students who enjoyed rapping and writing poetry and was not exclusive to African American students.

The CCSS place an emphasis on language, including speaking and listening, because for students to succeed after high school, whether they attend college or pursue a career, they must have the ability to speak and listen effectively. For example, the Common Core State Standards Initiative (2010) explains,

> The Speaking and Listening standards require students to develop a range of broadly useful oral communication and interpersonal skills. Students must learn to work together, express and listen carefully to ideas, integrate information from oral, visual, quantitative, and media sources, evaluate what they hear, use media and visual displays strategically to help communicative purposes, and adapt speech to context and task. (p. 8)

I became excited when I first learned of these expectations because, based on my own background knowledge and experience with African American culture, I realize how important the spoken word is and I understand that African American students are very creative with words.

ADAPTING SPEECH TO CONTEXT AND TASK

What stands out to me from the above CCSS quote is that students must be able to "adapt speech to context and task." This expectation is extremely critical. Most African American students speak what linguists have termed Black Vernacular English (BVE). Students learn to speak BVE from their immediate family, extended family, and cultural group members—and this vernacular has value within the context of culture; apart from culture, BVE is perceived, by many, as an unintelligible way of speaking and using words.

To teach language skills to African American students, without offending them or making them feel that their method of speaking is inferior, educators should become familiar with qualities of BVE. BVE has similar qualities and features as Standard English but has stark differences as well. Common features of BVE as described in Sattler (2008):

- Use *be* to denote an ongoing action: "He be going to school."
- Dropping linking verbs: "You smart."
- Shortening plurals: "Thirty cent."
- Dropping of some final consonants: "las instead of last"—"I did my homework las night."
- Substitution of some pronouns: "He got all the money."
- Substitution of /ks/ for /sk/ in final position as in "ax" for "ask."
- Substitution of past, present, or future verb form—as in "he goes" for "he went."

Because language is a core construct of culture, students who speak BVE are fluent with this form of vernacular, but many do not have the skills to code switch—or switch between two different languages. In other words, most African American students do not have the skillset to adapt speech to context and task, which is an expectation within the standards. Rather, students usually use BVE in all contexts—in the classroom, at home, within their communities, during job interviews, and so on. When they open their mouths to speak, BVE usually comes out—regardless of the context.

I should be clear in that many Black professionals use BVE outside of their workplaces. For example, social media have received a tremendous amount of attention over the years, and people are now interacting via Facebook (FB), among other social networks. I have many professional colleagues on FB who use BVE in their comments and posts but use Standard English on the job and in meetings; these professionals are skilled at adapting their speech to appropriate contexts. They may also use BVE on their jobs to emphasize a point or to illicit strong emotion.

To use an example, one day I made a comment on FB about Olive Garden's Zuppa Toscana soup. In the post, I explained that I was going to have to memorize the name of this soup so that I would stop embarrassing my wife. Because I could not remember the name of the soup—Zuppa Toscana—I would ask for the "potato soup." In the FB post, I explained that the waitress/waiter and I would laugh and that I would always explain that I had trouble memorizing the name of the soup. While explaining my difficulty memorizing the name of the soup, my wife would be on the other side of the table staring at me and shaking her head.

In response to my post, one of my colleagues, who is a nationally certified school psychologist and doctorate degree holder, stated, "Mr. Williams, I'm goin' to need you to get yo'self together!" Her comment was hilarious, and her point was clear. She received an array of *likes* from other professional Black men and women who read her comment and found it humorous. And it was! Although she would not write in this manner when creating reports or speak this way in IEP meetings, she adapted her language and writing to show expression; the context was appropriate and her use of words expressed perfectly what she meant. Her writing created imagery, and FB friends felt her expression. It is important to note, however, that orality and BVE are not synonymous; many Black Americans speak Standard English and do not speak BVE—but these same individuals might engage in characteristics surrounding orality, including the call-response themes of orality.

LINGUISTICS, LANGUAGE, AND EDUCATION

Michael Stubbs, a sociolinguist, explained that most people hold stereotypes and attitudes about language. He explained that it is impossible to hear someone speak without drawing conclusions about their background and status and that there is a direct correlation between socioeconomic status and language (Delpit & Dowdy, 2002). Stubbs's comments about evaluating language brings to mind a comment an 8-year-old African American girl made about an African American woman.

"Why She Talk Like That?"

One Sunday morning, as clergy professionals were preparing to start church service, my family and I were seated next to a young African American girl; the young girl sat next to her mother. While we, and the rest of the congregation, waited patiently for the praise team to prepare to engage us in worship, an African American woman walked past us while talking with her children. The way in which the woman spoke caught the attention of the young girl who sat next to me. The young girl watched in amazement at the Black woman and analyzed her method of speaking. After the woman walked away, the young girl turned to her mother and said, "Did you hear how she talk? Why she talk like that? She talk like she White!" I was intrigued at this young girl's response to the Black woman's speaking style.

Initially, I ignored the young girl's comments, but as her voice reverberated in my mind, it was difficult for me to refrain from asking what she meant, so I asked, "Hey, I heard what you just said. What did you mean by talking White?" In response to my question, the little girl said, "Oh, you didn't hear how she talk? She'on [she don't] sound Black. She soun' White. Why she talk like that? She should'n talk like that cus she Black!" Based on this statement, it was clear that this young girl had expectations about language; she had expectations about how Black and White people should speak. Not only did she value the manner in which Black people sound and speak, but also she believed that, if you are Black, you should sound a certain way. I was amazed at this experience—to learn that a young 8-year-old girl had expectations about race and language. Not only did she hold stereotypes about the manner in which people spoke, but also she held a certain type of attitude about language.

When I thought about her statement, I wondered how many other African American students thought that Blacks should sound a certain way. I had mixed feelings about her comments. I was excited because the little girl showed that she embraced and valued the way "Blacks speak"; she was comfortable with how she sounded when she speaks. But I was also concerned in that she did not realize that not all Black people sound like her or her family members.

This experience raises an important question, one that I eluded to earlier. What happens to the self-esteem and confidence of young Black students who embrace and value BVE—similar to the little 8-year-old girl in the above example—but are told that BVE is improper and a *bad* way of speaking? These students might begin to harbor negative feelings toward the person who made the evaluation about their speech because, in their minds, their speech is representative of an entire race of people—Black people, their people.

Before I transition into culturally relevant instructional strategies aligned with the CCSS, I will share one more example about stereotypes surrounding language and speech. Our understanding of language is fraught with stereotypes and social values, which Michael Stubbs referred to as "linguistic stereotypes" (Delpit & Dowdy, 2002, p. 67). To show how we perceive language through linguistic stereotypes, Stubbs provided an example, in which a teacher engaged her students in a discussion about speech dialects. The dialogue was recorded, and students had a transcribed script in front of them:

> Teacher: You can see on the bottom of your sheet, "We ain't got no money." That is typically a London accent—the tendency to drop the aitch off the front of words, d'you? It's a lazy way of speaking. (Delpit & Dowdy, 2002, p. 66)

In reference to the above lesson, Stubbs pointed out that the teacher provided a "confused and dangerous linguistic folklore" (Delpit & Dowdy, 2002, pp. 66–67). He explained that associating the dropping of aitch at the front of words with being "lazy" was damaging. Stubbs explained, "Dropping aitches is a linguistic stereotype which is believed to characterize London speech, and it is thought to be 'lazy' or 'slovenly'" (Delpit & Dowdy, 2002, p. 66). He went on to say that dropping the aitch is a linguistic practice used by most educators in the country.

Becoming aware of linguistic stereotypes, as Stubbs calls it, is critical to instructing students in the classroom. If teachers engage in linguistic stereotypes and deem their students' dialects or speech as lazy, inappropriate, or bad, these students may disengage in the classroom and become resentful toward their teachers; students may develop negative emotions about learning English and grammar.

When providing instruction in the classroom, it is critical that educators teach English grammar in a way that is nonoffensive and nonthreatening to students who speak BVE. It is vital that educators become conscious about their teaching methods, self-monitor, and remain cognizant of how their students respond to instructional comments and feedback surrounding *appropriate* and *inappropriate* ways of speaking. Engagement is key. When we offend students and make them feel inferior, students shut down. When they shut down, their grades tend to decrease, and over time, team members often attribute their students' failure to learning disabilities. Although many students shut down because they have been offended (D. D. Williams, 2012), educators interpret the shutting down and refusing to work as needing specialized services.

CULTURALLY RELEVANT INSTRUCTION ALIGNED WITH THE COMMON CORE STATE STANDARDS

Since it is vital that students develop code-switching skills, let's begin with Language standards. According to the Common Core State Standards Initiative (2010), "The Language standards include the essential 'rules' of standard written and spoken English, but they also approach language as a matter of craft and informed choice among alternatives" (p. 8).

An instructional strategy that has been effective with many African American students is comparing BVE to Standard English—while showing appreciation for both (Ladson-Billings, 1995a). This strategy is in contrast to teaching Standard English grammar while condemning BVE. To compare BVE and Standard English, educators will have to understand the features of BVE as described in the bullet points above. For instructional purposes, the following chart might be helpful in comparing BVE and Standard English.

Black Vernacular English		Standard English	
Usage	**Example**	**Usage**	**Example**
Uses *got*	*The girls got a cat.*	Uses *have*	*The girls have a cat.*
Omits *is* and *are*	*The cat in the wagon.*	Uses *is* and *are*	*The cat is in the wagon.*
Omits the third-person singular ending *–s* from verbs	*The man ask the boy what to do.*	Uses the *–s* ending on verbs	*The man asks the boy what to wear.*
Omits the *–ed* ending from verbs	*The dog get chase by the cat.*	Uses the *–ed* ending on verbs	*The dog was chased by the cat.*
Uses *do*	*The girl do pull the wagon to the boat.*	Uses *does*	*The girl does pull the wagon to the boat.*
Uses *be* in place of *am, is,* and *are*	*The big ball be rolling down the hill. He be going home.*	Uses *am, is,* and *are*	*The big ball is rolling down the hill. They are going home.*
Pronounces *th* at end of word as *f*	*In the baf, he washed his mouf and played wif a toy*	Pronounces *th* at the end of a word as *th*	*In the bath, he washed his mouth and played with a toy.*
Drops the final *r* and *g* from words	*My fatha and motha be talkin and laughin.*	Pronounces the final *r* and *g* in words	*My father and mother were talking and laughing.*

Chart used from Sattler (2008) with permission.

Note: There is much variability with how students use BVE. Not all students will say "baf" for *bath*.

I cannot stress enough the importance of appreciating our students' dialects when teaching grammar. Educators should know that linguists have identified BVE as a fully formed linguistic system that includes its own grammatical rules and pronunciation (Belgrave & Allison, 2014; Delpit & Dowdy, 2002). Researchers explain that an effective method of teaching grammar to African American students who use BVE—and value orality—is by starting instruction by showing how BVE has had a tremendous impact on English language. When students realize that the way they speak is accepted and has contributed to English, most become empowered and feel good about themselves. If educators are unsure of

how to strengthen their students' self-esteem about speaking or lack ideas
of how to show that BVE is valued within our society, they could begin by
reviewing these facts, as described by Emmons (1996):

> It [BVE] has enriched the fabric of American English. Black
> English is in jazz. Among the hundreds of the jazz world's words
> that have filtered into the American lexicon are "hip," "cool,"
> "gig," "jiving around," and "gimme five." Black English is in blues
> and soul, giving America expressive, often sensual, words and
> phrases like "hot," "baby," "mojo," "mess with," "thang," (as in
> doin' my thang), "take it easy," "slick," "rip-off," "cool-out" and
> "bad." Black English is in Negro spirituals ("Dat Ole Man River,"
> "Ah Got Shoes"). It is in gospel ("Aint No Devil in Hell Gonna Walk
> on the Jesus in Me") and through these mediums of expression
> has found home in the vernacular of the [B]lack church. (p. B9)

I recommend that educators google "*Black English Has Its Place, Los
Angeles Times*" to read Emmons's (1996) full article, which is very interesting and provides great ideas for instructional activities for the classroom.
The article also explains why it is important that Black students maintain
their ability to speak BVE. Although it is widely agreed that Black students
should maintain their BVE skills, many educators, during the school day,
identify BVE as a "bad," "inappropriate," and/or "incorrect" way of speaking. It is vital that educators understand that, grammatically, BVE is
incorrect compared with the grammatical rules of Standard English and
other forms of languages and vernaculars. Likewise, Standard English, as
a system of rules, is incorrect compared with the rules of BVE.

SPEAKING, LISTENING, LANGUAGE,
AND VOCABULARY EXPECTATIONS

Students are expected to adapt their speech to context and task, and
comparing BVE and Standard English is an excellent way of integrating
students' cultural skills with instruction; it is an excellent way of using
what they already know—and what they value—to meet reading and
writing standards. This instructional method is also perfect for teaching
speaking, listening, language, and vocabulary standards.

African American students are extremely creative at putting words
together. They come to the classroom with a wealth of vocabulary
words that are meaningful within their cultures and communities. The
words that African American students use—words that most educators

might identify as slang—could be used to teach new, novel vocabulary words. Educators could refer to sources like the Urban Dictionary to become familiar with words some of their students use. Let's use the word *turn up*, since it is highly used among youth and hip hop culture, as an example. This is how the Urban Dictionary defines the phrase *turn up*:

> (v) getting wild or excessively crazy. Typically used in the context of a party. It is normally followed by a prepositional phrase (For the party, In that place) and it is often used in the past tense (turned up). "Turning up" is almost never said. As far as I can tell, it is the 2011 equivalent of what "Getting Crunk" was in the early 2k's and late 90's. We turned up in Mr. Mitchell's class when he had a sub last week; I turn up every weekend. (Urbandictionary.com)

Based on the definition, it may be engaging to have students identify synonyms and antonyms of what it means to turn up; it would also be interesting to take the phrase *turn up* and create a sentence using literal and figurative meaning. Although the phrase *turn up* does not describe "Black culture," it does include orality, in that the phrase is used to explain emotion and excitement. It is not used to simply state an action. This example could be used when considering the vocabulary standards, which focus on "understanding words and phrases, their relationships, and their nuances, and on acquiring new vocabulary, particularly general academic and domain-specific words and phrases" (Common Core State Standards Initiative, 2010, p. 8). Students could learn new, academic, and domain-specific phrases by comparing and contrasting what it means to turn up and relating personal experiences to their academic content.

Considering these expectations, students might become engaged in the classroom if they are allowed to use their own words and learn new, academic terms that are similar in meaning as the words they use within their communities. This method is exactly what Ann Lewis used to increase engagement in her class. Ann Lewis is a White woman who Gloria Ladson-Billings—the researcher who coined "culturally relevant pedagogy" (Ladson-Billings, 1995a)—has described as "culturally Black" (p. 161). In describing the process of linking school and community experiences, Ladson-Billings provided examples of Ann Lewis's instructional strategies of using students' home languages to introduce new vocabulary words and to build grammar skills (Ladson-Billings, 1995).

Instead of criticizing students for using BVE in the classroom, Ann Lewis encouraged them to speak how they spoke within their communities. She used their ways of speaking to introduce Standard English. Students were allowed to speak and write in the method they were most comfortable; they were then required to "translate" their written or spoken expression to Standard English (Ladson-Billings, 1995a, p. 161). From this method, students not only showed progress but also were successful at code switching. More important, they were able to use both languages effectively. Ann used culturally relevant instruction to help students meet expectations.

What is most exciting about Ann's lessons is that she helped her students meet what we call Language standards by appreciating how they used language. This approach to teaching vocabulary and grammar helped students develop both BVE and Standard English. Ann Lewis provided culturally relevant instruction in that she introduced activities that integrated students' cultural values; she did not attempt to detach students from how they speak at home or within their communities. Because of Ann's instructional method, she bonded with her students (communalism) and formed valuable relationships. As Ann demonstrated, schools should be a place to further learning. It should not be a place to shame students' cultures or speaking dialects.

INSTRUCTION

As Ann Lewis did, educators could teach literary words and concepts by using phrases such as *turn up* and other words that students bring to the classroom. Educators could create lessons that integrate these words with poetry and Shakespeare readings to make classroom more engaging. If teachers hear their students use words that are expressive or words that reflect orality, they could ask the students to define the words and later, during instructional time, integrate the words with instruction and show how the words are similar to or different from key terms that were discussed within the lesson. This method would help students memorize new vocabulary words because students would have background knowledge to pull from and to help assimilate the new words.

Activities for Developing Speaking Skills, Grammar, and Standard English Using Orality

- Create activities where students can compare the speaking styles of news reporters and music artists, including hip hop and rap artists.
- Many teachers in New York City have allowed their students to identify a news reporter, take on the reporter's persona, and create news shows every day of the school year. It might be a powerful activity if students identify a news reporter who shares the same

race as the student: After the student performs, the teacher could say, "Good job speaking like Don Lemon. You did a great job and you would be a great anchor!" (Lemon is an African American male news reporter.)

- Allow students to role-play: Students can become news reporters and other students can role-play the music artists; when students role-play music artists, require them to translate slang or Black Vernacular English—while showing appreciation of Standard English and Black Vernacular English.
- Allow students to role-play drama productions so that they can get used to speaking Standard English.
- Allow students to perform profanity-free hip hop, rhythm and blues, or rap and have them translate certain words in writing.
- Allow younger students to create puppet shows and imitate super-heroes (as these heroes engage in hyper-correct Standard English).
- Allow local music artists to perform for students and help the students translate their music into Standard English.
- Allow your students to bring in samples of lyrics from nonoffensive rap songs. Allow the students to perform the songs, and as their teacher, you reproduce the lyrics on the overhead projector to discuss literal and figurative meanings, as well as components of poetry such as rhyme, scheme, alliteration, and onomatopoeia (Ladson-Billings, 1995a).

Literature, Writing, Grammar, and Orality Instruction

Students should know that rappers are poets, just as Shakespeare was a poet. Because rap and poetry include literary concepts, educators and students could have a discussion on the similarities between rap, poetry, literature, and writing. Educators could allow students to engage in

- Rhymed verse activities
- Free verse activities
- Rimes and rhymes (also known as word families)
- Activities that integrate singing

CHAPTER SUMMARY

Orality has been described as a hallmark characteristic of African American culture. The "spoken word" is valued among many people of color in general and students of color in particular. The CCSS place an emphasis on speaking and listening standards, and consistent with these standards, it is critical that African American students learn how to adapt speech to context; it is critical that they learn how to code switch. Educators who are familiar with the research surrounding orality are encouraged to differentiate instruction by incorporating language-based activities, including hip hop, rhyme, and poetry for students who desire them.

In the next chapter, I show how instruction that incorporates communalism, movement expressiveness, and orality creates a vervistic (taken from the word *verve*) classroom. In addition, I discuss how educators could use verve characteristics to increase engagement in the classroom and show how Charlotte Danielson's teacher evaluation system speaks to the importance of vervistic environments. Scenarios are provided to give concrete examples of vervistic instruction within the context of culturally relevant RTI models.

Verve, Evaluation Systems, and Instruction

21

At the school level, analyses of the current affairs find a tendency for student supports to be highly fragmented.

—*Howard S. Adelman and Linda Taylor*

In the previous chapters, I provided examples of how educators could integrate communalism, movement, and orality activities to engage students at the Tier 1 level. When these characteristics are integrated, they create engaging and entertaining experiences. These experiences are also known as vervistic experiences in that many activities occur at once, music is integrated with instruction to enhance learning, and students and teachers work together to achieve goals.

In this chapter, I will show how verve could be used to increase engagement among students of color in the classroom. As stated at the start of this section, I will discuss verve within the context of Charlotte Danielson's (2007) teacher evaluation system. It is vital that teachers do not get overwhelmed about current initiatives or teacher evaluation systems. I could show how verve fits into an RTI model—throughout tiers—but believe it would be more meaningful to show how RTI, the Common Core State Standards (CCSS), and constructivist approaches to learning (the theoretical model used in Danielson's evaluation system) align. I have decided to focus on Danielson's Domain 3, which emphasizes engagement in the classroom. Danielson (2007) explains that "the heart of Domain 3 is engaging students in learning" (p. 77). When considering engaging students in learning, an important question is, "How do we effectively engage students who come from culturally diverse backgrounds?" "How do we engage students who value Afrocultural characteristics?" This chapter speaks to how teachers could integrate communalism, movement expressiveness, orality, and verve into the classroom to enhance engagement with students who embrace traditional characteristics associated with African American culture.

ENGAGING STUDENTS AT THE TIER 1 LEVEL—AND THROUGHOUT TIERS

Important questions when considering verve and academic engagement:

- What are key elements of verve?
- Are there research-based studies that show the effectiveness of verve on academic performance among students of color?
- How do verve elements and Danielson's evaluation system align?

DEFINING VERVE

Prior to diving into a discussion on vervistic classrooms, I will provide a definition of *verve*, as described by Boykin, Tyler, and Miller (2005), to ensure that we are working from the same definition:

> Veve refers to a special receptiveness to relatively high levels of physical or sensate stimulation (Bailey and Boykin, 2001). Physical stimulation or sensate stimulation is understood in terms of intensity, variability, and density of stimulation. Qualities related to intensity are those having to do with volume and vibrancy of stimulation in one's behaviors. Variability has to do with the level of changeability or alternation among activities or stimulation elements in one's environment or induced by a person. Density has to do with the number of stimulus elements or activities simultaneously present in one's environment. It can convey (a) the number of distinct events occurring at the same time, (b) the simultaneous engagement in more than one activity, and (c) the focus on a given task while there is discernable background activity or stimulation present. (p. 531)

Physical, Observable Expression of Verve

Verve represents one characteristic, but the term embodies communal bonding, sharing, rhythmic movement, expressive orality, preference for music, and interdependent functioning. The integration of communalism, movement expressiveness, and preference toward rhythmic behaviors is what creates the verve characteristic. Educators could perceive verve as the integration of all characteristics—communalism, movement expressiveness, and orality. Verve refers to physical, bodily stimulation—but it also refers to stimulation sensed within one's environment.

Verve and Cognitive Breaks

The physical, observable component of verve that is often expressed in behavior could be measured in terms of (1) intensity, (2) variability, and (3) density of stimulation (Bailey & Boykin, 2001).

Intensity

Intensity refers to the *volume* (strength) and *vibrancy* (rhythmic orientation) of behavior. The volume or "strength" in behavior could be observed in voice pitches and bodily gestures. Vibrancy consists of lively or rhythmically oriented behaviors; volume and vibrancy refer to observable stimulation in one's behavior. Educators often perceive students as aggressive, offensive, loud, or hyper because of intensity of behaviors. Moreover, students who demonstrate high levels of intensity in behavior, when observed using traditional on-task/off-task measuring tools—and rating scales—are usually identified as off-task and disruptive (D. D. Williams, 2012). The reason students are identified as off-task is because most observation tools school psychologists and other educators use are insensitive to characteristics that reflect verve. Students who demonstrate high levels of intensity in their behaviors in the classroom place themselves at risk for being referred for specialized services (D. D. Williams, 2012); the reason is, classroom norms and school cultures are usually in stark contrast to these behaviors (D. D. Williams, 2013).

Variability

Variability has two components: a (1) physical, behavioral component and an (2) environmental component. The physical, behavioral component refers to "the level of changeability or alternation among activities or stimulation elements in one's environment or induced by a person" (Boykin, Tyler, & Miller, 2005, p. 531). I like to use examples that include making beats because these are common behaviors many students demonstrate in the classrooms. It is not uncommon to observe students who value vervistic qualities to work on their required assignment, take a brief break from their assignments to create a beat with their pencils, or make a beat with their feet. These behaviors reflect variability; students alternate from their assignment(s) to creating a beat or alternate from their assignment to singing or humming a song. These varied behavioral responses interrupt the monotony in mundane instructional activities. These varied behaviors allow students to take brief cognitive breaks from activities that require deep thought. Once students take such breaks, they usually return to their assignment. These experiences may occur throughout a given school day.

Density of Stimulation

Density of stimulation refers to one's tendency to engage in many behaviors at once. When I observe students who demonstrate vervistic behaviors, they might tap their foot on the floor in a rhythmic beat, nod their heads to the beat they create, express gestures with their mouths—all while completing writing or math assignments. When teachers who are unfamiliar with verve characteristics observe students demonstrate such behaviors, they often identify students as off-task. They explain, as I observed a teacher express to a student, "You can't possibly be paying attention to what you are doing if you are making beats with your foot and rocking to the beat in your chair!"

Many of our students work best under vervistic conditions, and educators should know that all African American students may not respond to such activities the same. To use an example, I become most motivated to write when I have music in the background. In fact, if the room is absent of music playing in the background, my writing experience usually concludes rather quickly, because I lose motivation. It is also more difficult for me to create and express ideas while writing without music in the background. On the other hand, my wife, who is also African American, must read, write, and study in silence. When she and I are studying in the same room, I usually listen to music through headphones to increase my motivation and engagement while reading, writing, and studying. This example shows that, even for students who come from vervistic backgrounds, they may prefer to learn in environments that are less stimulating.

Verve Expressed Within the Classroom

Density of Stimulation

Density of stimulation also refers to stimulation that takes place within the classroom or within one's environment as well; it speaks to the number of engaging activities that take place simultaneously. The best example of density of stimulation within the classroom is creating instructional activities that allow students to engage in workstations, with stimulating music playing in the background; if students in the classroom prefer not to listen to music while working, students could have the option to listen to music through headphones or earphones. The essence of density of stimulation within the class surrounds engaging in activities while integrating stimulating background elements simultaneously.

Variability

When considering the environment, variability refers to the change-ability or alternating activities within the classroom. Variability in the classroom is in contrast to requiring students to complete one task for the entire instructional period; it also is in contrast to lecturing at students the entire instructional time.

Essentially, verve speaks to high levels of stimulation within an environment; these high levels include physical behaviors expressed in bodily movement and language—as well as affection for group members within the environment. Vervistic classrooms speak to learning environments that incorporate music and opportunity for students to perform, act, and role-play.

RESEARCH-BASED STUDIES ON VERVE

The positive effect of vervistic classrooms on the performance of African American students is well documented, in that many students who come from homes that are vervistic not only prefer stimulating classroom environments but also perform better when their classrooms reflect verve experiences (Boykin, 1978, 1982; Boykin, Allen, Davis, & Senior, 1997; Boykin & Bailey, 2000; Carter et al., 2008; Tuck & Boykin, 1989).

DANIELSON EVALUATION MODEL AND VERVISTIC CLASSROOMS

Danielson (2007) speaks of the importance of creating classrooms that are conducive for learning. To this end, research shows that many African American students respond well to classrooms that are vervistic in nature, but this does not mean that all Black students will prefer stimulating environments; it also does not mean that White, Asian, or Latino students will oppose vervistic classrooms. An important question, when creating an environment that is conducive for learning, is, "In what conditions do my students learn best?"

In her evaluation system, Danielson (2007) speaks to the importance of creating classroom environments that are engaging—environments where students are engaged not because teachers are standing on their heads, turning tricks, or making themselves disappear during instructional time but rather by creating environments whereby students connect to the lesson. Danielson (2007) says this about the importance of the classroom environment:

> In a classroom with a strong culture of learning, everyone, including the teacher, is engaged in pursuits of value. Rather than an atmosphere of "getting by" or "punching the time clock," both students and teachers take pride in their work and give it their best effort. In such classrooms, it is "cool" to be smart, and good ideas are valued. The classroom is characterized by high energy, by a sense that what is happening there is important and that it is essential to get it right. (p. 67)

In contrast to valuing instruction that is provided in the classroom, many African American students treat instruction as "getting by." When interviewing a student who was failing four classes, he explained that he was "just not motivated to work in his classes." He explained, "Everything we do in my classes is boring. I just feel like I am sitting there waiting for the bell to ring. Class be so boring that I usually think about other stuff." When asked what could make instructional time more engaging for him, he explained, "Something as simple as listening to music while working." When I asked this student if he had shared his thoughts with his teachers, he said, "I explained this to one of my teachers, but she explained that she does not allow music in the classroom. She stated that I will have to find another way to get excited about instruction." Interestingly, this particular student earned a respectable score on his ACT but was failing in the classroom. His grade point average did not reflect his academic skills as represented by his ACT scores.

Danielson (2007) speaks to this young man's experience:

> Students who don't find a task engaging let their attention wander to more interesting matters. For example, high school students pass notes or discuss out-of-class events; a 2nd grader converts his pencil into an imaginary car and runs it around his desk, with appropriate sound effects. (p. 71)

When students find instructional time "boring," their minds wander to more engaging thoughts. They occupy themselves mentally while sitting in their seats, staring around the room.

ENGAGING ACTIVITIES THAT INCORPORATE VERVE

The following are examples of vervistic activities that educators could integrate in the classroom:

- Integrate hip hop music, culturally specific word games, and multicultural poetry to enhance reading skills (McQuiston, O'Shea, & McCollins, 2008).
- Select culturally relevant books and encourage paired reading.
- Ask interesting questions to gain student attention—"How do you believe African Americans have contributed to our national culture?"—and pair this question with interesting documentaries on inventions of African Americans.
- Create culturally relevant thematic units about Africa, in which students learn about music/art, math, social studies, literature, science, physical education (dance), listening, speaking, reading, and writing as they pertain to the continent of Africa (for an example, see Alber-Morgan, 2010).
- Interview students and parents about cultural background information and values and create thematic units surrounding cultural experiences.
- Create thematic units about African Americans and how African American culture has helped shape mainstream culture, including the impact the culture has had on rock-n-roll, country, pop, and hip hop music.
- For literature and grammar, allow students to bring in appropriate lyrics that relate to chapter content and identify literary terms from the music.
- Allow students to write raps and songs to chapter content and engage in "peer editing"—in which students read the lyrics and provide feedback, including how students could make the rap more relatable to chapter content.

These activities could be modified based on grade and skill level. I often explain that, when students explain that they do not like a particular subject, what they really mean is that they do not like how the subject is taught. If educators teach subjects and lessons in vervistic ways, students may be more prone to engaging throughout instructional time.

CHAPTER SUMMARY

When I train teachers on culturally relevant RTI (CR-RTI) models, many explain that they experience a high level of stress when they are told that they have to learn to implement "another" initiative. Many educators look at current practices, initiatives, and evaluation systems as fragmented. It is important to understand, however, that CR-RTI, the CCSS, and Danielson's evaluation system align. Danielson's evaluation system is rooted in constructivist theory. Domain 3 of her system aligns with the research on verve, in that instructional activities alone should be enough to engage students behaviorally, cognitively, and affectively. Danielson speaks of the importance of integrating instructional strategies that have the strength to engage students within the classroom and the importance of high-intensity activities. When educators create CR-RTI models within their classrooms and vervistic learning environments, they are better able to engage their most difficult students during instructional time; teachers place themselves in positions for better evaluations when being evaluated with Danielson's teacher evaluation system.

In the next chapter, I provide scenarios to show how a CR-RTI model might look in the classroom. I provide scenarios to show concrete examples of integrating communalism, movement expressiveness, orality, and verve with instruction at all three levels of the RTI model.

Tying It All Together Within an RTI Framework

22

It is not a question of how well each process works, the question is how well they all work together.

—Lloyd Dobens

In the introduction section, I explained that the purpose of writing this book is twofold: (1) to examine RTI in the context of culturally relevant instruction and (2) to discuss how educators might incorporate an RTI model that fits the cultural needs of most African American students. Within the covers of this book, I have

- shown how we have gotten to this place in education;
- explained the big idea surrounding RTI;
- shown *how* and *why* culture mediates learning;
- provided theory that supports a culturally relevant RTI framework;
- shown step-by-step examples of how to create culturally relevant RTI models;
- provided information surrounding evidence-based, process-focused instructional strategies that have been associated with African American culture; and
- provided practical examples of my experiences as a school psychologist who has worked with students of color at the primary and secondary levels.

Now that you are more familiar with the concept of culturally relevant RTI models, let's consider how a culturally relevant model might look!

Let's put all that we have learned through previous chapters to see how we could create a nurturing environment for students who value Afrocultural characteristics. In the following scenario, consider how Ms. Johnson prepares for the school year and how she integrates communalism, movement expressiveness, orality, and verve with instruction.

Scenario 1

During her summer vacation, Ms. Johnson was determined to learn more about culturally diverse students. She attended a seminar on creating culturally relevant RTI models and read books about culture and academic engagement. From the seminar and summer reading, Ms. Johnson learned practical strategies on how to integrate culturally relevant activities that have been associated with African American culture and was eager to share with her team and implement what she had learned.

Creating a Welcoming Environment at the Tier 1 Level

Upon her return from summer break, Ms. Johnson, a third-grade teacher at Springhill Elementary School, prepared for the school year by decorating her classroom. Unlike past years, she posted pictures around the classroom that reflected the racial and ethnic makeup of her students. In addition, she brought in a collection of music to play during instructional time to make her lessons more engaging.

During the first few weeks of school, Ms. Johnson stood at the door and greeted every student who entered the classroom with a high five and a smile. From the seminar that she attended and summer book readings, Ms. Johnson understood the importance of communalism among students of color and wanted to create a communalistic environment. To start this process, she would play the song, "We Are One," by Frankie Beverly and Maze, softly in the background as students entered the room. The theme from this song explains that no matter what we experience in our lives, *we are all one*. Once students entered the classroom and placed their belongings in their proper places, Ms. Johnson would have the students listen quietly to the song as she took attendance.

After taking attendance, and upon the first time playing this song, she asked, "Has anyone ever heard this song before?" To this question, Jermaine, one of her students who struggled in first grade with reading and who rarely engaged during instructional time, stated, "I have! I heard this song. We always play it at family cookouts!" To this response, Ms. Johnson learned that many of her students and their families listen to music and dance during family cookouts. She engaged her students in a discussion on why they believed their families "are one."

After learning why her students believed their families are one, Ms. Johnson showed the group a picture of Frankie Beverly and Maze and explained that many of their songs are about treating people fairly, equally, and working together to achieve goals. She then directed the students to sit in a circle on the floor and led the group in a discussion on what it means to "be one." Within this discussion, Ms. Johnson explained that, like Frankie Beverly and Maze's song, she and all students in the classroom are one and that they are like a big family. She explained that, throughout the school year, she and the students will be like a big family who works together to achieve goals.

When Ms. Johnson created her rules in the classroom, a few of her rules reinforced communalism. For example, one rule was, "We will treat everyone with respect, because we are a big family." Ms. Johnson was intentional about creating a communalistic classroom and reinforced communalistic behaviors by praising students for working interdependently within the classroom.

Periodically, Ms. Johnson would review the notes she took during her summer seminar. In her notebook, she quoted the presenter: "Educators should be intentional about creating communalistic environments. Examples of being intentional about creating communalistic classrooms include making and reinforcing comments such as,

- We are like a big family reaching common goals!
- We are one!
- We will help each other achieve goals!
- Helping each other achieve is one of our primary goals in this class!
- You will succeed because you have the help of everyone in this class!
- You all are like brothers and sisters—you need one another!"

Ms. Johnson was also familiar with the research on teacher-student relationship quality (TSRQ), which explains that often, the quality of relationship among teachers and students is a predictor of academic achievement (Iruka et al., 2010; Murray, 2009); in other words, if the relationship between a student and teacher is poor, then the student is likely to disengage in the classroom. If the relationship is positive, then the student is likely to engage and put forth effort. Based on her knowledge surrounding culturally relevant instruction, Ms. Johnson was intentional about creating a communalistic classroom that emphasized sharing, bonding, and interdependence.

Teaching the Five Big Ideas of Reading

Ms. Johnson was also excited about introducing reading instruction in a culturally relevant manner. She used the evidence-based program, Success for All, as her core reading curriculum and integrated entertaining activities to assist with building *phonemic awareness, phonics, fluency, vocabulary,* and *comprehension*—the five big ideas of reading. Since many of her students enjoyed music and attended the local church, she thought it would be fun to create a "children's choir" within the classroom, considering the majority of her students were in a choir within the community.

As a daily practice, Ms. Johnson and her students sang songs, chanted rhymes, blended and segmented words—and stomped to syncopated beats.

(Continued)

(Continued)

She divided the class by "sopranos," "altos," and "tenors" and explained that all had to contribute during instructional time so that the choir could sound its best. She also emphasized that, although they were individual singers, they were *one* choir helping each other to achieve the same goal. She did this to emphasize their *communal* theme. Ms. Johnson allowed Darnell to be the director, considering he was the most active student in the class. Darnell would dance in place as he sang and directed the We Are One Choir, which is the name they decided to use for their children's choir.

To prevent academic failure and identify students who might need additional support, Ms. Johnson provided evidence-based Tier 1 instruction, in which she used choral responding, response cards, and guided note taking to enhance learning (to review these strategies, see Alber-Morgan, 2010). She integrated cooperative learning, buddy reading, rhymed verse, riddles, acting, and role-playing to make instruction more meaningful and fun (to review these strategies, see Tompkins, 2006). She integrated these activities because they are consistent with Afrocultural themes. When Ms. Johnson found that students were nonresponsive to evidence-based instruction, even with lively and culturally relevant activities, she supplemented instruction by using peer-assisted learning strategies (PALS) for Grade 2, a scientific-based instructional strategy developed by Lynn and Doug Fuchs (D. Fuchs, L. S. Fuchs, Mathes, & Simmons, 1997); she also integrated peer tutoring, consistent with their "we are one" family theme.

Ms. Johnson bonded with her students and provided scientific, high-quality, culturally relevant instruction daily. Although Ms. Johnson could have monitored the progress of her students every 3 weeks, at the Tier 1 level (Jenkins, Graff, & Miglioretti, 2006), Ms. Johnson decided to progress monitor more frequently. She wanted to get a pulse on students who showed early risk signs but understood that early progress monitoring data could be inaccurate considering students had just returned from summer break. She monitored her students' progress every 2 weeks prior to the beginning of the year (BOY) screening, which allowed her to identify students who struggled and students who were progressing at appropriate rates.

After administering the BOY screening, Ms. Johnson identified students who were deemed at risk for academic failure. Instead of moving these students to Tier 2 immediately after reviewing their data, she worked with these students in small groups in the classroom and progress monitored for 6 additional weeks. She provided 6 additional weeks of progress monitoring at the Tier 1 level because she remembered learning, at the summer conference, that it is best practice to ensure that students truly need additional support (Compton, Fuchs, Fuchs, & Bryant, 2006).

Tier 2 and Tier 3

Students who continued to show limited growth were moved to Tier 2, where they received 30 minutes of additional research-based instruction, paired with the Tier 1 core curriculum; *process-focused* activities that consisted of communalism, movement/music, orality, and verve were used to engage students at the Tier 2 level. Interventionists provided systematic, direct, and ongoing feedback about student performance, and students had ample opportunity to practice reading skills. Students read books based on their reading level, within appropriate groups (see Vaughn & Roberts, 2007).

When students failed to respond to Tier 2 instruction, although having received culturally relevant, research-based support, they were provided Tier 3 supports. At the Tier 3 level, interventionists provided intensive support. They modified the pace of instruction, provided high-quality and frequent feedback, and worked with students one on one (Gersten et al., 2009).

One difference that should be noted within this model compared to the model in Chapter 2 is that, when students did not respond to Tier 1 instruction, Ms. Johnson, in this example, attempted to reach out to community leaders to get afterschool supports for her students. She reached out to parents and community leaders because she learned that RTI is all about providing more instructional time on task, in smaller groups. She believed if students could receive additional instruction outside of school, then this would provide more data to show whether her students had a true disability or whether they were slow learners. When students did not respond to Tier 2 and Tier 3 supports, including community-based interventions, team members either qualified the students for specialized services (no formal evaluation from school psychologists) or requested additional academic achievement measures to help assist with determining special education eligibility (formal academic achievement evaluation, conducted by school psychologist). Compare this process of implementing RTI principles to the model in Chapter 2.

Notice that, in this example, team members could confidently rule out that cultural factors were not the primary reason for the student(s) underachievement, for students received culturally relevant, research-based instruction throughout tiers. At the screening meeting, Ms. Johnson had a wealth of data to share with the team, including *skill-focused* intervention data and *process-focused,* culturally relevant intervention data.

CULTURAL EXCLUSIONARY FACTOR

Educational mandates speak to the need to engage all students in the classroom, including culturally diverse students. In fact, the newest learning disability criteria state that educators must *rule out* cultural factors prior to making a decision on special education eligibility (Individuals

With Disabilities Education Act of 2004 [IDEA]). In other words, special education law says that team members must ensure that the primary cause of underachievement is not a result of cultural factors.

Ruling out cultural factors for African American students has been difficult for many special education team members, including psychologists. For example, when I asked psychologists I know about their interpretation of the culturally relevant criterion related to eligibility, all have told me that they automatically check this box, indicating that culture is not a primary cause of the students' underachievement.

The most obvious variable of culture that affects academic achievement is language; hence, interpreting the cultural factor during the eligibility process is easier when evaluating Latino students who have or have not had language-based interventions and testing. It becomes even clearer for this population when educators consider the research on basic interpersonal communication (BIC) and cognitive academic language proficiency (CALP). But for African American students, the question related to cultural factors is usually answered in the same fashion across students: "No, culture is not a reason for underachievement." This is a common statement because most educators do not understand the effect of Eurocentric culture, or "school culture," on many students of color. Moreover, many educators are unable to answer this question intelligently because they do not understand and have not been exposed to the cultural backgrounds of children of color. This is no fault of teachers. Laws have been created (i.e., IDEA), but the federal government has not articulated how to truly interpret them. The cultural exclusionary factor is one example.

The reason most educators automatically assume that cultural factors do not play a role in African American students' underachievement is that these students speak and read English; as educators, we often believe that if Black students are present in the classroom and receive "evidence-based," skill-focused instruction/interventions, then they have received high-quality, appropriate instruction. Thus, from the educators' perspective, culture is not a factor. But this is far from true. As stated throughout this book, for many African American students, if culture is not embedded within their curricula, then we cannot say they have received high-quality or appropriate instruction, for culture mediates learning (Belgrave & Allison, 2014; Klinger & Edwards, 2006). We could definitely qualify them for specialized services, but we would be left wondering how engaged and motivated they would have become if they had received instruction that incorporated their cultural values. When students are engaged cognitively, behaviorally, and affectively, they process information and are more willing to learn the instructional material compared to when they are bored, unmotivated, and disengaged. Learning becomes much more difficult for many students of color when they do not have solid relationships with teachers and peers within the learning environment. Moreover, when their cultural values clash with the school or class culture, paired with poor relationships, we could predict, with high probability, how they will perform in the classroom.

Culture Mediates Learning

Prior to referring students of color for full case evaluations or qualifying them for special education services, educators should first rule out cultural factors, meaning they should ensure that the school and classroom culture do not contribute or, more specifically, are not the primary cause of the students' disengaging behaviors. With this, educators should seek to understand the referred students' culture by speaking with the students about what goes on within their community and home. The educator should also interview the students' parents to gain an understanding of how the students respond to outside activities, including church-related activities if they attend church.

Educators should also measure how students feel about racism, including institutional racism, as research shows that students of color may believe racism exists within their schools and that they are often targets of racism (Lynn, 2006). I have worked with students, as young as second grade, who believed their teachers were racist toward them. Many African American high school students—both high achievers and low achievers—believed that some of their teachers treated Black students different from their White counterparts. They would often say, "I hate to say it, but they treat Black students different." A 10th-grade student I worked with stated, "It seems like some of these teachers are racist, although I hate to say it!"

Many African American churches integrate African American cultural values throughout worship service, as members encourage communalism (bonding), movement (rejoicing, including hand clapping), expression of emotion, music, and entertainment. It may be beneficial for educators who are unfamiliar with Afrocultural characteristics to attend a church whose members are predominantly African American and whose services incorporate music, movement expressions, and communalism. From this, educators will experience the call-response dialogue between the minister and the parishioners, including other relevant and valued cultural expressions. Again, not all predominantly Black churches engage in these activities, so it would be helpful to ask around to find this experience.

TIER 2 AND TIER 3 SOCIAL EMOTIONAL LEARNING (SEL) GROUPS

When providing culturally relevant instruction at the Tier 2 and Tier 3 levels, students would receive additional time in smaller groups just as they would in traditional RTI models. I often encourage Tier 2 and Tier 3 social emotional learning (SEL) groups, considering students often underachieve because of socioemotional factors rather than true academic deficits. For example, many students may struggle with *self-awareness, social awareness, self-management, responsible decision making,* and *building relationships.* Socioemotional factors often interfere with student learning, and educators could easily attribute poor performance in the classroom to academic skill deficits—while overlooking social emotional factors.

In my practices as a school psychologist and education consultant, I integrate hip hop SEL groups to build socioemotional skills, as these skills have shown to increase academic performance, reduce drug usage, and increase graduation rates (CASEL; http://www.casel.org). I integrate "hip hop" to increase engagement and attendance. It is critical that psychologists and social workers implement SEL groups at the high school level, as many students who underachieve at this level do so because they are unmotivated, are bored in the classroom, or have not identified a career interest. SEL Tier 2 and Tier 3 groups could help students become more aware of how their emotions affect school performance. These groups could also challenge them to reconsider their thoughts about racism in the school system—and cope, if they are indeed targets throughout their day. This is important to mention, considering Neal et al. (2003) showed that teachers in their study believed Black students who were expressive needed special education classes—and White students who acted like Blacks were worse off than the Black kids.

Scenario 2

Conventions of Standard English and Culturally Relevant Instruction

Ms. Johnson is an employee within a school district that has adopted the Common Core State Standards (CCSS); her administrators have placed great emphases on the standards and engaging students of color. Because Ms. Johnson engaged in ethnographic practices and understood the cultural values of her students, she acknowledged that many of her students value movement-expressive and entertaining activities—and she differentiated instruction to include these themes in the classroom.

Because the CCSS allow teachers to provide their own judgment on how to teach the standards, Ms. Johnson decided to teach the conventions of English in a communalistic and "vervistic" way. To emphasize communalism, she was careful not to criticize or shame her students for speaking Black Vernacular English (BVE); in fact, instead of criticizing their ways of speaking—and explaining that the manner in which they spoke was bad English—she embraced their dialect and created activities where students could compare BVE and Standard English.

Ms. Johnson had read Gloria Ladson-Billings's (1995a) article, "But That's Just Good Teaching: The Case for Culturally Relevant Pedagogy," and was inspired by Ann Lewis's approach to teaching culturally diverse students (see Chapter 20 for a review of Ann's story). Ms. Johnson was also inspired by Patricia Hilliard's use of culturally relevant instruction in the classroom, as cited by Ladson-Billings. Instead of bashing rap music, Patricia allowed her second-grade students to bring in rap lyrics, and she used appropriate music/lyrics to teach grammar and literature. For example, she incorporated movement-expressive and entertaining activities such as allowing students to perform as if they were at concerts. Patricia then displayed the lyrics on an overhead to show the relationship between rap, poetry, and literature. She used their music to "discuss literal and figurative meanings as well as technical aspects of poetry such as rhyme scheme, alliteration, and onomatopoeia" (Ladson-Billings, 1995a, p. 161). Ms. Johnson re-created these experiences in her classroom, as many of her students came from communalistic backgrounds and enjoyed rap music.

Ms. Johnson placed an emphasis on differentiating instruction by culture. In fact, prior to planning her lesson, she contemplated the following questions: "How do I make all of my students feel welcome?" "What must I do to show my students that I care about them as young people, not just as students?" "How do I make students who have learning disabilities feel that they can indeed learn in my class; how do I make them feel safe?" "How do I continue to build on our communalistic theme?" Ms. Johnson used evidence-based instruction and integrated communalism, movement, orality, and verve activities to teach the CCSS at the Tier 1 level. Often, when Ms. Johnson's colleagues explained that they are unfamiliar with evidence-based instruction that is culturally relevant for African American students, Ms. Johnson did not hesitate to share with them the research surrounding communalism, movement expressiveness, orality, and verve. She did not hesitate to share with them the research surrounding Dr. A. Wade Boykin's work. During problem-solving team meetings, she encouraged team members to consider evidence-based, process-focused supports when moving students of color through tiers.

CHAPTER SUMMARY

For years, educators have ignored the sociocultural aspect of learning in the classroom. Based on research surrounding culture and academic engagement, culture plays a critical role in increasing the level of interest in a particular subject. Through ethnographic studies, if teachers find that their students enjoy music, come from communalistic backgrounds, and are passionate about language-based activities—such as poetry, rhyming (rapping), and so on—then RTI models should integrate these sorts of activities at each tier. When students are moved through tiers and provided culturally relevant instruction and strategies in the process, it is much easier to show that culture is not a primary cause of the student's under-achievement, which is a factor in qualifying students for learning disabilities (IDEA). The following question should be addressed at special education screening and eligibility meetings when culturally relevant strategies have not been used when moving students through tiers: Would the students have engaged at a deeper level if they had connected to curricula and strategies that were related to their culture, passions, and interests?

In the next chapter, I discuss RTI at the high school level and provide examples of strategies that educators could integrate with high school students.

RTI for Students of Color at the High School Level 23

Culture includes—way of thinking, way of life, and way of worship.

—*Pandurang Shastri Vaijnath Athavale*

RTI is relatively established at the elementary level, and things are getting better at the middle school level. The high school level is where RTI is still developing. An important question is, What should RTI look like at the high school level? If this is a relevant question, than a comparably relevant question is, What should RTI look like for students of color?

We have come to the knowledge that there is variability between and within groups. We now realize that differences in cultures are not deficits, and educational researchers regard differentiated instruction as one of the best approaches to instruction. Translation: All students are different, have culturally relevant learning styles, and come from unique backgrounds. An effective RTI service delivery model, then, will have as its foundation current research on differences within and between groups, including interventions for a vast array of learning styles and interests. This means educators will refuse to create a *standard* service delivery model for their students. Because of variability between and within groups, and because all students have unique culturally relevant learning styles, educators will use research-based instructions and interventions but deliver such instruction in a way that is most meaningful to students. I have shown throughout this book that simply implementing "research-based" instruction or interventions does not mean that students will respond to them solely because they are based on research. *How* educators deliver instruction is as important as the content delivered.

RTI WILL LOOK DIFFERENT AT THE HIGH SCHOOL LEVEL

It should go without saying that RTI at the high school level will look much different than RTI at the elementary school level. Teachers at the elementary level have an abundance of reading interventions and research to which they could refer to implement solid models. Although there are reading interventions for high school students who struggle with reading, there are not as many resources that show how RTI should look at the secondary level. As a school psychologist, I have provided services within a few different high schools and understand the difficulty of providing RTI at this level. One important factor that should be examined when considering RTI at the high school level is that RTI is a service delivery model to increase performance among all students. Educators often get caught up in how the model "should look" at the high school level. Rather than understanding how a model should look, it is most important for educators to understand the basis of RTI, its purpose, and what it entails.

RTI Is Much More Than a Schedule—It Is a Host of Services

Educators often refer to RTI as a *framework* or *model,* but it is actually a host of evidence-based services that should occur at the elementary, middle, and high school levels. These services should begin with teachers, at the Tier 1 level. Services include using pre-and-post measures to identify the current knowledge of students and progress monitoring over time, evidence-based practices, differentiated instruction, reading support for students who struggle, and more. In any class, the teacher is the most valuable player in the RTI model. The most important factor of RTI at the high school level—and any level, for that matter—is teacher knowledge of RTI. In my experiences with working with high school leaders, teachers were the least knowledgeable about RTI but were required to do the most surrounding implementing the model in the classroom. School psychologists and special education team members were usually responsible for RTI processes and met weekly to determine students who were failing to respond to classroom instruction. Teachers were provided very little training and often referred to others for questions, rather than receiving ongoing professional development and coaching on the purpose of RTI and how to integrate strategies and evidence-based practices within their classes. Although it would be nice to have an effective schedule to which teachers and students could refer regarding RTI, there is much more to RTI than a schedule of when students should receive interventions.

If high schools do not have schedules for students to receive intervention supports, they should move forward with identifying which interventions they have available for students and ensure that all teachers receive ongoing coaching and training on how to incorporate RTI best practices within their classes, practices such as providing evidence-based strategies, culturally relevant strategies, and pre-and-post measures. Dialogue surrounding the quality of teacher-student relationships—and how teachers could strengthen relationships that have gone awry— should be ongoing. Such practices as the use of peer-mediated instruction, response cards, white boards, and cooperative and communalistic groups have been shown to be effective for engaging students during whole-group instruction; professional development should occur on how to use these methods most effectively. For students who enjoy music, it would be beneficial to integrate music and ask students how they'd like to do that, based on their music interest.

Another important component of RTI is determining the effectiveness of current interventions. Thus, it is critical that educators evaluate the effectiveness of their current interventions (building wide) and determine, with the help of students, how they could "beef up" what they currently use. Often, interventions that are available for students throughout the building are ineffective, but schools continue to use them for the same profile of students. When students do not show up for the interventions or do not respond to them, team members document that the student doesn't attend and, consequently, explain that the student did not respond to the intervention. It is important to note that the student probably did not respond to the intervention because it may not have been *appropriate* for him or her. Interventions that are appropriate are those ones that engage students and are delivered in a manner that connects with the students' interests, passions, and cultural values.

In addition to solid reading supports for students at the high school level, many students who struggle academically will require effective social emotional learning (SEL) groups to increase academic self-esteem, academic motivation, resiliency, and emotional intelligence. Often, one reason why students do not make much progress throughout their high school years is because emotions surrounding school interferes with their success. Because most students who struggle academically had negative experiences at the elementary and middle school levels with learning, many come to high school to pass time; many will do the bare minimum to get by. Others look forward to the day they are old enough to drop out or can walk the stage, not to move on to postsecondary high school but to call it quits. Therefore, SEL programs and groups are critical for students who struggle. Thus, high schools should have solid Tier 2 SEL groups and afterschool programs that emphasize SEL, strengthening mind-sets, and emotional intelligence.

The purpose of this chapter is to raise awareness of basic needs of service delivery at the high school level with regard to RTI and to point out some critical components that must be in place; it is beyond the scope of this chapter to provide step-by-step processes of how to create effective RTI models at the high school level. However, it is most important that teachers use evidence-based strategies when providing instruction in the classroom and remain cognizant that RTI is all about appropriate instruction. Creating stimulating and engaging classrooms are most important for RTI procedures at the high school level because teachers do not have the opportunities that elementary school teachers have throughout the day. When students engage during instructional time and connect with their teachers, they will learn.

Culturally Relevant Activities at the High School Level

All students may benefit from culturally relevant approaches to learning, but students who lack academic motivation require such supports more than students who are intrinsically motivated. The reason is students who lack intrinsic motivation require additional, extrinsic factors to motivate them. Thus, it is most critical that educators at the high school level not only become knowledgeable about basic components of RTI but also receive training on culturally relevant instruction and training on how they could integrate culturally relevant strategies within their subject areas. In addition, educators must become familiar with culturally relevant behaviors that are demonstrated by students who come from culturally diverse backgrounds. Understanding that, in most cases, expressive behaviors are not intended to hurt or harm others but are demonstrated in response to excitement, for example, will reduce the tendency of sending students to the dean's office or writing referrals for such behaviors.

Often, I would stand in the school hallways and observe students interacting with their peers between passing periods or in the gym and during lunch. Actually, it is during these times that children of color demonstrate behaviors that may be associated with cultural values. The reason is clear: They are not required to remain at their desks (restriction of movement expressiveness), work in isolation (individualistic practices), and adhere to an unlimited number of strict rules (bureaucratic orientation). Thus, students of color are able to express themselves. Because they are able to express themselves during these moments, it is very common to see them

- engage in expressive movements such that their behaviors are extremely animated,
- speak to each other in performance-driven dialogues,
- dance or move in rhythmic patterns,
- bond with each other, and
- sing or rap music aloud while walking to class, eating lunch, or participating in the gym.

One morning as I was preparing for the day, I was in my office reviewing data. Suddenly, my attention was drawn to the secretaries' loud laughter. As the secretaries laughed, they clapped their hands, and one of them stated, "That boy is so funny! I love when he does that!" When I asked what the laughter was all about, they told me to "just watch." At that point, I stood up from my seat and noticed an African American male student walk past the window. As he walked, he dipped his head as he watched us and lowered his body as if he was walking down a case of stairs. Then, when I thought he was gone, his head reappeared, as he demonstrated walking back up imaginary stairs. He then came in the office and, while laughing, he said, "Y'all like that don't y'all!" One of the secretaries then said, "Boy, you know you don't have any sense!" The young man hit the countertop with his hands, expressively, as he laughed hysterically; the secretaries leaned in their chairs as they laughed, I laughed, and we all had an amazing moment. This all occurred around 7:30 a.m., just after the bell rang for the start of the school day.

It's important to say that this young man was often sent to the dean's office because of inappropriate behavior in the classroom. In fact, this is how the young man and the secretaries established their relationship. Now get this—if the secretaries were his teachers, I believe that he would thrive in the classroom. I believe this because of the rapport he and the secretaries had; because the secretaries found the young man amazingly entertaining, he would have received positive praise in their classrooms for his gifts and talents. Not only did they tap into his culture, but they also valued his culture as they reinforced culturally relevant behavior (such as bonding, communalism, etc.). This experience brings me to my next point.

Engaging many African American students at the high school level will require instances similar to the example above. Although many African American high school students value song and dance, they may not desire to dance while learning. But this does not mean that they will not desire movement in the classroom, verve (variability), and communalistic and engaging oral expressive activities.

From my experiences with working with students of color at the high school level, establishing a communalistic environment, whereby students are encouraged to depend on one another to achieve academically, has been the single most powerful intervention to increasing academic engagement and decreasing disruptive behaviors. A communalistic environment is one where students feel valued not only by their peers but also by their teachers. It is an environment such that students are comfortable asking for help from their peers and teachers and expect a valued answer. It is an environment where students and educators bond beyond the student-teacher relationship.

COMMUNALISTIC EXPERIENCES ARE KEY

An RTI model that integrates characteristics associated with African American culture will include, at the Tier 1 level, communalistic environments. This means, on day 1, educators will emphasize the importance of relationships and bonding as learners, just as Ms. Johnson did. The educator will express the importance of helping one another achieve; he or she will incorporate cooperative learning strategies as much as possible and encourage interdependence in the classroom. The educator will seek to engage their students emotionally, not just cognitively, as academic engagement is an emotional expression toward learning. And consistent with the idea of RTI, the educator will research evidence-based instruction on creating communalistic classrooms.

ENTERTAINMENT, MOVEMENT, AND VERVE IN THE CLASSROOM

In addition to communalism, an RTI model that incorporates Afrocultural characteristics will have at the Tier 1 level entertaining activities embedded in the curriculum. This may require educators to ask their students for help—to ask their students how they'd like to learn. In fact, asking their students for help may be viewed as a research-based method. Music, movement expressiveness, and verve—high levels of stimulation and entertainment—should be embedded in the delivery of service.

In one school district I worked in, the principal asked me to observe a self-contained classroom and to come up with interventions that would potentially engage the students. The majority of these students were diagnosed with emotional and learning disabilities. Upon entering the classroom, students were walking around the room, talking disrespectfully to the teacher, walking out of the classroom, and engaging in other noncompliant behaviors. Prior to leaving the classroom, I explained to the group that I would be coming in to teach a lesson and that I was looking forward to working with them.

When I entered the room upon my instructional day, I did not come empty-handed. Rather, I came with a radio in hand (the district did not have much technology to engage students). The presence of the radio was enough to silence the students upon my entrance. As they stared at me, I stared at them. When the room was quiet enough for me to talk, I greeted them and explained that we were about to have some fun. I gave a small talk about education and how it does not have to be boring but can be very entertaining and engaging. I then told them that I would prove my point. I then explained that there are a few things that I wanted to do with them, but that in order to do these things, I needed their cooperation. Their response was amazing. From my introduction, I had the students' undivided attention. When a student spoke while I was speaking, a peer would redirect him: "C'mon man, I'm trying to hear what Mr. Williams is saying!"

At the end of my talk, I explained that we were going to learn together, play academic jeopardy, and listen to music. The classroom was engaged for the entire hour I was in there; I went into the classroom for a week, and when students saw me in the hallway, they would come toward me with high fives and daps; they would tell me how they couldn't wait until I came to their classroom. This experience validated the research on entertainment, movement expressiveness, verve, music, and academic engagement.

MEASURING CULTURALLY RELEVANT BEHAVIORS IN THE CLASSROOM

Incorporating Afrocultural characteristics into the classroom requires educators to become familiar with both Afrocentric and Eurocentric cultural characteristics. This would require studying research on culture and contrasting traditional Eurocentric and traditional Afrocentric behaviors. After learning about Afrocentric cultural characteristics, educators could compare their teaching styles against these cultures to determine which is most prevalent in their classroom.

In addition to researching and comparing these cultures, educators might benefit from having an outside observer who is familiar with Eurocentric and Afrocentric cultures observe the classroom. It's important to note that just because someone is of a particular race does not qualify her or him as an expert on identifying Afrocentric or Eurocentric culture. Stated differently, an educator would not be qualified to determine the extent to which Afrocentric cultural characteristics are present in the classroom simply because he or she is Black. As mentioned earlier in this book, although many Black educators come from Afrocentric cultural backgrounds, many are unfamiliar with the literature on culture. The literature usually becomes more meaningful to these educators only after they reflect on the concepts and compare them to their childhood experiences. In addition, some Black educators have assimilated to mainstream (Eurocentric) culture to the degree that they no longer identify with Afrocentric characteristics, even though they may have grown up in such culture. In addition to reviewing data from outside observers, it would be beneficial if educators collect data from their students, information on the extent that students themselves believe certain characteristics are present in their classroom.

ENTERTAINING GAMES AND ACTIVITIES IN THE CLASSROOM

Because many African American children come from stimulating backgrounds and because many of them desire entertainment, these students may benefit from live performing in the classroom. Instead of having these students sit at their desks all day and read from textbooks, these students may benefit from acting out their curriculum.

History

Performance and entertainment for history may include the following:

- Allow students to role play historical events after having read the chapter.
- Pair visuals (movies, film, etc.) with reading materials as much as possible.
- Allow young, accomplished African American men and women within the community speak to the class and, perhaps, co-teach a chapter.
- Allow students to create songs and raps about the video and book they had previously reviewed.

Math performance and entertainment for math may include the following:

- Incorporate cooperative learning as much as possible.
- Instead of completing math sheets at their desks, allow students to create teams of five and allow them to learn by shooting spongy balls into some bucket. Once a student shoots a shot, other students, collectively, would have to add, multiply, or divide the shot by a number specified by the teacher.
- Ask students what they desire to pursue after graduating from high school. Introduce math problem solving and concepts based on their desired profession. Many male students desire to become rap stars or athletes. One activity would be determining how much it would cost to make a CD and how much money artists actually earn after they pay their labels. Allow students to compute how much athletes make prior to and after endorsements.
- Divide students in the classroom and allow one group to be the artists, one group the record producer, and so on, and allow them to make computations based on some amount.
- Divide students in the classroom into groups of four or five. Allow one person in the group to be the athlete and the remaining students the organization. Allow them to negotiate their salaries and, after negotiations, require them to use some math problem solving and computation strategy to understand what they'll eventually earn.

Language Arts/Written Expression

Performance and entertainment for written expression may include the following:

- After they have read a chapter in their literature books, allow students to write poems, songs, or raps about the chapter content. Allow students to speak, sing, or rap their art in front of the classroom if they desire.
- Allow students to research artists and print out profanity-free lyrics. Compare and contrast the lyrics with Standard English.
- Allow students to role-play their literature content—allow them to become the characters.

Students may respond better to academic instruction if educators incorporate performance and entertainment with standard objectives. This may not be true only of children of color but also of White children as well. Essentially, all children and youth desire entertainment. Young children are usually eager for recess and gym because they anticipate playing games, running, jumping, and chasing their peers. They come from recess and return to a classroom where, most often, they are required to remain in their seats, remain still, remain silent, and watch and listen to their teachers talk at them.

The above activities could be used to enhance learning at the Tier 1 level and throughout tiers; they highlight vervistic activities, but it might be helpful to ask students how they desire to learn standards and content in the classroom, rather than automatically assuming that all students of color will respond well to such activities and characteristics.

CHAPTER SUMMARY

When discussing RTI at the high school level, educators and researchers often explain that it is difficult to create a "schedule." At this level, it is most important for teachers to become knowledgeable about RTI and understand the components that make RTI work, including using pre-and-post measures, evidence-based and culturally relevant strategies, and establishing relationships. Effective SEL groups are critical components of increasing engagement at the high school level. Often, students disengage not only because they lack skill but also because they do not have the con-fidence to put forth effort. RTI is often referred to as a framework or model, but it is most accurate to identify it as *processes* or *strategies* that are rooted in best practices—practices that should occur at the elementary, middle, and high school levels. Even if high schools have not identified an effective "schedule" to use to implement RTI, it is most important that all teachers in the building understand the importance of high-quality instruction that is tailored to their students' needs, including cultural needs.

Reflections

Research has shown clearly that many children of color perform poorly in the classroom. Many educational researchers have attempted to explain why Black and Brown children underperform academically and why they leave school earlier than most White students. Areas that are rarely discussed within schools are (1) the impact of culture and (2) students' perception of racism in school on academic engagement.

This book supports the position that if response-to-intervention (RTI) models are going to be effective with increasing academic engagement and performance among children of color, then the models must incorporate ways to address institutional racism and cultural depravity in schools. Upon hearing this statement, many educators may say, automatically, "Well, our schools do not have issues with institutional or cultural racism. We all get along fine." Although educators may make these claims about their school's climate, research shows that many students of color have opposing views. Students may believe that educators treat them differently simply because of skin color, and for students, their perception is reality. This is critical considering that the quality of the teacher-student relationship is correlated with student engagement in the classroom.

This book also supports the position that if RTI models are going to be effective with Black and Brown students, then the models must represent an ecological model. This means it must include parents and community leaders in the process. Educators must create ways to include parents and community leaders in the process of establishing a solid RTI model; parents and community leaders must play vital roles in problem-solving teams.

Educational laws and initiatives explain that schools must consider culturally relevant pedagogy when educating students of color. But many educators do not know what culturally relevant pedagogy looks like for children who do not come from traditional Eurocentric backgrounds. This book contrasts Eurocentric and Afrocentric cultural characteristics and can be used as a starting point to incorporating culturally relevant activities in the classroom. Educators and parents could also use this book to spark dialogue about what institutional and cultural racism look like; they can determine if their school's climate engages in these forms of racism.

References

Adelabu, D. H. (2008). Future time perspective, hope, and ethnic identity among African American adolescents. *Urban Education, 43*(3), 347–360.

Adelman, H. S., & Taylor, L. (2006). *The school leader's guide to student learning supports.* Thousand Oaks, CA: Corwin Press.

Akbar, N. (1981). Cultural expressions of the African-American child. *Black Child Journal, 2*(2), 6–16.

Alber-Morgan, S. (2010). *Using RTI to teach literacy to diverse learners, K–8: Strategies for the inclusive classroom.* Thousand Oaks, CA: Corwin Press.

Albury, A. (1998). *Social orientation, learning condition and learning outcomes among low income black and white grade school children* (Unpublished doctoral dissertation). Howard University, Washington, DC.

Allen, B., & Boykin, A. (1991). The influence of contextual factors on Afro-American and Euro American children's performance: Effects of movement opportunity and music. *International Journal of Psychology, 26*(3), 373–387.

Allen, B. A., & Boykin, A. W. (1992). African American children and the educational process: Alleviating cultural discontinuity through prescriptive pedagogy. *School Psychology Review, 21*(4), 586–596.

Allison, B. N., & Rhem, M. L. (2007). Effective teaching strategies for middle school learners in multicultural, multilingual classrooms. *Middle School Journal, 39*, 12–18.

Ani, M. (1994). *Yurugu: An African-centered critique of European cultural thought and behavior.* Trenton, NJ: Africa World Press, Inc.

Asante, M. (1988). *Afrocentricity.* Trenton, NJ: Africa World Press, Inc.

Ashton-Warner, S. (1965). *Teacher.* New York: Simon & Schuster.

Bailey, C., & Boykin, A. W. (2001). The role of task variability and home contextual factors in the academic performance and task motivation of African-American elementary school children. *Journal of Negro Education, 70*(1/2), 84–95.

Barna Group. (2005). African Americans. www.barna.org/

Barna Group. (2009). Major faith shifts evident among Whites, Blacks, and Hispanics since 1991. www.barna.org/faith-spirituality/510-major-faith -shifts-evident-among-whites-blacks-and-hispanics-since-1991

Bartone, M. (2010, Summer). Cultural applications: Ideas for teacher education programs. *Perspectives on Urban Education*, pp. 91–95.

Belgrave, F. Z., & Allison, K. W. (2014). *African American psychology* (13th ed., pp. 31–62). Thousand Oaks, CA: Sage.

Bell, Y. R., & Clark, T. R. (1998). Culturally relevant reading material as related to a comprehension and recall in African-American children. *Journal of Black Psychology, 24,* 455–476.

Bender, W. N., & Shores, C. (2007). *Response to intervention: A practical guide for every teacher.* Thousand Oaks, CA: Corwin Press.

Berkeley, S., Bender, W. N., Peaster, L. G., & Saunders, L. (2009). Implementation of response to intervention: A snapshot of progress. *Journal of Learning Disabilities, 42*(1), 85–95.

Bodrova, E., & Leong, D. J. (2007). *Tools of the mind: The Vygotskian approach to early childhood education* (2nd ed., p. 3). Columbus, OH: Merrill/Prentice Hall.

Boykin, A. W. (1978). Psychological/behavioral verve in academic/task performance: Pretheoretical considerations. *Journal of Negro Education, 47,* 343–354.

Boykin, A. W. (1982). Task variability and the performance of Black and White schoolchildren: Vervistic explorations. *Journal of Black Studies, 12,* 469–485.

Boykin, A. W. (1983). The academic performance of Afro-American children. In J. Spence (Ed.), *Achievement and achievement motives* (pp. 324–371). San Francisco, CA: Freeman.

Boykin, A. W. (1986). The triple quandary and the schooling of Afro-American children. In U. Neisser (Ed.), *The school achievement of minority children* (pp. 55–72). Hillsdale, NJ: Lawrence Erlbaum.

Boykin, A. W., Albury, A., Tyler, K. M., Hurley, E. A., Bailey, C. T., & Miller, O. A. (2005). Culture-based perceptions of academic achievement among low-income elementary students. *Cultural Diversity and Ethnic Minority Psychology, 11*(4), 339–350.

Boykin, A. W., & Allen, B. A. (2001). Rhythmic-movement facilitation of learning in working-class Afro-American children. *Journal of Genetic Psychology, 143*(3), 335–348.

Boykin, A. W., Allen, B. A., Davis, L. H., & Senior, A. M. (1997). Task performance of Black and White children across levels of presentation variability. *Journal of Psychology, 131*(4), 427–437.

Boykin, A. W., & Bailey, C. T. (2000). *The role of cultural factors in school relevant cognitive functioning.* Washington, DC: Howard University and Johns Hopkins University, Center for Research on the Education of Students Placed At Risk (CRESPAR).

Boykin, A. W., & Ellison, C. (1995). The multiple ecologies of Black youth socialization: An Afrographic analysis. In R. L. Taylor (Ed.), *African-American youth: Their social and economic status in the United States* (pp. 93–128). Westport, CT: Praeger.

Boykin, A. W., Jagers, R. J., Ellison, C., & Albury, A. (1997). Communualism: Conceptualization and measurement of an Afrocultural social ethos. *Journal of Black Studies, 27*(3), 409–418.

Boykin, A. W., Coleman, S. T., Lilja, A., & Tyler, K. (2004). The influence of communal vs. individual learning context on academic performance in social studies of Grade 4–5 African Americans. *Learning Environments Research, 7*(3), 227–244.

Boykin, A. W., & Cunningham, R. (2001). The effects of movement expressiveness in story content and learning context on the analogical reasoning performance of African American children. *Journal of Negro Education, 70*(1–2), 72–83.

Boykin, A. W., & Noguera, P. (2011). *Creating the opportunity to learn: Moving from research to practice to close the achievement gap.* Alexandria, VA: ASCD.

Boykin, W. A., Tyler, K. M., & Miller, O. (2005). In search of cultural themes and their expressions in the dynamics of classroom life. *Urban Education, 40*(5), 521–549.

Bronfenbrenner, U. (1977). Toward an experimental ecology of human development. *American Psychologist, 32,* 513–531.

Brown-Chidsey, R., & Steege, M. W. (2005). *Response to intervention: Principles and strategies for effective practice.* New York, NY: Guilford.

Burns, M. K., Appleton, J. J., & Stehouwer, J. D. (2005). Meta-analytic review of responsiveness-to-intervention research: Examining field-based and research-implemented models. *Journal of Psychoeducational Assessment, 23,* 381–394.

Burt, C. (1937). *The backward child.* London, UK: University of London Press.

Byrnes, J. P., & Miller, D. C. (2007). The relative importance of predictors of math and science achievement: An opportunity-propensity analysis. *Contemporary Educational Psychology, 32*(4), 599–629.

Carter, N. P., Hawkins, T. H., & Natesan, P. (2008, January). The relationship between verve and academic achievement of African American students in reading and mathematics in an urban middle school. *Educational Foundations,* pp. 29–45.

Chatters, L., Taylor, R. J., Bullard, K. M., & Jackson, J. (2009). Race and ethnic differences in religious involvement: African Americans, Caribbean Blacks and non-Hispanic Whites. *Ethnic Racial Studies, 32,* 1143–1163.

Chimezie, A. (1998). Black children's characteristics and the school: A selective adaptation approach. *Western Journal of Black Studies, 12*(2), 77–85.

Civil, M., & Khan, L. H. (2001). Mathematics instruction developed from a garden theme. *Teaching Children Mathematics, 7*(7), 400–405.

Collier, C. (2010). *RTI for diverse learners.* Thousand Oaks, CA: Corwin Press.

Common Core State Standards Initiative. (2010). Common core state standards for English language arts and literacy in history/social studies, science, and technical subjects. http://www.corestandards.org/assets/CCSSI_ELA%20 Standards.pdf

Compton, D. L., Fuchs, D., Fuchs, L. S., & Bryant, J. D. (2006). Selecting at-risk readers in first grade for early intervention: A two-year longitudinal study of decision rules and procedures. *Journal of Educational Psychology, 98,* 394–409.

Cunningham, P. M. (2000). *Phonics they use: Words for reading and writing* (3rd ed.). New York, NY: HarperCollins.

Cunningham, R. T., & Boykin, A. W. (2004). *Enhancing cognitive performance in African American children: Infusing Afro-cultural perspective and research* (4th ed., pp. 487–507). Berkeley, CA: Cobb & Henry.

Daiute, C., & Dalton, B. (1993). Collaboration between children learning to write: Can novices be masters? *Cognitive and Instruction, 10,* 281–333.

Daly, E. J., Chafouleas, S., & Skinner, C. H. (2005). *Interventions for reading problems.* New York, NY: Guilford.

Danielson, C. (2007). *Enhancing professional practice* (2nd ed.). Alexandria, VA: ASCD.

Delpit, L. (2006). *Other people's children: Cultural conflict in the classroom.* New York, NY: New Press. (Original work published 1995)

Delpit, L., & Dowdy, J. K. (2002). *The skin that we speak: Thoughts on language and culture in the classroom.* New York: New York Press.

Deno, E. (1970). Special education as developmental capital. *Exceptional Children, 37,* 229–237.

Diller, J. V. (2007). *Cultural diversity* (3rd ed.). Belmont, CA: Thomson Brooks/Cole.

Ellison, C. M., Boykin, A. W., Tyler, A. W., & Dillihunt, M. L. (2005). Examining classroom learning preferences among elementary school students. *Social Behavior and Personality, 33*(7), 699–708.

Emmons, R. (1996, December 27). Black English has its place. *Los Angeles Times.* Retrieved May 31, 2014, from http://articles.latimes.com/1996–12–27/local/me-13049_1_black-english

Ensign, J. (2003). Including culturally relevant math in an urban school. *Educational Studies, 34,* 414–423.

Fletcher, J. M., Lyon, G. R., Fuchs, L. S., & Barnes, M. A. (2007). *Learning disabilities.* New York, NY: Guilford.

Fogle, T., & Jones, L. (2006). *Writing to be heard: Parents speak up and out about parents' participation in urban public high schools.* Philadelphia, PA: Research for Action.

Frazier, E. F. (1962). *Black bourgeoisie.* New York, NY: Crowell, Collier, and MacMillan.

Fredricks, J. A., Blumenfeld, P. C., & Paris, A. H. (2004). School engagement: Potential of the concept, state of evidence. *Review of Educational Research, 74*(1), 59–109.

Fuchs, D., Fuchs, L. S., & Compton, D. L. (2012). Smart RTI: A next generation approach to multilevel intervention. *Exceptional Children, 78*(3), 263–279.

Fuchs, D., Fuchs, L. S., Mathes, P. G., & Simmons, D. C. (1997). Peer-assisted learning strategies: Making classrooms more responsive to diversity. *American Educational Research Journal, 34,* 174–206.

Fuchs, D., Mock, D., Morgan, P. L., & Young, C. L. (2003). Responsiveness-to-intervention: Definitions, evidence, and implications for the learning disabilities construct. *Learning Disabilities Research and Practice, 18*(3), 157–171.

Fuchs, L. S., & Fuchs, D. (2009). On the importance of a unified model of responsiveness to intervention. *Child Development Perspectives, 3*(1), 41–43.

Gay, G. (2010). *Culturally responsive teaching: Theory, research, and practice.* New York: Teachers College Press.

Gay, L. R., Mills, G. E., & Airasian, P. (2005). *Educational research: Competencies for analysis and applications* (8th ed.). Upper Saddle River, NJ: Prentice Hall.

Gersten, R., Baker, S. K., Shanahan, T., Linan-Thompson, S., Collins, P., & Scarcella, R. (2007). *Effective literacy and English language instruction for English learners in elementary grades: A practice guide* (NCEE 2007–4011). Washington, DC: National Center for Education Evaluation and Regional Assistance, Institute of Education Sciences, U.S. Department of Education.

Gersten, R., Compton, D., Connor, C. M., Dimino, J., Santoro, L., Linan-Thompson, S., et al. (2009). *Assisting students struggling with reading: Response to intervention and multitier intervention for reading in the primary grades. A practice guide* (NCEE 2009–4045). Washington, DC: National Center for Education Evaluation and Regional Assistance, Institute of Education Sciences, U.S. Department of Education.

Gilmore, P. (1985). "Gimme room": School resistance, attitude and access to literacy. *Journal of Education, 167*, 111–128.

Gorski, P. (2009). What we're teaching teachers: An analysis of multicultural teacher education coursework syllabi. *Teaching and Teacher Education, 25*, 309–318.

Gottlieb, G. (2007). Probabilistic epigenesis. *Developmental Science, 10*, 1–11.

Guthrie, R. V. (1998). *Even the rat was white: A historical view of psychology* (2nd ed.). Needham Heights, MA: Allyn & Bacon. (Original work published 1976)

Gutiérrez, K. D., & Rogoff, B. (2003). Cultural ways of learning: Individual traits or repertoires of practice. *Educational Researcher, 32*(5), 19–25.

Gutstein, E., Lipman, P., Hernandez, P., & de los Reyes, R. (1997). Culturally relevant mathematics teaching in a Mexican American context. *Journal for Research in Mathematics Education, 28*, 709–737.

Hamre, B. K., & Pianta, R. C. (2001). Early teacher-child relationships and the trajectory of children's school outcomes through eighth grade. *Child Development, 72*(2), 625–638.

Hamre, B. K., & Pianta, R. C. (2005). Can instructional and emotional support in the first-grade classroom make a difference for children at risk of school failure? *Child Development, 76*(5), 949–967.

Hare, N. (1965). *Black Anglo Saxons.* New York, NY: Mangi and Mansell.

Hassell, S. H., Barkley, H. A., & Koehler, E. (2009). *Promoting equity in children's reading instruction: Using a critical race theory framework to examine traditional books.* Chicago, IL: American Association of School Librarians.

Haycock, K. (2001). Helping all students achieve. *Educational Leadership, 58*(6), 6–11.

Haynes, N. M., & Gebreyesus, S. (1992). Cooperative learning: A case for African-American students. *School Psychology Review, 21*, 577–585.

Herrnstein, R. J., & Murray, C. (1994). *The bell curve: Intelligence and class structure in American life.* New York, NY: Free Press.

Heward, W. L. (1994). Three "low-tech" strategies for increasing the frequency of active student response during group instruction. In R. Gardner III, D. M. Sainato, J. O. Cooper, T. E. Heron, W. L. Heward, J. Eshleman, & T. A. Grossi (Eds.), *Behavior analysis in education: Focus on measurably superior instruction* (pp. 283–320). Monterey, CA: Brooks/Cole.

Hierck, T., & Weber, C. (2014). *RTI is a verb.* Thousand Oaks, CA: Corwin Press.

Hilliard, A. G., III. (1992). Behavioral style, culture, and teaching and learning. *Journal of Negro Education, 61*(3), 370–377.

Hilliard, A. G., III. (1998). *SBA: The reawakening of the African mind.* Gainesville, FL: Makare.

Hood, P. D. (2003). *Scientific research and evidence-based practices.* http://www .wested.org/online_pubs/scientific.research.pdf

Howard, G. (2006). *We can't teach what we don't know.* New York, NY: Teachers College Press.

Howard, T. C. (2001). Telling their side of the story: African-American students' perceptions of culturally relevant teaching. *The Urban Review, 33*(2), 131–149.

Howard, T. C., & Reynolds, R. (2008). Examining parent involvement in reversing the underachievement of African-American students in middle class schools. *Education Foundations, 22,* 79–95.

Howard, T., & Terry, C. L. (2011). Culturally responsive pedagogy for African American students: Promising programs and practices for enhanced academic performance. *Routledge, 22*(4), 345–362.

Hughes, J., & Kwok, O. (2007). Influence of student-teacher and parent-teacher relationships on lower achieving readers' engagement and achievement in the primary grades. *Journal of Educational Psychology, 99*(1), 39–51.

Hurley, E. A., Allen, B. A., & Boykin, A. W. (2009). Culture and the interaction of student ethnicity with reward structure in group learning. *Cognition and Instruction, 27*(2), 121–146.

Hurley, E. A., Boykin, W. A., & Allen, B. A. (2005). Communal versus individual learning of math estimation task: African-American children and the culture of learning context. *Journal of Psychology, 139*(6), 513–527.

Iruka, I. U., Burchinal, M., & Cai, K. (2010). Long-term effect of early relationships for African American children's academic and social development: An examination from kindergarten to fifth grade. *Journal of Black Psychology, 36*(2), 144–171.

Jacob, S., & Hawthorne, T. S. (2007). *Ethics and law: For school psychologists* (5th ed.). Hoboken, NJ: John Wiley.

Jenkins, J. R., Graf, J. J., & Miglioretti, D. L. (2006). *How often must we measure to estimate ORF growth?* Unpublished manuscript, University of Washington, Seattle.

Jensen, A. R. (1969). How much can we boost I.Q. and scholastic achievement? *Harvard Educational Achievement, 39*(1), 1–123.

Jeynes, W. H. (2003). A meta-analysis: The effects of parental involvement on minority children's academic achievement. *Education and Urban Society, 35*(2), 202–218.

Jeynes, W. H. (2007). The relationship between parental involvement and urban secondary school student academic achievement: A meta-analysis. *Urban Education, 42*(1), 82–110.

Jones, J. (2003). TRIOS: A psychological theory of the African legacy in American culture. *Journal of Social Issues, 59*(1), 217–243.

Kerpelman, J. L., Eryigit, S., & Stephens, C. J. (2008). African-American adolescents' future education orientation: Associations with self-efficacy, ethnic identity, and perceived parental support. *Journal of Youth and Adolescence, 37*(8), 997–1008.

King, B. B., & Ritz, D. (1996). *Blues all around me: The autobiography of B. B. King.* New York, NY: Avon.

Kirk, S., Gallagher, J., Coleman, M. R., & Anastasiow, N. (2012). *Educating exceptional children* (13th ed.). Belmont, CA: Wadsworth.

Klinger, J. K., & Edwards, P. A. (2006). Cultural considerations with response to interventions models. *Reading Research Quarterly, 41,* 108–117.

Kozol, J. (1991). *Savage inequalities.* New York, NY: Crown.

Ladson-Billings, G. (1995a). But that is just good teaching: The case for culturally relevant teaching. *Theory Into Practice, 34*(3), 159–165.

Ladson-Billings, G. (1995b). Toward a theory of culturally relevant pedagogy. *American Educational Research Journal, 32*(3), 465–491.

Lee, C. (2001). Is October brown Chinese? A cultural modeling activity system for underachieving students. *American Educational Research Journal, 38,* 97–143.

Lewin, K. (1952). *Field theory in social science: Selected theoretical papers by Kurt Lewin.* London, UK: Tavistock.

Lewis, O. (1961). *The children of Sanchez.* New York, NY: Random House.

Lopez, R. (2011). The impact of involvement of African-American parents on students' academic achievement. *Journal of Multiculturalism in Education, 7,* 2–46.

Lynn, M. (2006). Race, culture, and the education of African Americans. *Educational Theory, 56*(1), 107–119.

Maheady, L., Harper, G. F., & Mallette, B. (2001). Peer mediated instruction and interventions and students with disabilities. *Remedial and Special Education, 22,* 4–14.

Marieb, E. N., & Hoehn, K. (2013). *Human anatomy & physiology* (9th ed.). Upper Saddle, NJ: Pearson.

Martin, D. B. (2000). *Mathematics success and failure among African American youth: The role of sociohistorical context, community forces and school influences & influence and individual agency.* Mahwah, NJ: Lawrence Erlbaum.

Martin, G., & Pear, J. (2007). *Behavior modification: What it is and how to do it* (8th ed.). Upper Saddle River, NJ: Pearson Prentice Hall.

McMaster, K. L., Fuchs, D., & Fuchs, L. S. (2006). Research on peer-assisted learning strategies: The promise and limitations of peer-mediated instruction. *Reading and Writing Quarterly, 2,* 5–25.

McQuiston, K., O'Shea, D., & McCollins, M. (2008). Improving phonological awareness and decoding skills of high school students from diverse backgrounds. *Preventing School Failure, 52,* 67–70.

McWhorter, J. (2003). *Authentically Black: Essays for the Black silent majority.* New York, NY: Penguin.

Mellard, D. F., & Johnson, E. (2008). *RTI: A practitioner's guide to implementing response to intervention.* Thousand Oaks, CA: Corwin Press.

Merriam-Webster. (2003). *Merriam-Webster's Collegiate Dictionary* (11th ed.). Springfield, MA: Author.

Meyers, A. B., Meyers, J., Graybill, E. C., Proctor, S. L., & Huddleston, L. (2012). Ecological approaches to organization consultation and systems change in educational settings. *Journal of Educational and Psychological Consultation, 22,* 106–124.

Mid-Atlantic Equity Center. (2009). *The over-representation and under-representation of minority students in special education and gifted and talented programs.* Arlington, VA: George Washington University Center for Equity and Excellence in Education.

Millis, B. J. (2009). Becoming an effective teacher using cooperative learning: A personal odyssey. *Peer Review, 11*(2), 17–21.

Milner, H. R., Flowers, L., Moore, E., Jr., Moore, E., III, & Flowers, T. (2003). Preservice teachers' awareness of multiculturalism and diversity. *The High School Journal, 87,* 63–70.

Mitchem, K. J., Young, K. R., West, R. P., & Benyo, J. (2001). CWPASM: A classwide peer-assisted self-management program for general education classrooms. *Education and Treatment of Children, 24,* 111–140.

Moe, T. M. (2001). *A primer on America's schools.* Stanford, CA: Hoover Press.

Moje, E. B., & Hinchman, K. (2004). Culturally responsive practices for youth literacy learning. In T. L. Jetton & J. A. Dole (Eds.), *Adolescent literacy research and practice* (pp. 321–350). New York, NY: Guilford.

Muellen, E. J., & Streiner, D. L. (2004). The evidence for and against evidence-based practice. *Brief Treatment and Crisis Intervention, 4,* 111–121.

Murray, C. (2009). Parent and teacher relationships as predictors of school engagement and functioning among low-income urban youth. *Journal of Early Adolescence, 29*(3), 376–404.

Nasir, N. (2000). Points ain't everything: Emergent goals and average, and percent understanding in the play of basketball among African American students. *Anthropology and Educational Quarterly, 31,* 283–305.

The National Commission on Excellence in Education. (1983). *A nation at risk: The imperative for educational reform.* Washington, DC: U.S. Department of Education.

National Center for Culturally Responsive Educational Systems (NCCRESt). (2005). Cultural considerations and challenges in response-to-intervention models: An NCCRESt position statement. www.nccrest.org/PDFs/rti.pdf?v_document_name=Culturally%20Responsive%20RTI

National Center for Education Statistics. (2003). *Status and trends in the education of Blacks.* Washington, DC: U.S. Department of Education Institute of Education Sciences.

Neal, L. I., McCray, A. D., Webb-Johnson, G., & Bridgest, S. T. (2003). The effects of African-American movement styles on teachers' perceptions and reactions. *Journal of Special Education, 37*(1), 49–57.

Ogbu, J. (1985). *A cultural ecology of competence among inner-city Blacks.* Hillsdale, NJ: Lawrence Erlbaum.

Osborne, J. W. (1997). Race and academic disidentification. *Journal of Educational Psychology, 89*(4), 728–735.

Oyserman, D., Coon, H. M., & Kemmelmeier, M. (2002). Rethinking individualism and collectivism: Evaluation of theoretical assumptions and meta-analyses. *Psychological Bulletin, 128,* 3–72.

Pai, Y. (1990). *Cultural foundations of education.* Columbus, OH: Merrill.

Patterson, J. A., Hale, D., & Stressman, M. (2007). *Cultural contradictions and school leaving: A case study of an urban high school.* Chapel Hill: University of North Carolina Press.

Payne, R. K. (2001). *A framework for understanding poverty.* Highlands, TX: aha! Process, Inc.

Perry, T., & Delpit, L. (Eds.). (1998). *The real Ebonics debate: Power, language, and the education of African-American children.* Boston, MA: Beacon.

Polakow, V. (1993). *Lives on the edge.* Chicago, IL: University of Chicago Press.

Porter, M. (1997). *Kill them before they grow.* Chicago, IL: African American Images.

Ramose, M. B. (2003). The philosophy of ubuntu and ubuntu as a philosophy. In P. H. Coetzee & A. P. J. Roux (Eds.), *The African philosophy reader* (pp. 230–238). New York, NY: Routledge.

Randolph, J. J. (2007). Mete-analysis of the research on response cards: Effects on test achievement, quiz achievement, participation, and off-task behavior. *Journal of Positive Behavioral Interventions, 9,* 113–128.

Rathvon, N. (2008). *Effective school interventions: Evidence-based strategies for improving student outcomes* (2nd ed., pp. 142–144). New York, NY: Guilford.

Reiter, A. B., & Davis, S. N. (2011). Factors influencing pre-service teachers' beliefs about student achievement: Evaluation of a pre-service teacher diversity awareness program. *Multicultural Education, 19*(3), 41–45.

Response to intervention: A model for dynamic, differentiated teaching. (2012). http://cw.routledge.com/textbooks/9780415503815/data/Response-to -Intervention.pdf

Richards, D. M. (1994). *Let the circle be unbroken: The implications of African spirituality in the Diaspora.* Trenton, NJ: Red Sea Press.

Rogoff, B. (2003). *The cultural nature of human development.* New York, NY: Oxford University Press.

Salend, S. J. (2001). Differentiating large- and small-group instruction for diverse learners. In A. C. Davis & G. Marsella (Eds.), *Creating inclusive classrooms: Effective and reflective practices* (4th ed.). Upper Saddle River, NJ: Merrill.

Sattler, J. M. (2008). *Assessment of children* (5th ed.). La Mesa, CA: Jerome M. Sattler.

Schorr, L. B., & Schorr, D. (1988). *Within our reach: Breaking the cycle of disadvantage.* New York, NY: Bantam Doubleday Dell.

Schultz, K., Buck, P., & Niesz, T. (2006). Authoring "race": Writing truth and fiction after school. *The Urban Review, 37*(5), 469–489.

Seiler, G., & Elmesky, R. (2007). The role of communal practices in the generation of capital and emotional energy among urban African-American students in science classrooms. *Teachers College Record, 109*(2), 391–419.

Shade, B. J. (1991). African-American patterns of cognition In R. Jones (Ed.), *Black psychology* (3rd ed., pp. 231–247). Berkeley, CA: Cobb & Henry.

Shade, B. J. (1997). *Creating culturally responsive classrooms.* Washington, DC: American Psychological Association.

Shapiro, E. S. (2004). *Academic skills problems workbook* (3rd ed.). New York, NY: Guilford.

Share, D. L., McGee, R., & Silva, P. D. (1989). I.Q. and reading progress: A test of the capacity notion of I.Q. *Journal of the American Academy of Child Adolescent Psychiatry, 28,* 97–100.

Slavin, R. E. (1983). When does cooperative learning increase student achievement? *Psychological Bulletin, 94,* 429–443.

Spencer, M. B., Noll, E., Stoltzfus, J., & Harpalani, V. (2001). Identity and school adjustment: Revisiting the "acting White" assumption. *Educational Psychology, 36*(1), 21–30.

Stage, S. A., Abbott, R. D., Jenkins, J. R., & Berninger, V. W. (2003). Predicting response to early reading intervention from verbal IQ, reading-related language abilities, attention ratings, and verbal IQ-word reading discrepancy: Failure to validate the discrepancy method. *Journal of Learning Disabilities, 36,* 24–33.

Stanovich, P. J., & Stanovich, K. E. (2003). *Using research and reason in education: How teachers can use scientifically-based research to make curricular and instructional decisions.* Washington, DC: U.S. Department of Education.

Stauffer, R. G. (1970). *The language experience approach to the teaching of reading.* New York, NY: Harper & Row.

Sternberg, R. J. (2003). *Cognitive psychology* (3rd ed.). Belmont, CA: Wadsworth.

Stewart, E. (2008). School structural characteristics, student effort, peer associations, and parental involvement: The influence of school-and individual-level factors on academic achievement. *Education and Urban Society, 40*(2), 179–204.

Tate, W. (1995). Returning to the root: A culturally relevant approach to mathematics pedagogy. *Theory Into Practice, 34*(3), 166–173.

Terry, C. L. (2010). Prisons, pipelines, and the president: Developing critical math literacy through participatory action research. *Journal of African American Males in Education, 1*(2), 73–104.

Tomlinson, C. A. (1999). *The differentiated classroom: Responding to the needs of all learners.* Alexandria, VA: Association for Supervision and Curriculum Development.

Tomlinson, C. A. (2000). Reconcilable differences? Standards-based teaching and differentiation. *Educational Leadership, 58*(1), 6–11.

Tomlinson, C. A. (2001). *How to differentiate instruction in mixed ability classrooms.* Alexandria, VA: Association for Supervision and Curriculum Development.

Tompkins, G. E. (2004). *Teaching writing: Balancing product and process* (4th ed.). Upper Saddle River, NJ: Prentice Hall.

Tompkins, G. E. (2006). *Literacy for the 21st century: A balanced approach* (4th ed.). Upper Saddle River, NJ: Prentice Hall.

Trawick-Smith, J. (2006). *Early childhood development* (4th ed.). Columbus, OH: Pearson.

Tuck, K., & Boykin, A. W. (1989). Verve effects: The relationship of task performance to stimulus preference and variability in low-income Black and White children. In A. Harrison (Ed.), *The eleventh conference on empirical research in Black psychology.* Washington, DC: NIMH Publications.

Tucker, C. M., Zayco, R. A., Herman, K. C., Reinke, W. R., Trujillo, W., Carraway, K., et al. (2005). Using curriculum-based assessment and curriculum-based measurement to guide elementary mathematics instruction: Effect on individual and group accountability scores. *Assessment for Effective Intervention, 30,* 15–31.

Valentine, C. (1968). *Culture and poverty.* Chicago, IL: University of Chicago Press.

Valeski, T. N., & Stipek, D. J. (2001). Young children's feelings about school. *Child Development, 72*(4), 1198–1213.

VanDerHeyden, A. M., & Burns, M. K. (2005). Using curriculum-based assessment and curriculum-based measurement to guide elementary mathematics instruction: Effect on individual and group accountability scores. *Assessment for Effective Intervention, 30,* 15–31.

Varnum, M. E., Grossmann, I., Kitayama, S., & Nisbett, R. E. (2010). The origin of cultural differences in cognition: Evidence for the social orientation hypothesis. *Cultural Directions in Psychological Science, 19,* 9–13.

Vaughn, S., Linan-Thompson, S., & Hickman, P. (2003). Response to treatment as a means of identifying students with reading/learning disabilities. *Exceptional Children, 69,* 391–409.

Vaughn, S., & Roberts, G. (2007). Secondary interventions in reading: Providing additional instruction for students at risk. *Teaching Exceptional Children, 39,* 40–46.

Vellutino, F. R., Scanlon, D. M., & Jaccard, J. (2003). Toward distinguishing between cognitive and experiential deficits as primary sources of difficulty in learning to read: A two-year follow-up to difficult to remediate and readily remediated poor readers. In B. R. Foorman (Ed.), *Preventing and remediating reading difficulties* (pp. 73–120). Baltimore, MD: York Press.

Viney, W., & King, D. (2003). *A history of psychology: Ideas and context* (3rd ed., pp. 391–394). Boston, MA: Allyn & Bacon.

Vygotsky, L. S. (1978). *Mind in society: The development of higher psychological processes.* Cambridge, MA: Harvard University Press.

Watkins, A. F. (2002). Learning styles of African American children: A developmental consideration. *Journal of Black Psychology, 28*(1), 3–17.

Webb-Johnson, G. (2003). Behaving while Black: A hazardous reality for African-American learners. *Beyond Behavior, 12*(2), 3–7.

White, J. L., & Parham, T. A. (1990). *The psychology of Blacks* (2nd ed.). Englewood Cliffs, NJ: Prentice Hall.

Wijeyesinghe, C. L., Griffin, P., & Love, B. (1997). Racism curriculum design. In M. Adams, L. A. Bell, & P. Griffin (Eds.), *Teaching for diversity and social justice* (pp. 82–109). New York, NY: Routledge.

Williams, C. (1974). *The destruction of Black civilization: Great issues of a race from 4500 B.C. to 2000 A.D.* Chicago, IL: Third World Press.

Williams, D. D. (2009). *A closer look at Ruby Payne's culture of poverty theory* (Vol. 28, 2nd ed.). Las Cruces, NM: Trainers Forum.

Williams, D. D. (2012). *An RTI guide to improving performance of African-American students: What every teacher should know about culture and academic engagement.* Aurora, IL: Tier 1 Educational Coaching and Consulting Services.

Williams, D. D. (2013). *A cultural awareness manual: What every teacher should know about characteristics associated with traditional African American culture.* Aurora, IL: Tier 1 Educational Coaching and Consulting Services.

Wilson-Jones, L., & Caston, M. C. (2004). Cooperative learning on academic achievement in elementary African American males. *Journal of Instructional Psychology, 31*(4), 280.

Wood, F. B., Felton, R. H., Flowers, L., & Naylor, C. (1991). Neurobiological definition of dyslexia. In D. D. Duane & D. B. Gray (Eds.), *The reading brain: The biological basis of dyslexia* (pp. 1–26). Parkton, MD: York Press.

Wood, S. J., Murdock, J. Y., Cronin, M. E., Dawson, N. M., & Kirby, P. C. (1998). Effects of self- monitoring on on-task behaviors or at-risk middle school students. *Journal of Behavioral Education, 8,* 263–279.

Woodson, C. G. (2006). *The mis-education of the Negro.* Trenton, NJ: Africa World Press.

Yilmaz, K. (2008). A vision of history teaching and learning: Thoughts on history education in secondary schools. *The High School Journal, 92,* 37–46.

Index